EACH ONE
TEACH ONE

UP AND OUT OF POVERTY
Memoirs of a Street Activist

by
Ron Casanova
as told to
Stephen Blackburn

CURBSTONE BOOKS
NORTHWESTERN UNIVERSITY PRESS
EVANSTON, ILLINOIS

Curbstone Books
Northwestern University Press
www.nupress.northwestern.edu

Printed in the United States of America

10   9   8   7   6   5   4   3   2   1

ISBN 978-0-8101-4505-4 (paper)

The Library of Congress has cataloged the original, hardcover edition as follows:

Casanova, Ronald, 1945–
    Each one teach one : up and out of poverty ; memoirs of a street
    activist / by Ron Casanova ; as told to Stephen Blackburn.—1st ed.
        p.   cm.
    ISBN 1-880684-37-3
    1. Casanova, Ronald, 1945–. 2. Homeless persons—United
    States—Biography. 3. Social reformers—United States—
    Biography. 4. Recovering addicts—United States—Biography.
    I. Blackbum, Stephen. II. Title.
HV4505.C34   1996
362.5'092—dc20   96-9248
[B]

This book is dedicated
to the homeless people of the world,
and to the memories of Terry Taylor,
Keith Thompson, Spider and Barbara,
Willie, and Ed Rutter, my Polish brother.

But people are always speculating—why am I as I am? To understand that of any person, his whole life, from birth, must be reviewed. All of our experiences fuse into our personality. Everything that ever happened to us is an ingredient.

Malcolm X

For I was an hungred, and ye gave me meat: I was thirsty, and ye gave me drink: I was a stranger, and ye took me in: Naked, and ye clothed me: I was sick, and ye visited me: I was in prison, and ye came unto me.

...

Verily, I say unto you, Inasmuch as ye have done it unto one of the least of these my brethren, ye have done it unto me.

Jesus of Nazareth
(*Matthew* 25:35-36, 40)

CONTENTS

EACH ONE
TEACH ONE

CHAPTER 1
Rabbit Blood

Now I cannot recall all the names because it was too long ago and too many things have happened. I use my art work as a way of escape and a way of remembering. I paint Christmas cards and tigers and cartoon characters, but also scenes I've remembered from my life. I have the picture in my mind. You want a picture, I'll give you a picture.... I can close my eyes right now and see my tent. I see the tents of a hundred other homeless people. I see the farm field where we stayed on the march to Washington out under the stars, warm around our fire. Then I see a lot of smoke, I see flames coming out of a tent, people running. I see smoke in the sky, helicopters and helmeted police on horseback riding in among my friends who are trying to hold onto what little they possess. Every time I close my eyes it still hurts. I have been homeless for most of my life, but today I believe it is not coincidental that my name is Casanova. The English translation of Casanova is "New House." And that is what we are fighting for.

I never had any intentions of becoming an activist. I was born on June 11, 1945, and my earliest clear memory is of being put into the orphanage at the Mission of the Immaculate Virgin for the Protection of Homeless and Destitute Children, Mount Loretto, Staten Island, when I was three years old. Years later I found out that the name my parents gave me was Renaldo, but at the orphanage it was changed to Ronald. Ronald was the name I grew up with.

Mount Loretto was a big old orphanage in the middle of the suburbs on the southeast side of Staten Island, in the beach area. To me the orphanage was huge. The rest of the suburban houses weren't all that close. You needed transportation to get to them. The orphanage looked like a college campus, with one big boulevard right down the center. One side was all male and one side was all female. Male and female separated by the boulevard.

It seemed there were thousands of other kids. The orphanage was under the control of Franciscan priests, but the nuns of the order of the Immaculate Conception ran the place. There was a row of junior dormitories for boys from three years old up until early teens. They called them "cottages," but that was just a name. The buildings were very institutional. Two-story, red brick. From First Cottage all the way up to Sixth Cottage were straight buildings. All identical. In fact, from the right angle it looked to me like one big building. They had the same thing on the female side.

The area around the orphanage was beautiful. On the female side there was the beach. On the male side was the farm, where the orphanage got corn and milk and eggs, and then the football and softball fields and the woods. It was a long way across the boulevard to the cottages where the girls were. You had to go through a big wheat field.

Inside the dormitory where I lived were rows of beds in a big, beige room like a barracks. There was a front area for recreation. A nun's office off to the right. I remember how the uniforms smell, how their habits smell, of starch and mothballs. The dorm smelled like nuns.

The mess hall and the school were separate from the dormitory cottages. The mess hall was a huge, huge building where everyone went to eat. All the males, that is. As I said, the females were on the other side of the road. At the orphanage the routine was mess hall for breakfast by six o'clock, then you would go to school. You'd go to school, you'd eat again. They had everything set up and you did the conveyor belt type of thing. Then at a certain time in the evening, after showers, the nun would come out.

"It's time to go to bed," she would say, and everybody went to bed.

Sundays we went to church.

It was several years before I even knew I had any brothers or sisters at the orphanage. When we did finally meet, I found out I was the youngest of eleven kids. Two of my brothers and two of my sisters were in the orphanage with me: Philip, Richard,

Sonya and Marie. The five of us had been left there together when our mother had died. Richard was about two years older than me, Philip about four years.

I thought about it a lot, but I couldn't truly remember seeing my mother. All I had was a vague memory of sharing an overcrowded room with my sister and some of my brothers and a lady who was probably my mother. I never asked what my mother had died from. It didn't seem important. What difference did it make how a person died? She was dead, what else mattered? I don't remember seeing my sister Marie much at all, although sometimes I was allowed to go over and visit Sonya. In reality, we had no firm bonding as a family in the orphanage.

Many of the kids at the Mount Loretto orphanage had family, mostly extended, but their families were having problems making it themselves. Nevertheless, on Sunday, which was visiting day, a lot of kids got visits from sisters and cousins and uncles. From my brothers and sisters at the orphanage I knew I had relatives, family outside of Mount Loretto, so I wondered why I was at the orphanage. How come it was so rare that I got any visits? In fact, I can only remember two visits in all. Vaguely I recall that my sister Norma visited me once. I have a better, though still hazy, memory that another sister, Carmen, came to see me once, too. All I remember is coming out of the building and seeing her walking up with a kid in a baby carriage. We had a visit. It was awkward, but it meant a lot to me. I have a sense that she had the intention of hopefully seeing me again, but it never happened. To this day I don't know why. I was very lonely as a child.

One thing they insisted on teaching at the orphanage was etiquette. Though I don't know how to set up silverware, I do know how to say "thank you," how to open a door for a woman. I left the orphanage with good manners. Yet the disturbing truth is that the nuns put so much emphasis on courtesy, they didn't teach anything about life outside of that, which can be damaging. They did not put enough emphasis on individuals and their humanity. If you were in trouble, then they would get to know your name, but other than that, if you weren't an outstanding troublemaker, then you were simply part of the statistics. Let me put it this way: they knew my name.

***

As a child you look at people and they remind you of something. Sister Monica Denise reminded us kids of a bird because of her sharp features and because she was fidgety. So all the kids called her "Tweety Bird," mostly behind her back. One of her main faults, as far as all the kids were concerned, was that she was the kind of nun who would always hit people's hands with a twelve-inch wooden ruler with metal edges when they did something wrong.

In class one day, Sister Monica Denise stood with the map down, pointing at different cities and towns. Some kid got rambunctious and, as usual, got beat by the ruler. Watching that nun smack the kid's hands, I worried that sooner or later it would be my hands under that ruler.

"Tweety Bird, if you live by that ruler," I said, "you are going to die by that ruler."

Some of the boys laughed at my wisecrack. Sister Monica Denise snatched me and hit me with the ruler. Then she took me down the hall to an office. Inside, a black priest stood up, the only black authority figure I ever saw working in the orphanage. He didn't say very much. He was the punisher.

The priest took me into a room where there was what we boys called the "horsey," a sawhorse. He put me over the sawhorse and took my pants down. Then he pulled off his garrison belt, went back to the end of the room, came back and got to my butt with a running start. That's all I remember of the first and last time I ever saw him.

Another time I got in trouble when I was six or seven, a nun took me to a room where there were two chairs. One of the chairs had the middle slat of the back missing. The nun instructed me to take down my pants and stick my head through where the slat was missing. I did it. We kids were pretty much trained.

The nun had this stick called the "cat o' nine tails," and the name was indicative. It was a stick with nine leather strips, with thorns on each tail, like the stations of the cross thorns, like the thorns on Jesus Christ. I don't know if they were plant thorns, but I know those suckers hurt.

If the nun called me names, or if she called on the Lord and all that, I really don't remember. I didn't listen very well. I didn't hear what she said. That was one of my faults before I became an activist: I did not pay attention. The only thing I paid attention to was the beating. It made me very bitter.

Nevertheless, life at the orphanage was not all bad. In those days there were a lot of groups that harmonized together. Philip and Richard, my brothers in the orphanage, were part of a singing group of teenagers that used to go in the stairwell of one of the buildings on the Senior Side at the orphanage. They liked singing in the stairwell because they could get the acoustics they wanted for their sound. The hollowness made their singing sound better than in a normal room. I used to go along with Philip and Richard and two or three other guys when they would practice. I would sit on the sidelines and watch the older boys and listen. Occasionally they would bring something to drink, mostly beer. I'm not sure where they got it. If you walked far enough from the orphanage, there was a town called Tarkensville. Or maybe they got somebody to pick it up for them in Pleasant Plains.

One night while the harmonizing was going on, I sneaked a beer and drank it. I don't even think they knew I'd done it. It was my first taste of alcohol.

From time to time the nuns would take some of the kids shopping in Pleasant Plains, a town not too far from the orphanage. On one of the trips, a kid convinced a nun to buy us a jar of marshmallow fluff. I had never had marshmallow fluff, but one of the kids told me about how good it was on peanut butter sandwiches. When we got back to the orphanage we made some peanut butter and fluff sandwiches, and I found out the kid hadn't been exaggerating. I was hooked, and after that sometimes I'd even go into town on my own to buy the tasty fluff.

When I heard about the privileges and prestige altar boys got, I became an altar boy for a while. Sometimes I even liked the services. I liked to hear people talk, and I liked knowing that people had things they believed in. I guess I believed at the time, but I was inclined to be rebellious about religion because it was part of the orphanage program. They didn't give me any choice in the matter of what I did or did not believe. Besides, all that kneeling and all that jumping up and down made me weary.

Every Sunday I was reminded of what I did not have. As I watched all the other kids getting their Sunday visits and hugs from their brothers and sisters and mothers, I became even more curious about family relationships. Seeing those visits both showed me examples of family life and made me feel my lack of family even more sharply.

I remember watching a game one Sunday at the orphanage baseball diamond. All around me other kids and their visitors were talking, eating, laughing, having a good old time. I didn't feel too good because I didn't have anybody there. The longer I was in the middle of other people's happiness without being able to share in it, the worse I felt. I ended up leaving the game and going out to the woods on the orphanage grounds, where some of us boys hung out and smoked. A lot of other Sundays I'd go away and sit in the hay barn alone and eat a jar of fluff.

Despite my dislike for the institution, the orphanage was where I learned to love all colors, all races. That feeling wasn't really formed at that time, but the seed was planted. There was rarely prejudice at the orphanage. In an orphanage you're all on the same ground. A lot of the kids at the orphanage had been taken away from their parents due to abuse or lack of funds. Racially, it was a pretty well-mixed orphanage as far as the orphans were concerned. We all felt the same, until visiting family members would make a comment, or a teacher would accidentally slip out a slur as we studied ancient history. Remember this: children are open. We don't get these prejudices unless they are instilled in us. Even though the people in charge of the orphanage were nuns and priests, their job, as is the case with too many institutions, seemed to consist mostly of maintaining the status quo and keeping the statistics on the people living in the institution.

Even though the nuns and priests at the orphanage professed to be caring people, and they officially tried to instill that into the residents, they would come to work at eight o'clock and they'd go home at five o'clock. That was the type of attitude. I never had anyone sit down and talk with me, which I needed because I had a lot of anger and confusion. I didn't understand what I was doing in the orphanage, so I was angry at everything. Even as an eight-year-old in the orphanage I felt I could do a better job than the nuns, priests, and civilian social workers there. I didn't think they understood. An antisocial introvert, I had in me a seed of ambition to work with people, to become a social worker, if only to do a better job helping people than the clock-punchers who controlled my life.

One warm day in 1953, I ran away from the orphanage. It was to become a habit. I had rabbit blood and wanted to run. I felt I should be with my family. I was curious, not only about them, but also about life outside the constant impersonal rules and harsh discipline of the orphanage.

I went out to the woods and followed the commuter train tracks down to the ferry. The Staten Island Ferry was only five cents at the time. Cars lined up and rolled on and filled the big wide-open, two-tiered boat. In the center of the ferry was a passenger cabin where people would get out of their cars and go get coffee up on the second floor. Standing in the wind on the front of the ferry, I faced New York.

CHAPTER 2

Stray Dog

I had only a vague idea of where to find my family, but I felt I belonged with them. From my older sister Sonya I knew that our oldest brother Gino lived in New York around 104th Street and Central Park, so that's where I headed. Along the way I found a stray black and white cocker spaniel, and the dog stayed with me.

When I found my way to 104th Street, I just started asking strangers if they knew where my brother Gino Casanova lived, or my sister Norma. By the time it got dark, I hadn't had any luck. I remember going into a building and sleeping in the hallway. In the morning when kids came out of their apartments to go to school, they stood looking at me there with the black and white cocker spaniel. That made me uncomfortable, so the next night I started going all the way to the top landing to sleep, where the landing leads to the roof, because I thought it was safer and out of the way. People left me alone, all right, but one morning I woke up and there was food for me on a plate on the floor. I ate it hungrily, sharing with the dog.

Basically I was a loner, used to being by myself in a crowd, but I was also a scared kid, so I went about making friends that summer. First I'd get up in the morning and I'd go down and hang out in the street. I'd hang on the stoop and after a while the kids got used to seeing me there. They'd be across the street playing handball or stoop ball. One day I got over where they were and asked if I could play. They said yes and it turned out we were kids who liked being with each other.

Tom and Richard Wright became my best friends. The Wrights lived one flight up at 608 West 104th Street, the building where I was sleeping. Any time I went there, I could eat. They had three sisters, Emily, Betty, and Maxine, who used to hang out with us. Their mother was a big old tall generous country woman from down south somewhere. Come suppertime, Mrs. Wright didn't treat me different from her own kids. It was "Come on in, let's eat." They were all friendly, so I ended up eating with them a lot. I don't really know what Mr. Wright's profession was, I didn't see him all that much, but I know he had something to do with fish because we ate a lot of fish. That, and corn bread and collard greens, black-eyed peas and chitlins. Down-home food.

One day I was standing on the stoop at 104th Street with Thomas, Richie, their sisters, and some other kids from the neighborhood, when a light-skinned dude with straight black hair came down the street, stopped at our stoop and looked us over.

"Ronnie?" he said.

It was my oldest brother, Gino. Somehow he had heard that I was out of the orphanage, and he had come looking until he found me. Well, by that time I wasn't really looking for him anymore. I was more into hanging out on the stoop with my friends, but my brother picked me off the stoop and took me home.

In those days Gino was living at 103rd and Riverside Drive or West End Drive, I can't remember exactly, with his wife Peggy, who was Italian. Gino's apartment was on the ground floor of a clean building. It had been a fairly well-to-do area at one time. His apartment had three rooms: a living room that we shared as a bedroom, a small kitchen, and a small bathroom. Before I showed up, Gino and Peggy had just had a baby, Junior, and the baby had fallen on his head. By the time I got there, he'd already been taken care of, but he had a very soft part of his head. He cried a lot, and you had to be very careful with him, which made me nervous. But Peggy was pretty cool. She really loved Gino and the kid, and even liked me and the rest of the family.

For money, Gino did a lot of Johnny-on-the-spot odd jobs and labor pool jobs, mostly unloading trucks or working in industrial areas. When he was home, Gino sketched in the living room with both pencil and charcoal. To me this was fascinating, and I liked to sit and watch Gino draw. When I found time alone, I began trying my own hand at drawing, copying pictures from magazines with charcoal I had taken from Gino. I didn't show anybody my first attempts.

Even when I was watching him draw, my brother and I didn't have much conversation, although one day I worked up the courage to ask him about our family.

"Our mother and father were Puerto Rican," he said. "Mama's name was Carmen Quiñones."

Gino sketched a while longer.

"What about our dad?" I asked. Gino sketched without answering.

"Pop's name is Marcelino Trinidad Casanova," Gino said at last. "Like me. That's why I'm also called Gino, or Junior."

"What happened to him?" I asked. "Where is he?"

"Drunk somewhere," Gino said, and then he wouldn't say any more.

Gino and Peggy had a tv, and I soon learned that my favorite dude on tv was Peter Gunn, a detective. He had a part on the left-hand side of his head with his hair combed to the sides. I liked the way that looked.

That was the era of "The Process," when a lot of black folks were processing their hair, straightening their hair, conking their hair. Gino had a conk, and he introduced me to the style. He did my first conk. I can understand Malcolm X's concern about this style because when I got my hair processed, I had it done like Peter Gunn. I tried other styles, but Peter Gunn was always my favorite. But even though I was emulating a white man, the conk also kept my Puerto Rican-ness more visible. I spent a long time in my life figuring out who I was. Most of my life I grew up around black people, but I always wanted to emphasize the Puerto Rican in me, too. So I guess that had something to do with my favoring the process.

Only one time did I have a process done in a barber shop. I went to a barber shop around 114th or 115th and Lennox Avenue or 8th Avenue. The day I went in Sugar Ray was there with Cassius Clay, who would later become Muhammed Ali. I could hardly believe it.

"They come here a lot," a man told me. "Just come down to say hello to everybody." Everybody else was shaking hands with them, so I went over and shook hands too.

The process, which involved lye, never hurt until I tried to do it myself for the first time. It burned and stung like the devil, but it looked real good. It stayed perfect; I never had to comb it. In fact, I couldn't have combed it if I had wanted to because it was hard as a brick. When I was processing, I forgot to use the oil that gets it soft. It was as if I had placed a solid helmet of hair on my head. It was like some hard wig. Only problem was, it was up there permanently.

The only way I was able to get my hair back to being loose and soft was using mineral oil. I kept rubbing that oil into my Peter Gunn. After two weeks or so, it loosened the hair and took out the scabs. That's what happens when you try to be somebody else.

One day Gino took me to see Uncle Pete, my mother's brother. Uncle Pete was still on 112th Street, where he had lived when my mother was alive. On the way Gino pointed out a storefront on the block that had big-paned windows and a middle entrance.

"This looks like the restaurant our mother had," he told me.

"She had a restaurant?" I asked.

"Yeah."

"What kind of food?"

"Puerto Rican food, what do you think? Chicken, *chuletas*, *arroz con* beans, *pasteles*, that sort of thing."

I peered through the window and tried to imagine my mother in there cooking the tasty-smelling dishes. My Aunt Alice was the only one who had a picture of my mother. She showed it to me once. My mother was short, a dark-skinned and straight-haired Indian-looking woman of medium weight. I don't remember her smiling in the picture.

At Uncle Pete's I remember sitting underneath a table where Uncle Pete was playing dominoes with Gino and they were drinking Rheingold beer. A case of it was under the table with me. Listening to them click the dominoes as they played and talked, I learned that my father and Uncle Pete used to live together at one time. As I snatched one of the Rheingolds to drink later, I also heard that Pops had fallen downstairs the day before.

While working as a mover, Uncle Pete said, Pops and some other Spanish guy had been carrying a refrigerator. My father had the bottom part of it coming down the stairs and the other guy had the top. The guy at the top was having difficulties. Pops saw this, so he said, in Spanish, "I got it."

But Pops was drunk, so when the other guy let go, Pops fell down the stairs with the refrigerator. Apparently no damage. No physical damage.

"Maybe the alcohol made him movable," suggested Uncle Pete, "more flexible."

The next day Gino and I went again to Uncle Pete's, and I saw standing on Uncle Pete's stoop a tall man, light enough to pass for white. I stopped where I was. Even though I had never seen him prior to that, I knew it was my father. We have Italian in our family, Gino had told me, and you could see it in the senior Marcelino Trinidad Casanova. All through my life most people have considered me black, whereas Pops had naturally straight hair and looked more like an Italian than a black man. But he came from Puerto Rico, he was a *jíbaro*, which means a country boy, a country person. This was the man who my sisters and brothers said used to beat my mother. This was the man who let alcoholism take control of his life and so I got left in an orphanage.

I was scared of him.

He acted distant when he saw me. I went up to him and put out my hand.

"*¿Cómo está?*" I said. That was about all the Spanish I knew. He didn't speak a word of English. We had that shyness and uncertainty that comes any time a person meets another who doesn't speak the same language. We didn't understand each other beyond the fact that we knew that we were blood. So we didn't get very far.

I felt love for him even though I didn't know him. The fact that he was my father was enough for me, I thought. But anger was rising up, too. I couldn't really love him the way you'd love a father who had been there for you the whole time. Why had he left me in the orphanage? That's what I would have asked him, but I did not know the Spanish words. I looked at him and saw a vivid image of him living in a small room with no windows, just enough room for a bed. And empty beer bottles. Empty wine bottles. Empty rum bottles.

I just walked away.

***

Staying with Gino was all right, but I learned soon enough that he was going through problems of his own. He and Peggy were having a rough time getting along. They had male-female problems, they had money problems, and there was the baby crying. And me, one more mouth to feed. So after a while I would just come in to go to sleep, then get up and leave the next morning. Anytime there was an argument at Gino's, or even if I sensed one coming, I hit the streets. Living in the orphanage had trained me to feel that conflict was something to avoid. It was something I could not face.

While staying with Gino I had met another one of my older sisters, Pauline, so I tried staying with her a few times. Pauline was shorter than me, heavyset. She seemed jubilant whenever I saw her; unfortunately, it was due to alcoholism. She had a boyfriend, and they had a very small room. I have a memory of their icebox always being full of food and drink, but it was close quarters where they lived. Again, lots of nights it was just easiest to take off. Sometimes I felt more at ease sleeping in Central Park, or in the hallway of Tom and Richie's building, than anywhere else.

To tell the truth, there was another reason I felt uneasy at Gino's. See, I had taken to stealing from them, my family, on my first visit. Not necessarily money. They never had any money to steal. Not that I knew of, not that I could get to. I would take small things, like an ashtray, and go out and sell it to some dude on the street. One time I ran off with a transistor radio that I kept instead of selling.

Then one day I was rummaging around in Gino's living room for something I could sell. In the drawer of a small table with a lamp on it, I came across a big beautiful knife, like a dagger. I held it and looked at it. I felt uneasy about my thefts, yet at the same time, from what I had seen of the world, everybody had to look out for themselves. I believed Gino was happy when I would leave because then I wasn't in the way. But he had given me a key, even though there was somebody home most of the time.

I put the knife back in the drawer. The simplest thing for an eight-year-old boy like me was to run.

There used to be a lot of supermarkets on the West Side. On 104th there were two grocery stores on the same block. A&P's was on 104th Street between Manhattan Avenue and Columbus, and right on the corner of 104th Street and Columbus Avenue was the Met food store or supermarket. The Met was the smaller of the two. It had big windows in front, but it was a dark supermarket. A&P was well-lighted, you could see in there, but the Met is the one that I went to the most. One day as I stood outside I saw a woman come out with a whole wagonful of stuff and it seemed like it was heavy.

"You need some help?" I asked.

"I sure do," she said. I pushed the cart, took it to her home, and up to the house. She gave me some money. From then on I basically lived off the money I made from supermarkets, delivering people's groceries home for tips. I delivered groceries from lots of supermarkets all over the area, depending on where I was at the time.

***

Winter was coming on and I had stopped sleeping in the park because it had gotten too cold to sleep outside. The Wrights had given me some extra clothes, but even in the hallways with the dog it was cold. One morning I woke up on the landing and the radio I had taken from Gino was gone. Even my bag of leftover groceries from the night before had been taken. I looked at the cocker spaniel. Some watchdog. The thief probably paid him off with a share of the food.

I decided to turn myself back in to the orphanage. I knew I couldn't take care of the dog at Mount Loretto. What I ended up doing was taking it to a downtown luxury building. There was snow on the sidewalks. I tied the cocker spaniel to a banister so a rich person could find it and take it in.

When I got back to the orphanage, it seemed like my running away had not made much difference to anybody. No one ever questioned me about why I ran away. There was simply no counseling. Only punishment.

CHAPTER 3
Living in the Notch

They sent me to a special room in a big building on the Senior side. It was a big empty room like an army barracks, with a lot of windows, a high, vaulted ceiling, and a wooden floor. There was no furniture in the room except a desk and chair for whichever nun was monitoring us. I remember their being anywhere from six boys to seventeen or more being punished at one time for various infractions. All you did was stand there with your arms crossed all day long, and that's how you would stand for as many days as they said you should be there. The only time we sat down was to eat or to go to bed. Other than that you would just stand there. Looking back, I don't know how any of us could have accepted that kind of treatment. Yet until I was 44 years old, defending my home in Tompkins Square Park against the police, I believed all this was the normal way of life.

I didn't exactly feel a sense of injustice because this treatment was what I knew. I actually expected it. But still, although the room was cold and I was shivering, an anger simmered inside of me. At the age of eight I made up my mind: I'd show them. I would be a social worker when I grew up. I wouldn't be a clock-puncher; I'd work to find out what made a person tick, what made them hurt.

Little did I dream that far down the road I would actually live up to that angry promise. Of course, at that young age I had no idea how to go about it.

Instead, my sense of separateness grew. It got to be a pattern at the orphanage that I didn't eat in the mess hall with the others. I would go steal a chicken or pick some corn from the farm on the orphanage and go to the incinerator in the back of the institution to cook it. That's where I ate because I didn't want to be in the mess hall. Independence was what I wanted, and so, barely a few months into 1954, I had run off again.

***

The Stoop at 104th Street between Central Park West and Manhattan Avenue became the place I would go to first every time I ran away. And from there, everything and everybody else caught up. All of the kids I knew then lived in that block. I have a picture in my mind of that block on 104th Street, and that specific stoop; it's just a matter of getting it down on canvas.

In the street we would play stickball, stoop ball and one-wall handball. That and marbles, but we really didn't play marbles all that much. Stoop ball is the same thing as stickball, just without a bat. The so-called "batter" throws the ball at the stairs of the stoop, hits the stairs at a certain angle at the back part of the step. The ball bounces off the bottom part of the stoop and out into the street, and the batter tries to run the bases.

One day Tom and Richard and I went exploring in Central Park, which was right across 104th Street. We came to a hill the brothers knew about. There was a wall around it, and on the hill was a little cliff. Up there I noticed a good place I might be able to use, with a notch in the rock. Down from that was a tunnel.

We went in to look around. Inside the tunnel we came to a big rock.

"Check it out," Richard said.

"Looks like Frankenstein's tomb," said Tom. We all laughed. From then on the rock was Frankenstein's Tomb.

Once the weather warmed up, I started sleeping in the park at the spot I had noticed on the hill with the cliff. That's where I cooked, in the notch in the rock. Waking up in Central Park on Easter Sunday 1954, I had a view of beautiful flowers and green leaves. I woke up to this beauty.

Somebody, I don't remember who, gave me a wooden basket with candy and some hard-boiled eggs for an Easter basket. That afternoon, I walked through the park, and I was going through the tunnel with my Easter basket. Right at Frankenstein's Tomb they jumped me. Several boys. I didn't know any of them.

"What gang you with?" they demanded, checking out my Easter basket.

"I ain't part of no gang," I said.

"Good, then nobody will bother when we beat your ass!"

I asked them not to.

"Give me the basket," one boy demanded. I handed it over, thinking that would satisfy them. Instead, I had given them a weapon. The boy beat me over the head with the basket, laying open my scalp. So on this Easter Sunday that had started out so wondrously beautiful, I ended up being beaten with an Easter basket in front of Frankenstein's Tomb. I had to go to the hospital to get stitches in my head. Two paintings I've done of that Easter are hanging now at Dignity Housing in Philadelphia in the main office. One is the beautiful scene of Easter Sunday morning. And one is the bad scene that same day's afternoon.

From the hospital I went back to Gino's house. I remembered the knife I had seen there, the one like a dagger. I went straight to the lamp table, opened the drawer and took the knife. I was ready if anybody tried jumping me again.

Later I was hanging out on the stoop with the other kids when I saw Gino coming.

"Give me back my knife," he said, and held out his hand. The other kids sat back and watched. I pulled out the knife and handed it back to him. Some of the kids laughed. To them getting caught stealing was no big deal. Most of them were doing similar things. Gino didn't hit me; he just turned around and walked away. Nothing direct, like "Get out of my house and the hell with you!" But it was implied. I felt I could no longer stay at his house, so I didn't go back there for a long time. In fact, I would go through a lot of changes and grief before Gino and I really got back together again.

***

As it happened, 1954 was also the year I found my sister Norma. Norma was the oldest sister of my family. She had a husky build and the mannerisms of a strong-willed woman. She could be very forceful; she was the one you wouldn't mess with. But I never had any problem with her. In fact, once I knew where she lived,

I used to go and stay with her the most because she was the one in my family who always had room for me anytime I showed up at her door. She lived in various places during my youth. At one point she lived in a three-story house in Brooklyn that I think she was renting. When I visited her, I stayed in the basement. It was pretty nice there—clean, homey. I loved all her kids. But Norma's husband cut out at some point. I guess she was getting a welfare check because she had a good number of kids she was supporting. Maybe that's why she didn't visit me at the orphanage.

Norma, and even Gino, must have known I had some kind of problem when I'd come and stay with one or the other of them for a couple of weeks and then disappear, sometimes without even saying good-bye. Norma was my big sister, whenever I allowed it to happen. She was the one whose shoulder I would cry on.

"Where are you living?" Norma would ask me. "What are you doing? How are you eating?"

They were the same questions Gino sometimes asked me, and later Sonya and Philip would ask me. But I just didn't have any answers for them or myself. By then I never liked depending on anybody, so it was very rare I would tell anyone about my problems. My brothers and sisters had their own worries, and I didn't like being one more. Teenagers are known for being troublesome, but looking back, I guess the orphanage brought that out in me early on because from the time I was eight and started running away, I rebelled against any rules. Maybe I also held some resentment against my brothers and sisters for not getting me out of the orphanage. But I think anybody who is forced to do something that they don't really understand will rebel against it in some way. When I ran off from the orphanage, it was to find my family, but it was also to get away from having to follow somebody's orders on how to live, where to live, what to do, when to do it. By the time I left the orphanage it seemed it was too late for me to stay put anyplace: I was a runner. That was the way I saw myself. I looked at the situation and knew I was a street kid who preferred being outside. But my brothers and sisters didn't understand that, and I saw they shouldn't really have to bear responsibility for me because I was so wild. I had a hard time believing that anybody, even my family, would honestly want to help me. So I convinced myself I didn't want family relationships. Still, I could not bear to tell Norma I was sleeping in hallways.

***

The stoop is where I got my first real introduction to wine, when I was nine. "Hombre" wine. On the label the Hombre wine had a Mexican wearing a sombrero. I guess that might have been the attraction. First time I got drunk I remember a lot of dizziness. To be honest with you, I liked the high. But I threw up. Man, did I throw up.

Sometimes members of the Assassins would come hang out with us and drink too. They were the main gang in my area of the 104th Street neighborhood, a gang of kids mostly our age and early teenagers.

The parents didn't like what was happening. They tried to stop us, but what were they going to do, stand there 24 hours a day? They couldn't do that. If they came to the stoop, we would go across the street or into the park.

Part of me still didn't understand what I was doing, why I was here with all these kids. Now I understand that I was still a scared kid. I needed some friends, so I drank along with everybody else. Sometimes after drinking I would sleep in between floors if I got so drunk I couldn't make it all the way upstairs to the top. There was one time in particular that I recall sleeping right there on the floor with four apartments all around me. I did a drawing of it.

Mostly, however, Tom and Richie and I and the guys spent our time hanging out to talk with the girls in the neighborhood. Today I find it unfortunate that we didn't do much talking about anything other than trying to get to the girls. I don't remember having any intellectually stimulating conversations, that's for sure. Our view of the world did not go much past that stoop and that block. We just hung out. But the playing and talking with girls and hanging out, that was all in the daytime. At night they went home, and I went to a hallway or a park where I could get to sleep. I have tried to capture those days of the 104th Street stoop on canvas, but it didn't come out right, so I whitewashed it over.

But Tom and Richard had become more than just my friends; we were like brothers, only they had a home and I didn't. Summer ended, and they went back to school while I spent my days in the park. They looked me up after they got home from school one day.

"Come on and spend the night," Thomas said. "Let's talk to my mom, man, and see what's happening."

I was resistant, but their mother agreed, so I started spending the night in their apartment every now and then. Their mother was like my mother. Their kitchen was where I would eat. Their room was where I got clothes. Betty, Maxine, and even Emily were more family, too, than girlfriends, though I admit I tried to get them to fool around. I believe Thomas and Richie were halfway trying to adopt me. But it didn't pan out. The Wrights were overcrowded already. They had a total of seven people living in that apartment, enough family of their own to where they couldn't take on another kid. I realized I couldn't stay there all the time, and it wasn't just my rebellious attitude telling me that. The parents had problems with alcohol, which had them arguing a lot. I didn't want to have anything to do with that. It made me feel uncomfortable, very uptight. As always, if any type of confrontation started, or if I even felt a vibration, I was gone.

CHAPTER 4

Ricochet Kid

During the periods each year that I spent back at the orphanage, I always did pretty well in school. Don't ask me how. I guess that was particularly surprising to the nuns, considering how much time I spent missing classes. But I turned out smarter than they expected. Math stands out as a subject I liked, but it was boxing that really caught my attention.

Boxing became important to me from the time I was nine years old until I was eleven. In the intervals when I was at the orphanage, I boxed on the school team for three years. I'm not a very rambunctious person, but as I have said, I was a very angry kid. I wanted to get *something* out of my life, so I liked the idea of the attention and the fighting. Boxing channeled the anger I had.

From what I can recall, there were about six of us on the team: a couple of Spanish boys, myself, a guy named Cooper and two white kids. At the orphanage there were guys I hung out with, but no one I really considered a close friend. The only boy that stands out in my mind is Cooper. Cooper stood about the same size as me but was darker, pitch black, with short-cropped hair. He and I didn't really hang out; it was more that we were forced to spend a lot of time together because we were on the team. Nevertheless I felt that Cooper and I were a clique, so to speak, off to the side of the rest of the team.

Nick, the coach, was a good dude. He did the training, made us go through the exercises. Our workouts consisted of a lot of push-ups, a lot of chin-ups and jogging. We boxed in Cottage Six, in a ring set up in the recreation area. Sometimes we boxed against St. Joseph's, which was another orphanage on Staten Island. Mt. Loretto was always in competition with St. Joseph's in sports. But mostly we boxed among ourselves.

Cooper was good, but so was I, and eventually we were matched up against each other in the school championship. Now in actuality, Cooper was better than me, but I was unpredictable as a boxer. A lot of times I'd punch with my eyes closed. What you might call a windmill style. That's probably what gave me the edge on him because I ended up beating Cooper. For my prize I got a little toy boxing man. When you pressed a button underneath the base, he would dance.

The next season, Cooper and I were set up in a boxing rematch, and this time Cooper was much better than me. This time he was more prepared and he beat me up. Cooper had beat me fairly. He did a good job as a boxer. But who wants to get beat? I was young, and I guess my pride was hurt, because I went and grabbed a broom and climbed back into the ring and hit him. They stopped that pretty fast, but I got off a few licks before I got chased out of the cottage.

When I ran, I ran toward the woods and the train tracks, but nobody followed me out there. I was scared. I was also angry, but I was more scared than anything. For some reason I didn't take off for New York. Maybe it was because I had started to pay attention to the Female Side of the orphanage.

By then I had a fair amount of experience sleeping in hallways and whatnot, but that was my first experience living in a tree. You know how a tree goes up and has some forks, a branch sticking up. That's where I was at night, right between the branches, sleeping, nervously. Actually I didn't do too much sleeping—more of a balancing act than anything. There were still animals in the trees, bugs anyway, but it was better than the mice and rats on the ground.

The next day I headed to the orphanage farm. I liked the hay house, the barn. I used to just go hang out in the barn, jump around in the hay. I even had a stash of marshmallow fluff in the barn. So after Cooper beat me and I hit him with the broom, I hid out at the barn. When nobody was around, I spent a lot of time swinging off the rope onto the hay and eating fluff out of the jar. Fluff to me was better than a steak.

A couple of days later I went back into the orphanage because I was hungry and tired. I needed a bath and clothing. When I went back I was accepted. Nick the boxing coach was very glad when I showed up. Looking back, I'm sure he must have been aware of what tree I was sleeping in. To tell the truth, had they come and pulled me out of that tree, things might have gone a lot worse because I hadn't yet learned how to compromise, how to admit a mistake. I hadn't learned to say, "Okay, it's over, now let's move on." I didn't understand that kind of reasoning at the time. I guess that incident cost whatever friendship I had with Cooper because I don't remember him after that.

As I said, the Female Side had caught my eye by the time I was eleven, and that may have been what kept me from going back to the streets right after my boxing defeat. Delayed my annual sprint from the orphanage. It was the procedure for all the boys who wanted to visit the Female Side to go there with the priests on weekends. The Female Side had a big center where boys and girls played ping-pong, listened to music and just generally congregated and hung out. My brothers and sisters would be there too sometimes.

By that spring of 1956, my sister Sonya was old enough that she was getting ready to move out of the orphanage to live with a man she had met. "Carol" was Sonya's name in the orphanage. She hung around with a lot of black girls. Rather than calling her "Sonya," they called her "Carol." I guess "Carol" sounded more black.

The girls lived on the beach side of the orphanage, so we went to the beach a lot as well. At the beach after dark we cooked marshmallows and people told ghost stories. Although I thought of myself as a loner, I found I liked these outings. They were cool, a better way to share companionship and meet girls than sitting around the orphanage. We went on weekends with the priests, but we also began sneaking out of the dorms at night whenever we felt like it and going on expeditions to the beach and to visit the girls.

I enjoyed going to the beach, although the first time I went wading I nearly drowned. I was out splashing around by myself. There were other people around, but I went out too far and I got cramps and started drowning. Fortunately somebody pulled me out. You might say it was an early lesson in how being a loner isn't necessarily the best way to survive.

There was a white girl with dark brown hair who was friends with my sister Sonya. One day when all of us boys were in the recreation area at the girl's side, Sonya introduced me to this girl. Unfortunately, I can't remember her name, though at the time I was glad of the opportunity to meet her.

The next time I laid eyes on the brownhaired girl was some weeks later. Sonya had by that time gotten out of the orphanage. Some of us kids were going out on the bus for an official weekend home visit. The brownhaired girl was going to her mother's house; I was being allowed to go visit Sonya, who was now living with her boyfriend at 115th Street and Morningside Drive in Harlem.

The brownhaired girl and I were riding the bus, sitting side by side. She was wearing a kind of blouse that wasn't really low-cut, but open at the top. She didn't show me her breasts on purpose. She made the mistake of bending over and I peeked. There they were, and I was hooked.

We became boyfriend-girlfriend. After that I would get together with her at the orphanage youth center, play ping-pong, hang out, or she and I would go to the woods. Sex and any education about sex was taboo at the orphanage. But we didn't go all the way at that time. Our making out was more curiosity than anything like love. I had never been with a girl, and she had probably never been with a dude. But it was a passing phase of discovering womanhood and manhood; it happened and it was over with and done. It lasted only six months, if that long. When summertime came, I went back to the streets.

Sonya and her boyfriend offered to let me stay with them, so I tried that for a while, too, but they lived in a one-room apartment. They slept on a bed, and I slept in the same room on a fold-up bed. As you can imagine, it only took a short time for that arrangement to wear thin. However, they also had an army cot in case anybody else they knew happened to be a guest.

"Give me the cot," I suggested to them one day. "Let me take it to the park to sleep."

Sonya argued, but not much. They needed their privacy. She knew I would leave anyway, and that if they didn't give me the cot, we might never see each other again. So she gave me the cot and let me go. I took the cot up to my hill at the notch and slept there.

Once I had that incident with the gang in the park, I had decided I would become a member of the Assassins. I had hung out with members of the Assassins before that. We had shared bottles of wine and done a few bad things together. I was a bad enough kid that I didn't really have to go through an initiation. After I had been a member for a while, I actually became the so-called "war counselor," although, to be honest, there weren't really any wars. A few times we fought other gangs, but mostly we were kids who broke into a lot of stores. We used to break into places real early in the morning, like two or three or four o'clock, so it would still be dark out. Though we mostly did burglaries just for the excitement, we always had an ulterior motive because every place we broke into had food or candy or alcohol.

Tom and Richard were not gang members. When I was a gang member, that was a different association. But I can remember one night when Richard, Tom and I sat out late on a park bench, talking into the night. Then we broke into a store for tootsie rolls and tootsie pops. In the daytime, though, we were usually too busy being kids to do much damage.

During those hot summer days, I'd be hanging out or playing handball with the kids from the stoop and one of my sisters would show up looking for me, and depending on how I felt, sometimes I would go stay with them for a while. Probably Norma and Sonya were making an attempt to look after me, to include me in the family. The problem was that every time I would get to their homes, I'd realize they had separate families of their own. Just like when I had been staying with Gino, I felt they couldn't really take care of me. Also, from being in the orphanage I had a rebellious attitude toward any rules. For a kid like me, it was easier to be in the streets than to be responsible to someone else.

Norma even made an attempt to get me steady work at a gas station in Brooklyn. I didn't have to do anything mechanical, mainly just cleanup, but as soon as I got my first check I went back to the street. That had become the pattern of my life: I'd run away from the orphanage, then run away from my brothers and sisters. Yet I can't say I fully understand what I was doing, why I was doing it. Maybe I was suspicious of their sincerity. After years of leaving me in the orphanage, why should my family now give a damn whether I came or went? Maybe they really were wanting and trying to build the family unit or relationship that I had always longed for. But you can want something and not be able to do it. They may have wanted the relationship with me, but they were also very busy worrying about food and clothing and rent and a lot of children of their own. But I had no appreciation for that when I was little and in the orphanage wondering why I had to stay there and why I didn't get visits. While I hated the rules of the orphanage, I didn't yet grasp the give-and-take necessary to live with people in a household. A wall of distrust had already started to form.

I liked my independence, however poor that may have been. To me it was preferable to the risk of closeness that comes from living in a family. I had a fear of that relationship. So that wall which had come up was building higher and thicker with each passing year. In fact, it stayed with me pretty much all my life, at least until I awakened to being an activist.

In those years when I got fed up with being out on the streets, I would turn myself in to the police station, knowing I would end up back in the orphanage. Or I'd take myself to a detention center that was over on 103rd Street and Central Park East. I used to turn myself in there, and a truant officer by the name of Mr. Butler would come to pick me up. Mr. Butler was a slim white dude with graying hair. I was a little bit intimidated by him as an authority figure. But he was really kind of mellow, just doing his job.

Sometimes I wouldn't make it directly back to the orphanage. Sometimes the court would send me to the Bronx Youth House, another juvenile detention center, which was on

Spotford Avenue. Youth House was supposed to be the port of entry back into the system of so-called normal society. In reality, the detention centers were a kind of training school: they trained you for prison. That may not have been their intention, but that's what happened.

More and more I would mentally shut out figures of authority. Here were people who could play a major part in how you formed your life, and they did nothing to help that happen other than run you through the regular impersonal routine and procedures. As far as getting involved with you and finding out what makes you tick, they didn't do that. So in return, I stopped paying any attention to them. I had no respect for them. Whether it was the orphanage or the detention center or juvenile court, I would resign myself to the fact that I had to be there and I would go along with their program for as long as I could take it. When I could take it no longer, I would run.

After a while the authorities got tired of my running away from the orphanage. In '57 or '58 they decided I couldn't stay at the Immaculate Virgin orphanage anymore. I pretty much busted that cord, and they sent me on a bus to Pope Pius the Twelfth in Orange County in upstate New York, around Beacon, Syracuse, in that area. Pius Twelve had just boys living there, and I was one of the first. They were trying a new concept, a new idea for getting kids out of the status quo orphanage. Pius Twelve was more like living on a farm. It had a manmade lake, horses and red cottages. School was taught in one of the log houses. All in all, it was cool, but once again, I felt the rabbit blood in me. I couldn't stand living by the institutional rules, so I ran away from there, too, but God if I remember how I got back to New York.

***

I lived day to day. I was able to go a long time without eating. Sometimes I even did it on purpose, as training for when I would not be able to buy or get food. That was the only thought I had for the future. When I was a kid, eating was a bar of candy or something like that. Food wasn't my main concern. What concerned me was the weather.

Movies were one of the things I liked to do. It was a way to get out of the weather. I would hang out at the theater on 125th and Morningside Drive, the Morningside Theatre. Forty-second Street was also one of the places to go. That's where the money was. I would go in one movie, see all they had, and then I'd go to the next one and the next one, all day long. Among my favorite actors was the guy who played Peter Gunn, Steve Craig. I remember Richard Burton, when he played Alexander the Great. I remember Sammy Davis and Sidney Poitier. And the old Superman, George Reeves, stood out. I might see about five or six different movies, and the last one I ended up in I probably never even saw because I fell asleep.

I lived there. I would scrounge up enough money to get hot dogs and stuff like that. Now in my memory those times appear just like a fast movie projector, going from movie to movie, movie to movie, movie to movie. Most of the theatres were grungy, filthy places that smelled bad. I wasn't the only one that used to sleep there. There were other homeless people who also went to the movies to go to sleep. Sometimes the management would roust me or some other sleeper, but not very often.

I soon learned another way to beat the weather. When I was about 13 years old, I had sex for the first time. I had been sleeping in some apartment building hallway when I ran into the mother of a guy I knew at that building. She invited me to her place. Nobody else was there, and one thing led to another.

This became another way of surviving, to sometimes be a male prostitute. I had to do certain things, not so much for money as for a place to get in out of the inclement weather, get a place to sleep and maybe a meal or two. Generally I went with women in their twenties and thirties, poor Harlem women mostly, who would see me hanging out at 104th Street and Broadway. Other times I'd get picked up down on 42nd Street, another big hangout. We would talk and they would end up taking me off the streets. Their intention in the beginning wasn't necessarily to get me in bed, but I was a youth with a strong curiosity. Young people are still doing the same thing today, even though now it's a much more dangerous situation with AIDS and HIV.

One of those encounters stands out. I was with a lady in her mid- to late-20s. "You're going to be a leader," she told me. "You're going to be a good leader." Her words always stuck with me, though I had no idea how her prediction might come about.

***

The next time the authorities either picked me up or I turned myself in, I don't recall which, they put me in the Warwick State School for Boys in Orange County, New York, not far from Pius the Twelfth. In fact, you could see Pope Pius the Twelfth from Warwick.

At Warwick the boys lived in dorms that were called cottages, like at Mt. Loretto. Maybe that's an orphanage thing. The house parents in my cottage were husband and wife, both of them black. I never did learn their names, but I remember the woman was medium height, good-looking, with long straight black hair. Her husband was tall, slim, and light-skinned, what was known as a "high yellow" in those days.

Every day before supper all of us boys had to sit on the floor in a long long hall, while the houseparents sat at one end of the hall. One day one of the boys gave the housemother the notion that I was looking up her dress, even though I wasn't. The woman told her husband and he came and snatched me. The other kids watched as he took me into the shower room. He pulled out a radiator brush, a long-handled brush of wood and bristles they use to clean the radiator heaters. He started beating me with that brush, on my ass, my legs, all over except for my face. I'm sure all the boys must have heard me yelling and screaming. When he got done, I had to go back out to the hall and sit and wait for supper.

Now there were a few guys in the ward who had epilepsy. I think most of those were legitimate. When somebody has a real seizure, they don't pick their spot, they fall down wherever they are.

A number of times I was there when a boy had a seizure. I had to watch because I had never seen any behavior like that. The epileptic would shake on the floor, arms and legs fighting, eyes rolling back. I tried to help as much as possible. They told us not to hold the person's limbs, only their face, slanting it so the epileptic wouldn't swallow his tongue. Then they would stick a spoon with tape wrapped around it into his mouth also to keep him from swallowing his tongue. After that, they would take the kid to the hospital ward and you wouldn't see him for a couple of days. I watched and learned.

The norm in Warwick was going to school, getting in line. All my life it had been "Get in line! Get in line! Do that! Do this!" I grew up in a statistical world that had no room for my feelings, with the result that I always internalized my anger, kept it forced inside. I kept all my feelings to myself. I never even argued. I ran if I could, but if I couldn't, I still needed an escape.

One day the pressure of my anger against institutionalization swelled up in me, and almost without thinking about it, I fell to the floor and began thrashing my arms and legs the way I had seen it. I rolled my eyes back. I was performing an epileptic seizure.

It must have been convincing because they stuck the taped spoon in my mouth and took me to the hospital ward. They gave me a shot to calm me down. The relief that went through my body was really tremendous. I felt the anger drain out of my body.

Over the next few days, I found the hospital had a freer atmosphere than the rest of the orphanage. There was less ordering around. And I enjoyed having the nurses concerned about me. Growing up I'd never had any attention really paid to me. I needed a way to let out my intense anger without it jeopardizing me, without it causing me any trouble.

I believed I had found a solution. I began performing seizures whenever it suited me. I knew that after every seizure they'd put me in the hospital, so that guaranteed me the nurses and the attention that came after the seizure. As I "recuperated" they would give me work assignments, so I became part of the staff in the hospital, cleaning up or helping somebody to bed.

Unfortunately I did such a convincing job of pretending to be an epileptic that the line between reality and acting blurred. In the beginning I knew I was performing, but gradually I started forgetting what I was doing. One time I woke up and found I had actually gone into a state of blackout, yet my body had still performed the seizure. That scared me, not knowing what was happening. It stopped being just a performance.

I spent a lot of time in the hospital at Warwick because of the seizures. The doctors gave me three different types of drugs: Phenobarbital, Dilantin and Librium. These kept me fairly inebriated. Both the seizures and the medication became habit-forming. Eventually I actually needed these drugs in order to go on.

***

One day they put me on a bus from Warwick, and then on a train. The authorities were sending me to meet a married couple interested in becoming my foster parents.

Their names I have forgotten. I don't remember the father, but I do recall that the mother was a heavyset lady, a light-skinned sister, black. The mother was nice, she tried to make me feel at ease. They lived in Queens in a two-story house, not big, but comfortable. Two other boys, and two girls, all adopted, were also living in the house with the couple.

When I got there, the mother fed me a nice meal. I was given a bed in a room the boys shared. The two girls, I think, shared one of the other bedrooms. I guess the kids were nice. I don't really know—they were as shy as I was. But here was somebody who really wanted to adopt me. That was cool, I thought. I stayed there one day to see how it was and then went back to Warwick to wait until the paperwork was done.

The weather was turning warm by the time they finally sent me out to live with this family that was adopting me. Maybe the warm weather got to my blood, or maybe I just wasn't comfortable with the idea of living there permanently. I no longer remember the reason, only the result. Once again, it turned out

I couldn't handle the actuality of living with a family. I stayed overnight, and then the next day ran away from my adopted parents.

I didn't have any direction. If any situation got too stressful, I'd fall into a fit. Naturally I had some concern about where I as going to get food, but I knew that I could get it carrying people's groceries, or by knocking on a friend's door when they were eating.

Throughout my early teenage years in the late 1950s, I kept up my interest in drawing. Along 42nd Street they had adult movie houses and bookstores. I used to go there for magazines and little comic books that had cartoons of big-breasted women. Sometimes I would steal the book because I had no money. Then, sitting alone in the park, I would copy the drawings, doing the contours of the females. That's all I drew for quite a while. My art today is about power, it's about fear, it's about love, it's about passion, it's about humor. Back then, however, my art mainly consisted of bodies of women. I guess you could call that *my* study of anatomy.

My friends liked the drawings. After all, they were pictures of women with huge breasts. I would also draw some of the guys I knew, depending on their features, if their features were pronounced. Like if they had a big nose. I could copy almost anything, but mostly I drew the nudes. I liked to draw. Every time I looked at a picture I had made, and saw that I could draw, it tingled. Like nothing else in my life, I felt the comfort and potential there.

CHAPTER 5

Jitterbugging

In those days I had a dog, and often we would wake up in the morning at an old hotel on Morningside Drive where Sonya lived every now and then with her boyfriend. The hotel was a brownish brick building, old, but in good shape. The hotel clerk knew I was Sonya's brother, so he never hassled me when I came in. But instead of bothering my sister, I would take the dog up and sleep in a hallway or better yet, the rooftop landing. Next morning the dog and I would get up, and if there was something to eat right then and there, a bag of cookies or whatnot, we would eat. Then we hit the street.

Back at the stoop you'd run into the Assassins. People had taken to calling me "Lover Boy" because of my last name, and then simply "L.B." When it came to girls I did a lot of talking, like all the guys, but to tell the truth, I was mostly an introvert. The sisters Emily, Betty and Maxine would often be there on the stoop. They were growing up nicely. Betty was the tall one, tall and slim, dark complexioned. Emily had a lighter complexion. Maxine seemed the more serious one. Emily was my favorite. She had the best shape, was closest to my age, and had a bubbling personality. But they were all teasers to my mind. Of course, when I was that age, they didn't necessarily have to say anything to make me horny, they just had to be there. You'd swear there had been flirtatious eye contact, yet anytime I tried to react to that, they would get away somehow. I tried, but never did get into their drawers. I did have some consolation, though.

I used to jump up to the fire escape and do pull-ups showing off for the girls. Right across 104th Street on the corner of the street called Central Park West, there was this big huge high-rise, what we would call a condominium these days. Rich folks, rich white folks lived there. Now one day I was hanging from the fire escape, and through an open window across the street I saw a woman taking off her clothes. Next day, I jumped up and grabbed the fire escape, doing my showing off again. I wasn't the only one. When I looked over at the high-rise, there she was again, standing in the window with no clothes on. So from then on, every time I'd be doing chin-ups, I wasn't only doing it for the exercise.

From the stoop, the Assassins would go on our activities. "Go jitterbugging," that was the slang term we used for it. We had some fights and took part in a lot of burglaries. Actually, jitterbugging is more when you're out showing off. Sometimes that meant "playing the dozens," which is sounding on somebody's mother. It went back and forth. If one dude sounded on another guy's mother, the second guy would sound on the first dude's father or some other family member. Unfortunately we thought that kind of disrespect was a good way of playing; we considered it a joke.

We did our burglaries and stuff outside of the neighborhood. The rich areas, that's where we did our crimes. We would go downtown to 42nd Street, in that area, where all the stuff was. We broke into stores to eat. We broke into stores to get candy. We flirted with the women. Our territory was home base, where you could sit down and not have to worry about your back. We used to hang out at the YMCA at Columbus Avenue or the Frederick Douglass Center. Not with their consent, you know, but we would meet in the yard or on the playground. Drink, get high, party, share. It was a family-type thing. Gang members were brothers and sisters. Even though not blood brothers and sisters, we were family. Our territory was our home. Every now and then the police would come down and get bombarded. Every time police came on our block we hit the roofs. There were always garbage cans up there filled with bricks and ashes, and bottles filled with water. We made sure the stuff was always there; it was a permanent thing. Any time the police came, all we had to do was go up and dump.

Even in fighting with the other gangs there was some kind of comradeship because the gangs we fought were all from the same neighborhood. In other words, no gang from some other part of the city could come in and pick a fight with one of the gangs in our neighborhood or they would have all the gangs of our neighborhood to deal with.

This was something that was passed down through generations. Although fathers usually didn't like gang activity after they got out of the gang; nevertheless, they pretty much tolerated it.

We were macho and all, but the Mau-Mau Chaplains were more of a gang than we Assassins were. The Assassins, we were kids. The Mau-Maus were really out there fighting. They killed. They did that kind of damage.

Gang fights in my time were not about drugs. Mainly they were the fight for territory, the expansion of the organization, of the gang. Just like a real estate concern. You know what the Assassins did with new territory? We hung out. Danced, partied. The Mau-Maus were more into "this is my territory and you don't belong here. You don't come, or you get killed."

The Mau-Mau Chaplains were mostly black, but there were Latinos as well. Who came up with the name "Mau Mau Chaplains," I'm not sure. In the fight for freedom against the British or English people who took over Africa, there was a lot of slaughter done by the Mau-Maus, and vice versa. Therein might be some of the reason why the name was picked by the gang, although I don't know if these young men really knew the history of the African Mau-Maus. But they knew the name sounded bad.

One of my sisters, I think it was Carmen, lived in Brooklyn, at the Fort Green Projects. The Mau-Mau Chaplains were the gang that controlled the Fort Green Project area. So you either became friends of the Chaplains, or you didn't come to the territory. When I was 14 or 15, I used to every now and then go visit her and her kids and her husband Frank.

Carmen knew some of the members from the gang, and in that way I met the Mau-Mau Chaplains one night at a YMCA dance. Dances were the time when a lot of gangs showed up with their colors, so there used to be a lot of fights at those dances. But I met a few of the Mau-Maus, and we talked, we mingled, we got along. I guess I had a reputation. I never was initiated, never an actual member of the Chaplains, I just ran with them. I dealt with them, but I didn't get real tight with those guys because of guns.

Sometimes other gangs would come to the Fort Green Projects to fight the Mau-Mau Chaplains. The Chaplains used handmade guns and knives. I never saw anyone get killed in one of these gang fights. I would see stabbings and blood, but I didn't always know the results of that, because once that started happening, and the police started coming, everybody dispersed. If you saw somebody the next day, you knew they were alive. If you didn't, you pretty much thought they were dead or at least in jail.

West Side Story is a prettied up version of gang warfare. Many Puerto Ricans don't like that movie. It's not a favorite movie unless it's seen at a very early age, when they can still see the romance in it. But when they become active, more politically aware, they dislike the movie.

The weird positiveness of gang life was just being with people, because often I was alone. Being in the Assassins or hanging with the Chaplains provided a certain amount of protection that came from being with other people. If you were with each other, no one was going to bother you...aside from the opposing gangs. I stuck around enough for the prestige and protection of knowing Chaplains. Remember, I had learned my lesson when I got beat up in Central Park for not being a gang member. Mostly, however, I hung out with the Assassins, smoking and drinking. To be honest, I had no intention of getting shot or beat up. Rather than going out and hurting someone or getting myself hurt, I continued having epileptic-style seizures in certain situations, foaming at the mouth and growling and throwing myself on the ground. In this way I was able to get away from a lot of frustration, a lot of anger, and a lot of danger. Again, however, the problem lay in the fact that I had convinced *myself* I was an epileptic. No longer was it a put-on act. It turned out to be a reality that would end up giving me trouble.

Despite hanging out with the Assassins and the Chaplains, I was not a follower, and at times I couldn't be a social person.

I had to get away from the gangs sometimes, so I would go deeper into Central Park, or I would go uptown, around 125th, all the way up there. If I knew a neighborhood, it was okay to sleep in the hallways. I was afraid to sleep in strange hallways or in an area where I didn't know anybody. But at times I needed to get away from the gang. This need to get away on my own stuck with me so much that later, even in the 1980s, every now and then I would still go uptown to 125th Street and sleep in those hallways.

As I said, I used to make money for food by delivering groceries for people, carrying people's packages to their homes. I did a lot of delivering and that is pretty much how I got money for my food, but I didn't make enough for money in the pocket, so one night I committed a burglary somewhere downtown and stole some appliances. Next day I sold them on the street. Thus I began breaking into radio and tv stores. Burglary became the way I supported my eating habit, and my drinking as well. But when I was doing these burglaries, it was not as part of the gang. It was part of individual survival.

Around that time, I met a kid named Spivey. His last name was Spivey. I never called him by his first name; in fact, I don't remember ever hearing his first name. I don't even know if Spivey was his real name, but that's what he told us kids. Spivey had a fairly good build and was about my height. Usually I didn't hang out with people too much taller than me. I didn't know much about his background. We just used to meet in the street. I don't think I ever even went to his house. We used to party together, be with girls together. We did a lot of things together, but he wasn't so much a real friend as a guy you'd hang out with to do mischief with.

Spivey became one of my crime partners. After a while it got to where I would go in these big appliance stores and pick out particular items because I would already have customers lined up for the merchandise. So when Spivey and I went to do the burglaries we stole specifically for our customers we had waiting. These customers were not gang members, they were neighbors, just people who needed a tv. Once we found out what they needed, we would go steal it to sell to them. The burglaries made me more popular with the gang because I always showed up with money.

***

Finally the child authorities tried sending me to Gino's on an arranged visit, with the idea of making it an official and permanent arrangement. So for a time I went back to staying at Gino's house again with Peggy and their son, Junior. It turned out my older sister Marie was also staying there. By that time she had been out of the orphanage for a while.

It was a small apartment. Marie was very friendly, but she was into alcohol. She had been drinking a long time, before I even knew about it, and so much so that the relationship was very shaky and difficult between Gino, his lady Peggy, and my sister Marie, so I didn't last too long there.

Later I heard Marie had gotten her own place in Brooklyn. Around Christmas I went to visit her there one evening. She fixed us both some eggnog with Bacardi in it. We had a pretty good time.

Not too long after that, Sonya came around the streets looking for me. At that time I wasn't living with anybody.

"Where the hell have you been?" she said.

"Happy New Year to you too," I said.

"Ronnie, Marie died," she said.

"What?" I had seen her so recently.

"She died from cirrhosis of the liver," said Sonya. Marie couldn't have been more than 23.

"She going to get buried?" I asked, but I didn't want to go to the funeral. I had never been to a funeral.

"She's already buried," said Sonya. "We couldn't find you."

***

One night when I was 16, me, Spivey, and some other dude committed a burglary. We had found some people who wanted tvs. I had checked out this radio and tv store around 50th and

Broadway in advance, going down there a couple of days earlier during store hours. We went down there around midnight. There was nobody on the streets. I was in shorts.

We started taking the grates off the windows. We didn't have the right tools; there was no finesse. All we knew was that we needed to get in there.

I was working on the grate when a policeman showed up at my side. Came up silently, no noise whatever. Spivey and the other kid had disappeared without saying anything. They were gone. Spivey and the other dude had seen the police officer and never said anything to me, just ran and left me there while I was trying to break in.

The officer shoved me. I fell and I hit my face on the sidewalk. As a cop car pulled up, the officer almost grabbed me but I took off. They came after me on foot and with the cop car.

When you're running from the cops, you're trying to zig-zag out of sight. We had no plan for escape because we never got caught before. I guess we thought we never would.

As I was running, the 47th Street train station popped up into view.

I ran down the stairs and jumped the turnstyle. A shout, and then a big Port Authority guy who takes money for the tokens grabbed me. It just so happened that Spivey had just been arrested at the same turnstyle. The big transit cop called on his walkie talkie, and the police who had been at the store showed up at the train station.

"So you like to run, huh? So you like to steal stuff?"

I was cuffed and stuffed into the patrol car.

I considered Spivey and the other dude rats because they did not say anything when they saw these police coming. They just left me there. And when the police questioned Spivey, he told them, yeah, that I was one of the ones in the burglary attempt. So that made him a rat twice, as far as I was concerned.

In a sense I had no qualms about being arrested and going to jail. I was an institutional kid, so it was like going home. I had no real fear. The cops were running their mouths to me about various things. To me, that's all they were doing, running their mouths. I had an attitude, so I said a few things I shouldn't have said to the cops and got my ass kicked for it. But I knew that no matter what they said, I had to go to jail, so I focused on going to jail and what I would have to do to survive. I didn't pay any attention to the cops because no matter what they said, I figured nothing changes. Inevitably I would to go back to an institution of some sort.

Prepared as I was, it still felt like degradation. You get arrested, they slap you around, they handcuff you, they fingerprint you, they strip you naked. Yet even though this was my first time to be arrested, in a sense I'd been there before.

All three of us boys ended up in the same joint together. Spivey didn't like that. I got him behind a mat in the gym and beat him up. After that I left him alone. We stayed away from each other.

The legal aid worker assigned to my case was young, white, and already very well versed in the bureaucratic style. He would have fit in well with the orphanage clock-punchers. Orphanage social worker, cop on the beat, legal aid lawyer, six of one, half dozen of the other. Authority, period. Whatever "the suit" said, that was bible, that was gospel. Nothing I said at any stage was going to change anything anyway. The legal system works like this: they give you a legal aid, he pleads you guilty, and you go to jail. No real dramatics. Spivey went to prison too, but I don't know which prison. I never saw him again.

CHAPTER 6

Coxsackie

When I got arrested for burglary the first time in 1961, at age sixteen, they sent me to the Coxsackie Correctional Facility, in West Coxsackie, New York, a youthful offender prison that opened for business in 1935. The only difference between Coxsackie and an adult prison was the word "youthful," not the actual prisons. They were both the same. You weren't treated any different as a youthful offender than you were treated when you were an adult.

Coxsackie looked to me like a fort, the way forts were made in the 1600s. As I approached the gates I felt a mixture of fear, and, I hate to say this, gratefulness, because there were three meals and a cot. So in that sense I looked forward to jail.

At Coxsackie, because I was on record as an epileptic, they put me in a ward instead of a cell. In the ward they had about 30 metal-frame beds for boys with medical problems or who were sick. It might have been part of the hospital, but I'm not sure.

Some of the people in Coxsackie I knew from the streets. To that extent, being in there was not much different than the orphanage and the training schools. Now the institution itself was a different story altogether.

My first real experiences with prejudice happened at Coxsackie. In the yard you were more apt to deal with prejudice than you were at any other time because the yard was separated into different blocks. You weren't allowed by the inmate factions to walk in certain areas of the yard because the inmates themselves kept it very segregated. The blacks were here in one corner, the Latinos there in another, the whites over there and so on, with the punks in the middle. The punks were not necessarily gay. They were the new guys or the guys who wouldn't join or the guys who were soft.

You were not allowed to cross these boundaries. If you just so much as stepped on somebody's line, you were apt to be beaten. It was pretty tense. There were fights, always somebody throwing a hassle. When I first went into Coxsackie I even walked the middle for a little while because I didn't believe in segregation. But as a means to survive, once again I decided I'd better join a group.

That's when the problem arose. I'm a Puerto Rican with a black background. If I tried hanging out in the black area, I had problems. They considered me Puerto Rican. When I went to the Puerto Rican area, I couldn't speak Spanish. It was kind of difficult. I was alienated. All the prejudices of outside culture were in there but it was more concentrated, more dangerous in the prison setting. But, as it turned out, I didn't stay at Coxsackie long enough to get involved in it.

The doctors started putting me back on Phenobarbital, Dilantin and Librium. They gave me so much medication that I was almost constantly in bed sleeping. I ate and I slept. The guards would assign me to clean a bathroom. I would do that and go directly back to bed. Nine times out of ten I wouldn't even eat.

They kept me so drugged up for epilepsy I wouldn't talk to anybody. Consequently a lot of the other inmates started thinking I was antisocial. They didn't understand I was drugged. They didn't realize that the medication had me so out of it that all I could do was sleep.

One day we got a new correctional officer, or C.O., on the ward, a young guy. Of course, the first time he came in the dorm he didn't know who was who, nor anybody's record or background. He started listening to the other inmates who thought I was being antisocial to them. They began instigating him against me. One night he came to my bed and shook me awake.

"Get up, Casanova. You have to measure the beds."

"What?" I asked. "The bed? Do what?" I was in no shape to deal with him. I could barely get my eyes open. I couldn't understand what he was getting at. He handed me a measuring stick

"Measure how far apart these beds are."

I didn't get it, but I began trying to hold the stick between the beds to measure the distances. Some of the other inmates were awake now. The instigators were snickering.

"Over here, Casanova!" the C.O. said. "You missed these beds!"

I trudged over and measured the space between those beds.

"How far between beds?" he asked. "This is important!"

I couldn't remember.

"Then damn it, you'd better start over!"

"To hell with that," I said, more awake now. I threw down the yardstick. "I ain't doing nothing."

He slapped me, I slapped him. He slapped me again, so I hit him with a chair. The C.O. cried out and before I realized it, the Goon Squad rushed in. They beat me up and threw me in a cell.

The cell was very small and dark. It had a mesh-fenced window and the same kind of window in the door. I didn't have anything but a mattress on the floor, a pot for my bowel movements and something to eat. I don't know how long I was in the cell. At least a couple of weeks.

The same officer who had me measuring the beds would come by my cell with his buddy, taunting me each night.

"Hey Nigger," he would say through the little window. "You spic. Your mother's a whore."

He kept calling me "nigger" and "spade" and "faggot" night after night. He just kept doing it and doing it and doing it and doing it, to the point where one night I couldn't handle it any more. I invited him in.

"Come on inside," I said. "Come on, man. Come into my room. Come on in."

He unlocked the door.

"Get your white ass in here!" I said. He came in, I took my pot and hit him with my bowel movements.

They beat me to a pulp then. I was bruised all over, except my head, and I remember them pouring this stinging, burning medicine into my open wounds. Then they took me to a different cell, and put me in there and tied me in a straitsheet bed. That is a metal-frame bed that has the same kind of material used for the straitjacket. I was bound to the bed with this straitsheet from thigh to head.

Here it gets hazy in my memory. I believe they put headphones on my ears, although I may have imagined that part. At that time I was on the verge of insanity. I was 16 and really really really close to quitting because everything was piling up, and I didn't see any way out of it. There is no question that it was their treatment of me that pushed me to the edge. Whether through headphones or not, I distinctly remember being tied in this bed and hearing the same repeated insults as when I was in the other cell.

"Ah you fucking nigger! Hey nigger, you stink! Hey faggot! You motherless bastard!" It seemed like it was right in my ears, in my head. On and on and on. I was inches away from being insane. I did a picture about this called "The Brainwashing," but I didn't paint that until years later. There wasn't any time for art in Coxsackie.

After they tied me in the bed, I was left that way for over a week. Naturally, I shit and pissed in the bed. After I had been that way a couple of days, a white, middle-aged doctor, a psychiatrist, I believe, came in the cell and sat down and talked to me with a patronizing attitude while I was lying tied in the bed stinking of my own waste.

Finally I realized this wasn't going to work. I had to devise a plan for getting out of there while I still had some shred of sanity. Even a week in a straitjacket or a straitsheet can drive you crazy. The pain from the straitsheet was getting to be a little bit more than I could handle. If I didn't get out of it soon, I would blow it, I knew I would crack.

Originally I had been put in the straitsheet for fighting with the C.O. Asking them to take me out of it wasn't working, so at the time I thought that the only way I could get out of the straitsheet was to act insane so they could let up and start doing things a lot differently.

In the cell there were a lot of fuzz balls under the bed. When the doctor came in, I nodded at the dust ball.

"Hey, look at that monkey. Look at that horse!" I said, thinking they would put me in a hospital, like at Warwick, where

I'd get treated well. I didn't know of any mental institutions at the time. The truth didn't dawn on me until later.

Before the doctor came the next time, the C.O.s took me out and put me in the shower, but then it was back into the straitsheet for my session with the shrink. While I was doing my fuzz ball thing with this doctor again, the officer I had hit with my bowel movements came by.

"So you're headed for Matteawan," he said. "You think you're going to get away by going there. Well, nice knowing you." He didn't say it in a loving attitude.

Later, one of the trustees who was cleaning the hall looked in on me. "You think you're getting a sweet deal," he said to me as I was lying there. "Matteawan's where they kill people."

I began to fear this transfer. I had figured a hospital meant comfort. This was a mistake. I have done a painting of my frame of mind when I realized what I was getting myself into. All you see is the back of me in my shirt and you see the big word "Mattawan" (sic) dripping blood through a light and dark blue haze.

A few days later they cleaned me up, dressed me, put me in shackles and handcuffs, and hustled me into a station wagon. Then they drove me to Matteawan State Hospital in Dutchess County, Beacon, New York.

CHAPTER 7

Matteawan

They called it Matteawan State Hospital for the criminally insane, so it was supposed to be a place for people who have mental problems and they're supposed to be working on the so-called mental problems. That wasn't what was happening at Matteawan.

It was a storage bin.

In addition to people who were truly insane, people who were not in favor with society were also stored in Matteawan State Hospital. Also some people went there to beat their crimes, you know; they pled insanity.

Just walking in the door meant you got beat up. That was the usual initiation to the institution. As they were walking me in, the C.O. kept telling me to hold my head up. Of course, they had me doped up on anti-seizure medication, so I couldn't hold my head up. They decided I wasn't cooperating, so they took me in the door to the admitting area and beat on me with their fists and kicked me. My body still had bruises and sores from my beating at Coxsackie and under this new beating my skin tore open in some places. They would not mess with your face too much so you wouldn't look bad for any visitors.

Following the beating they stuck me in a shower of scalding water. They used the hottest water possible to clean me, but what they were doing was working on the bruises I already had from their beating. They poured alcohol or some burning medicine into my open wounds. And all the time I was cursing them and screaming. Probably I did sound insane, but who wouldn't under those conditions?

They took me to Ward 5. The ward was long, with over a hundred beds in it. Ward 5 was the transition ward, a place where they observed you and figured out what ward you really belonged in. Although by that point I myself wasn't completely sane, many of my fellow inmates were very sick, were in much worse shape than I was. Some of them didn't even realize where they were.

One Flew Over the Cuckoo's Nest was a good story, but it wasn't factual, it wasn't complete. It didn't show the brainwashing the way it was. If you were to compare *One Flew Over the Cuckoo's Nest* with my two years and ten months at Matteawan State Hospital, you would see a completely different picture. I enjoyed seeing the movie, but as I sat there watching it, I was thinking "you are not telling it all." If you want to make a true movie about a place like that, don't wash it, don't clean it. The movies I've seen don't show the extent of the brutality and the mental brainwashing that goes on in these institutions. Geraldo Rivera had a good idea in making a documentary. He went into the institutions themselves and explained it more than the movies. But even he was given a cleaned-up version because though he may have surprised them, he is a public figure, and as long as he was in the building they were on good behavior.

At Matteawan you got all your food in the same bowl, so if the menu was, say, bread, beans, beets and coffee, it all went into your one bowl. One inmate, a young brother, used to sit in the corner every day. He would have a bowel movement and then eat his own crap. The C.O.s didn't even pay any attention to him. That was the atmosphere I was living in.

What they called the "Rec Room" was a big open day room where inmates were left. It had chairs and books and magazines and a tv. Off this room there was a room where they kept all the shoes and coats. Some of the inmates there could take advantage of the facility, but for a lot of them, recreation meant standing in one place for hours, or sitting and staring at nothing, or making sounds and rocking back and forth.

Several times late at night there were sexual rapes of inmates in the dormitory. To my knowledge, these went unreported. I saw a man in a straitjacket jump at the big plate-glass window in the recreation room. His head broke through the glass and his weight forced a shard up through his throat, and he bled to death. Sometime later I saw another inmate kill himself this way.

The C.O.s at Matteawan were sadistic. In one instance I witnessed the officers take a patient and wrap towels around his neck. Then they proceeded to drag him down the long ward until he was dead.

Another time an inmate had some kind of difficulties with an officer, so they decided he was going to get shock treatments. Now with shock treatments you are not supposed to eat anything beforehand. Yet first they took this man to breakfast and made him eat a couple of bowls of cereal. Shoved coffee down his throat. So the dude refused to go to get the shock treatment. They took him to the office and stood on his neck until they killed him.

They wanted me to carry his body upstairs to the hospital where the morgue was. What the hell, I refused. I was 16 and afraid of the dead. I didn't feel like carrying a dead body. Because of my refusal, they started beating me again. I ended up fighting them, but it was a losing cause. They hauled me to a cell and put me in a straitsheet.

All this time the doctors were reporting these deaths as heart failures. The families, being upset and naive, never thought to check to find out exactly what happened.

Eventually they let me out of the straitsheet, and I was assigned to Ward M, which was the ward where they put residents who did not need severe watching. A Mr. Charis was the head C.O. in charge of Ward M. He was a white man in his middle 40s with dark hair and a stocky build who looked like a police officer. He looked like one of the mean dudes, but surprisingly, he turned out to be a good guy. I can't say the same about the other C.O.s.

In the beginning of my stay in Ward M, I didn't have any assigned job, so I did a lot of hanging around, watching tv in the recreation room and reading. *The Tropic of Cancer* by Henry Miller was going around the dormitory, people reading it, and one day it was my turn to read the dog-eared old paperback. At one time it had been banned in the United States for its sexual content, and it contained very explicit sex.

One day an officer saw me reading *The Tropic of Cancer*. He snatched the book and slapped me. I was hot. Like a fool I challenged him to a fight.

"Come into the shoe room," I told him. "Me and you. Let's get this over with."

We went in one door of the shoe room. About four or five other C.O.s came in the other door. They beat me and threw me in a straitjacket and sat me in a chair in the rec room.

A straitjacket puts you in one constant position. They pull it as tight as possible, so that it hurts your shoulders and the muscles of your arms. There's no movement. When you start feeling a cramp, you can't do anything to stop it. I don't think you could find another pain to top that, other than an excruciating toothache.

I had been in the jacket for a few days and began to be afraid. Were they ever going to let me out of it? By that time I wanted out of that jacket no matter what. Now I understood why those men in straitjackets had jumped through the windows.

However, I had no intentions of killing myself, but I did have intentions of getting out of that straitjacket. So when I jumped through the window I twisted my body to where I didn't come down on the glass. I only nicked my throat. I lucked out. Someone must have been watching over me.

This move convinced them to take me out of the straitjacket. They took me to another room and removed the straitjacket, but from there they walked me down a corridor of cells and put me in a solitary confinement cell. From one extreme to another. But even that was preferable to the pain of the straitjacket.

Years after I got out of Matteawan, I saw an article in the *Daily News* with a photograph that showed a cell in Matteawan State Hospital. It showed a bed with a spread and lamp and chairs. This infuriated me because in there was no such thing as a cell like that. We didn't have anything in our cells except a torn mattress on the floor and a pot for the bathroom.

After a long while in solitary confinement, things got a bit confusing for me. But one day Mr. Charis's head appeared at my cell door, which was a big metal door with a little window in it.

"You'll be all right," he said. "Rest up. Be calm."

For some reason or another, Mr. Charis of Ward M had taken a liking to me. Yeah, I'll remember Mr. Charis very well. He pretty much helped me keep reality about me and hold on to my sanity. Periodically he would just come by and do that for me. He would come by and help me get over the humps.

The institution's use of epilepsy drugs on me intensified. They continued feeding me anti-seizure pills to the point where I couldn't walk and I wasn't eating. They were over-medicating me. They finally realized that I was getting weaker and weaker and that I wasn't going to eat any food. I couldn't even sit up.

It was decided I should be transferred up to the medical ward. They put me in a wheelchair and strapped me in. I kept nodding over against the restraints. I was trying to sit up, but because of my weakness and the overdose of epilepsy drugs, I kept slipping down. One officer took it upon himself to make me sit up straight.

"Keep your head up!" he warned me.

He punched me in my stomach and my head popped up. I used all my willpower trying to keep my head up, but my body would not allow it. My head sagged down again.

Boom! The officer punched me in the stomach again. My head went up.

"Keep it up!"

That's the way it went. He'd punch me in my stomach and my head would stay up for a moment and then roll down again. So he'd sock me in the gut again. Up and down, up and down all the way to the hospital ward. Once in the hospital, I stayed pretty much unconscious for a long time. I guess they finally backed off the dosage on the medication.

When I got out of the hospital and back to my cell, Mr. Charis read to me and talked to me. We talked together, so he pretty much knew where I was coming from.

Mr. Charis began talking to people about getting me back on the ward. He told them I just needed to be left alone. Eventually he got me a job and I was able to keep my head above water; otherwise I would probably have been there until they closed down Matteawan. Mr. Charis got it arranged so I could work on his ward and work on the recreational area. My job was to clean the porch and empty the butt cans.

During that period I hung out with another patient, I can't remember his name today, but he was a young Spanish brother, a Puerto Rican dude, my best friend at the time. I remember him as about my height, same build. I don't think he was mentally impaired. I think he was another kid who had been caught up in a bad social environment and was there because he did things to survive that society thought were unusual, and so they call it insanity or stupid or crazy. He knew I wasn't insane. Mr. Charis knew it, too. Actually I suspect most of the staff knew that, only they didn't consider that their concern. They couldn't care less if we were crazy or not. We were treated as if we were, regardless. We were there and that's all that mattered.

The only visit I got while I was there came more or less by accident. My sister Norma had a friend who had a brother in Matteawan. It just so happened that her friend's brother was my Puerto Rican friend.

One time Norma came along with her friend, and in the visiting room, her friend introduced my sister to the brother as Norma Casanova.

"Say, my best friend's a dude named Casanova!" he said.

Voilà! Norma realized that her brother was here in this mental prison. She had them call me, and I sat down with her and had a visit. Maybe she always knew I was there. It's hard to say because, as you know, my family wasn't much on visiting relatives in institutions.

I was at Matteawan two years and ten months. For my original crime I had a three-year sentence, so when they decided I was sane enough to leave there, they had to send me back to Coxsackie for the rest of my time. I was sane enough for prison; I was one of the fortunate ones.

In 1964, when I was getting ready to come out of Matteawan, I remember a guy that was in his 60s or 70s who was also getting ready to come out, only he was going directly back into society. I never met the dude before the day it was time for him to leave. They were getting ready to release him, and we ended up being on the same ward for processing us out.

The old guy had been put into Matteawan in his early teens. "Horse and buggy times," he said.

He was watching tv, now, as we waited. From the tv he saw that we had miniskirts and big fast cars.

"I've never been out there with all that kind of stuff," he said to me. "I don't know how I'm going to make it."

I was going to say they wouldn't let him go if they knew he was crazy, but this isn't true: they do this too. At any rate, he was sane enough to realize the fact that if he went out there he was liable to get killed by a car. He was in dreadful fear of going out. All he had known for 50 years was the institutional way of life. To be catapulted into society terrified him. He had gone into Matteawan when there were still horses and buggies, and now there was mass transit. He had outlived everybody in his family. So there was nobody to go to. How was he going to take care of himself after 50 years? So I was one of the fortunate ones.

Coxsackie was a very prejudiced place. Not only were there guards against the inmates, but also the inmates against each other. You lived under that pressure all the time. But I was lucky to one extent because I had just left a crazy house. When I came back to Coxsackie from the Matteawan State Hospital for the criminally insane, I walked anywhere I wanted to. Matteawan had a reputation, so those last two months of my sentence were pretty easy for me.

CHAPTER 8
Playing in the Village

When I got out of prison in 1964, I was fucked up. At the time I had a lot of prejudice in me from being in Matteawan. I became prejudiced against white folks because the officers who were killing people in Matteawan were all white. They had the controls, they were the dominating people in there.

I was so adamant in my hatred towards white folks when I got out of that place that one day I took a bike chain in my hand and went to Broadway. After walking a while I noticed a white dude walking down the street by himself. Suddenly I knew what I was going to do. I went over and hit him with the chain, and then ran off and hit somebody else. I ran up and down Broadway and actually beat people with that chain—not even stealing, just striking out. I misdirected my anger in this way three or four different times along the stretch from 96th and Broadway to 125th Street, injuring about four people each outing. This did succeed in getting rid of some of my anger, though I have always regretted my striking out.

Getting a job after coming out of prison is no easy matter. They say you shouldn't lie when you fill out a job application. That's ridiculous. Why should you tell the employers stuff you know will keep you from working, that will get you cut off? That was one of the first lessons I learned out of prison because no one would hire me.

Once again I had to live outside an institution, so I went back to doing burglaries. I didn't steal because I liked it; I stole because coming out of prison I had no money and no job, and I needed something to eat. I stole out of desperation.

I ended up living for a while in an apartment just off Broadway on 104th Street and Manhattan Avenue with a couple of dudes I knew. Every now and then I would still have seizures, but in the meantime I kept taking medicine for the seizures that my parole officer helped me get.

After three years away, I had lost track of my brothers and sisters, most of whom had moved once or twice during that time. Eventually I found them by just asking around. People in the streets knew more about my family than I did. Fortunately, it turned out that my brother Philip was living not that far away, on 106th between Manhattan Avenue and Central Park. Philip turned out to be the hard worker among my brothers. He was always the one who had a job. Me, Richard and Gino were always questionable as far as labor or work was concerned. Philip was the go-getter and hustler of the Casanova men, the legal worker maintaining a family with a job.

Philip was working as a shoemaker. He had started out shining shoes and now he got me into bootblacking. I liked bootblacking. I got money and I didn't feel I had to steal any longer. I didn't have that pressure.

Then word got around the neighborhood that they were taking applications for employment at the World's Fair, which was in Flushing Meadow Park in 1964. I went over with two or three other guys to fill out the application. Of course, this time I didn't put down on my application that I had just gotten out of Matteawan Facility for the Criminally Insane. Hell, no.

As it happened, they hired me to work in the French Pavilion of the World's Fair. I worked from nine in the morning to nine in the evening. My job was to dress nicely in a shirt and tie, wear a black French beret, and make sandwiches—heroes and hot meatball sandwiches. Chefs cooked the fancier meals, but I was the sandwich monsieur. I also waited tables and cleaned up. A Jacques of all trades.

Even though I was 19 years old and had done time, in many ways I was very naive. I was a kid still. Because I had spent so much time simply surviving, I didn't have a full understanding of all that was going on in the world. I never even knew Kennedy was president until he got killed and I saw it on the tv in Matteawan's rec room. So the job at the World's Fair was great for me. It was a good job and paid good money. I liked wearing nice clothes. But one of the best things about it was that I got to meet people. I met a lot of different kinds of people everyday.

There was conversation, there was prestige, there were women.

After work I liked visiting the Spanish Pavilion and I especially liked going to the Caribbean Pavilion. Joe Cuba used to play there, and I went just about every night. Cuba sang one song in particular that I liked, called "I Wish You Love." Originally it was done by Gloria Lynn, but at the Caribbean Pavilion they did it with a Latin beat.

They got to know me at that pavilion after a while, and any time I came in there with a date or a friend, Cuba would say, "We're going to play this next song for Casanova and his friends," and then you would hear "I Wish You Love" start up.

I really enjoyed working at the World's Fair. Things seemed to be going well. Back in Harlem I was paying my own rent by myself, and I was going with a young lady named Brenda, who lived on 105th Street. I worked there every day I could, all the time. Then they closed the pavilion and that was that. Being young, I had not had the foresight to save a thing. I had used every cent I earned.

Around that time, in 1965, I started coming down to Greenwich Village. In Harlem, the Village had a reputation even in those days. People said it was about beatniks, that kind of atmosphere, with a lot of women, a lot of women and a lot of women. So I went to check it out. Imagine a 20 year-old who has scarcely been out of either Harlem or rigid institutions where the people themselves helped keep each other segregated, who goes to the West Side, to Washington Square, and sees a clean, fresh-air park where friendly people of all colors are sitting around socializing, communicating in a very open and trusting way. My eyes and my mind began to open. It was a variety of cultures, and that's what made it interesting to me. I lived a little bit more whenever I came to Washington Square Park.

Then my drinking got me into trouble. One night in an alcoholic haze of jealousy I beat my girlfriend Brenda badly. I don't even remember what or who I was jealous about. That night I didn't feel any sorrow for what I had done, only jealousy, insecurity. Alcohol was just a fuel to these emotions. I know that now, but I didn't know it then.

Next day Brenda's face got all swollen. By that time I had sobered up, and I didn't like what I had done, but neither did I want any repercussions from Brenda's family, her brothers, so I stopped living in Harlem. I just split. I had already visited the Village enough to know where I was going to sleep. There was a place over a bowling alley where I had seen homeless teenagers sleeping. From there I soon switched to living underneath the stairs in one of the buildings near Washington Square Park.

When I left Harlem, I left a whole lot of stuff there, including the epileptic seizures. Up there in Harlem it was a different world. It was more about raw survival in Harlem than it was in the Lower East Side. All the robbery and gangs and violence I had experienced in Harlem didn't happen downtown at that time. Sleeping in a hallway was much easier and safer in the Washington Square neighborhood.

As you entered Washington Square Park from 5th Avenue, there stood a statue of George Washington and a stone arch. I heard the park had been used as a training ground for Union troops during the Civil War. But now was the good era, the love era. The Village smelled of incense in those days, it smelled carefree and happy. It was nothing to see a group of people dancing and singing for the entertainment, period. The neighborhood bars played softball against each other, and the neighboring restaurants used to cook up extra food, and people from the restaurants would bring out gigantic pots of soup or stews with fresh-baked bread and they would feed the people in the park like a big community picnic. It was just the thing to do on nice sunny days.

It seemed everybody was coming to Washington Square Park. People from all over the world and all colors came to this community of free-feeling people, where a person could come and not be inhibited. That's what attracted people to it; that was the object. You could go down there and throw your shoes off if you wanted. Relax, be yourself.

I remember I had started wearing a Cuban straw hat with my processed hair. One afternoon, a skinny, dark-skinned brother I had recently met, who went by the name Wigfall, came up to me.

"Let me see that hat," he said.

He took the Cuban hat off my head and put his fist through it.

"You ain't gonna be needing that no more down here. Or that conk."

"Okay," I said. "Cool."

I knew he wasn't doing it to be derogatory; that's just the way it was in the square. Down there, you just let everything grow natural. That's what Wigfall was telling me. So I went along with it. I left my conk behind in Harlem with everything else. I let my hair grow natural and found I liked it.

You could be yourself in the Village and yet be amongst people of varying nationalities. There had been white people at Central Park, but I never really had any dealings with them. At the World's Fair I had started experiencing white people, but in Washington Square Park I was living with them, and it was cool. The Village was a way of life I had never envisioned before. After that I didn't like to go anywhere with only one color of people. That's when the Village was the Village. People enjoying life, a time of sharing good vibrations with each other. My growing as a caring person didn't really begin until I hit the Village.

I even went back to Harlem and saw Brenda. She had a new boyfriend and they were engaged to get married. Brenda seemed happy to see me, though. I said hello and apologized, but it was done, nothing I could do to change it.

Wigfall became one of my best friends for a while. He showed me where the shelters were and introduced me to the women he knew. Until that time I had never experienced drugs other than what the doctors gave me for my seizures. I believe Wigfall was the one who introduced me to marijuana. We used to get stoned together. I was part of the scene.

My enjoyment of music started with my experiences when I first moved to the Village. Down there, there were a lot of jazz joints and clubs. Everybody down there knew Bob Dylan from when he still used to sing in the park like a lot of the rest of us. Everybody used to sing in the park. The huge circle fountain had steps around it, and in the fountain in the summer there were always kids taking baths or swimming or playing under the jet of water as it shot high up into the blue sky. Around the fountain there were always different types of music. If you walked toward one part of the circle, you'd hear a banjo playing. Walk to another part, there'd be congas, or somebody else banging on drums, or somebody else strumming a guitar.

I found I loved the sound of an alto flute and taught myself how to play. I never took classes; I just started blowing the flute. I used to sit and play flute in the park whenever I could. Other people would play congas—not for tips or anything, just playing for the playing.

One time somebody had been playing a flute for a while, and needed to take a break.

"Let me try your flute," I asked him, and he handed it to me.

I began playing, and apparently one man in the crowd saw me and liked what he heard because about a week later this dude came up and handed me a heavy flute made of cast-iron.

"Here," he said. "I made this for you."

"How come?" I asked.

"Because I like the way you play."

That was the kind of atmosphere that existed in the park then. On one of those many days when we were in the park, probably a Saturday or a Sunday because I remember tourists were all around us, I stood among the people listening to some musicians play. I had my flute in my shoulder pouch, and a peacock feather sticking out of the flute.

"Look at that crazy dude," I heard a guy behind me say. I didn't think too much about it.

"Baby, look at that fool with a damn peacock feather coming out of his flute."

I had to turn around. I saw this dude with his lady. His face was lit up.

"Ronnie!" he said. I knew him then.

"Gino!" We laughed as we greeted each other with a hug and pats on the back. I was already living in the Village before Gino moved in, but he'd been going down there longer than me. I hadn't seen him since I went into Coxsackie. I learned that after years together, Gino and Peggy had finally broken up. But he still saw her and the kids now and then, and Gino was painting a lot of pictures now, and he would sell them or give them away in the park.

They had employment agencies in that area, and through them around 1966 I went to work at a Jewish retirement home in New Jersey called Mount Freedom. It was a retirement resort for Jewish people. Their kids couldn't keep them at home anymore, so they put them in the resort. These retirement homes were called resorts because everything you needed for a resort was right there: it was on the beach, there were handball courts and tennis courts. It was very nice. The resort job was pretty good although it didn't pay too much. My first job was dishwasher. I worked there for about six months the first time.

I met a nurse in Washington Square named Miriam and we started living together on Ludlow Street. At the time I was doing a little bit of work at a steel factory. Manpower Temporary Services had sent me there to help move steel pipes. Around the time Miriam became pregnant with our child, we moved to Ludlow Street.

Miriam and I liked going down to this bar on 110th and 8th Avenue. One night when we had been partying there, we came out of the bar and were getting ready to hail a cab when we saw a bunch of dogs running loose. One of the dogs was a tan Great Dane. Miriam flagged a cab, I snatched the Great Dane and we put it into the taxi with us and took him home. He was a cool dog. We named him "Duke" after John Wayne.

We also used to go to a place called the Kettle of Fish, on MacDougal Street. MacDougal was the nightclub street. You couldn't go anywhere in those blocks without running into another nightclub. Mostly jazz, although there was also folk music. I don't think rock and roll was ever very big down there in those days.

I had never been to the Kettle of Fish until Miriam took me there. It was an all-out friendly place. It was always a full house down there, and I didn't get the paranoia of the bar scene the way I would in Harlem.

They had the bar up front where I think they served food, although I never went there to eat. You walked through to the back area, which opened up more spaciously, with a place for the band, a piano, tables and chairs. That's where we saw Bob Dylan playing one night. We didn't go in specifically to see him. At that time, Dylan's commercial career had started taking off. He used to be a regular hippie from the Village, just a person that used to play down in the parks, and then he started playing the clubs. Apparently he had something to say. I didn't hear it at the time. I was more in awe of the whole Village scene than caring what Dylan specifically sang about.

I liked Bob Dylan, but I'm a jazz freak. I love jazz, although I never really paid attention to it before I started going to Washington Square and hearing the bands playing by the fountain. I like to use my own imagination, and with jazz, as long as nobody's singing, if they're just playing the instruments, you can use your own imagination. I love Dave Brubeck, Lionel Hampton, Dizzie Gillespie. I like my jazz from the middle 1940s. Back then I found I could listen to Lionel Hampton on the vibes, and he wouldn't be singing, but his feelings were in there. With him you feel your own rhythm.

One day around five p.m. I went into the Five Spots club over on 2nd Avenue and St. Marks. I liked the Five Spots and used to go there a lot. It was a jazz nightclub, but you could hear jazz there in the daytime as well. That afternoon when I went in, Thelonius Monk was playing the piano. I ordered a drink and sat listening to him play, enjoying his music. In the middle of a piece he stopped playing and went into a nod. About a minute or so later he came out of it and continued playing the piano as if he had never stopped, picked up the song right where he left off. He was high. Apparently he had done some heroin.

Through Gino I became reacquainted with my brothers, and we would hang out together. We would always drink, mostly Bacardi dark rum. Understand that we had never really been together before, and yet we were trying to be brothers. I don't know where they picked it up, but at some point my brothers Gino, Richard and Philip started calling themselves Gino, Mino and Dino. Richard was "Mino" and Philip was "Dino." That was their so-called hip name which we had fun with.

Unfortunately, it seemed like every time we got together there was a fight. There existed at that time a feud between Philip and Richard. And they were always fighting with each other. I don't even really remember what these fights were about. It may have been because Philip was the hard worker of the group and Richie was more like me, a rolling stone. And there was often fighting between Richard and Gino. I guess part of that was machismo, but alcohol played a very prominent part in it. The fights would begin as my brothers would start at each other with snide remarks. That was my signal. As always, anytime I sensed an argument coming, I was gone. I didn't need that.

When it came time and Miriam began having labor contractions, let's put it this way: I panicked. I raced us to the hospital and it turned out to be a false alarm. We got there and Miriam wasn't ready, so we had to go back home.

I panicked the second time, too. We got in the cab and I had that guy speeding. The police didn't stop us, but the patrol car pulled alongside the cab.

"Got a woman here ready to have a baby," the cabby shouted to the police.

"We've got to get her to a hospital!" I shouted to them.

The police turned on their siren and led the way. We made it, and this time Miriam gave birth to a baby girl we named Yolanda.

Gradually we started coming over to the East Side. We began hanging out in Tompkins Square Park. Even that park was very nice in the '60s. We would go there on a regular basis.

The next season I went back to Mount Freedom and moved up to busboy. At various times I worked there as a cook, elevator operator and chamberman, depending on what they needed and if I could get it. I finally worked my way up to chamberman, which I liked the most because I got to go into the rooms and meet the people. I got to be a favorite to many of the residents. They gave me bigger tips when I was a chamberman than I got working any other position. They would also give me clothes. Once I was even given a color tv.

When I'd get off work, residents or guests would invite me to come to the courts to play handball or they would invite me to swim with the guests. Once I had Miriam and Yolanda come out, and we went to the beach there. I was doing a lot of alcohol at the time, but never at work.

Unfortunately, I rarely gave Miriam anything but a hard time. Alcohol had taken precedence over my relationship with Miriam and Yolanda. I loved Miriam, but I would steal her money and go get drunk. Looking back, I realize that by the time she and I got involved together I was also too used to running the streets for our relationship to work.

After about two years of living together, Miriam and I broke up. I went back to the streets of the Village. Miriam took me to court and the judge said I had to give her some money, but we never followed through on that because although I was looking for work, I never really got a solid job. I was working Manpower and Johnny-on-the-spot jobs, mostly, loading and unloading trucks, or working at textile places, setting up the material for the women to use on the machines.

I ended up in the park with Duke, our Great Dane. For a while, people gave me money to feed him, but finally I couldn't afford to take care of him any longer. So I made a "for sale" sign I hung around Duke's neck and sat under the arch at the park with him. In the end I sold Duke for 20 dollars.

Around that time I met Mama Bang-bang, who had that name for obvious reasons. She was white, with blonde hair and one finger missing on her left hand. She was one of those girls who hung around bikers. One day she invited me up to her place to take a bath.

She was living on the third floor with about ten people in a five or six story brick building over on 3rd Street between Avenues B and C. There was a landlord, but nobody was taking care of the building. When I got there, my brother Richie was there and so we had a reunion. I ended up living there.

My relatives called me a black Puerto Rican hippie. I just considered myself a free thinker. Gino was the real hippie of the family. He had started calling himself "Hundu" because he was into the Indian thing. He leaned toward Indian philosophy, the

Asian-type Indian. In fact, he was an all-around Indian freak. He used to like Iroquois Indians, too. From somebody in our family he got some background and told me about our family.

"Our family, our real family," Hundu said, "came from the *Borinqueños*, the original Indians who lived in Puerto Rico."

My brother went on to explain that the Borinquins no longer existed as tribes, but the blood lived on in the mountain country people, the *jíbaros*. He told me that the Casanova family came to the U.S. in the early '40s from Puerto Rico as part of the immigration for the labor force the United States was building up in New York and other East Coast cities.

Hundu was the beads, he was the bellbottoms, he was the artist. With him around, I started my own drawing and painting again.

Occasionally I would go back to Miriam to say "hi," and to see Yolanda. Miriam and I still had feelings for each other, so sometimes I would end up spending the night. My second daughter Tonya was the happy result of one of those periodic visits.

One beautiful, misty afternoon, I went to Central Park with Miriam. I had dropped some acid, and as we walked I heard saxophone music. Miriam and I were sitting on a bench, and I thought I was watching Charles Mingus sitting on a hill practicing with his horn. To this day I don't know if it was really Charles Mingus, but the acid had me thinking it was.

***

The Blue Note club was around the corner from Washington Square, and I used to go by there when I was working at a club called the Electric Circus. Later, after I split up with Mama Bang-bang, I worked for a while as a bouncer at the Village Gate. They had too many doors there, so my job was to protect one door and not allow anybody to sneak in. But I made more money letting people in than keeping them out.

That's where the jazz was. It was a good jazz spot. I saw Miriam McKeever play there, and Herbie Mann. Mann became an inspiration for my own flute playing. When I had a break, I'd go to watch him and listen. That job ended the same way too many of my jobs ended—I'd get paid, go out drinking, and end up drunk. Then I wouldn't go back to work because of a hangover.

When I was working as a short-order cook at a place called the Cave, Hundu and a lot of people I knew frequented the place. There were five or six of us who were hanging out together on the Lower East Side. Well, my brothers and I had a reputation. Remember, I was "L.B."—Lover Boy. At that time I used to believe in the name Casanova. We had a lot of women in those wild days. In fact, I, myself, was dating three women at once and all of them knowing it. Then somebody came up with "The Casanovas" as a name for all of us guys who hung out together. It became our name, and it fit. For a time Richie and I wore our hair cut Mohican style, and we wore big black capes, like Dracula capes, with collars. I don't know why. We thought it looked good, I guess. The Mohawk twins.

We got to know the guy who owned the Cave, a tall black dude, and we got along with him and gave him a lot of business. Quite a few of the Casanovas ended up working at the Cave.

Hundu located a building on the Lower East Side where there was a vacant apartment on the top floor. The street dead-ended into an old school that was still in use. There were people paying rent and living at the address, but the place was falling into disrepair. We just moved in. First I stayed with Hundu and his ladies. Hundu was going now with another Italian woman. I think he was getting SSI (Supplemental Security Income) at that time. The Italian woman had a sister named Margie, and she and I became friends.

Hundu and I set about renovating the apartment. We found that the apartment next door was also vacant, so we broke down the wall between them to connect the two apartments. We put up a beaded curtain in our new doorway.

After looking around the building, Hundu and I discovered that there were a lot of empty apartments in that building. Margie and I moved into an empty apartment on the second floor along with two other families. Nobody ever said anything to us about just moving in. So Hundu and I got Richie and some of the other guys in the Casanova crew to move in. There were three buildings on that block that we went into. We started fixing them up.

We were hustlers, so we would go out and find the materials to fix the building, or find people who would give them to us. We rigged up some plumbing and we figured out how to hook up electricity. We'd get it from the next building and from the street lamp. It was mostly the hippies that did the electrical stuff. They had done this before. Nobody called them squatters at the time. They were just people living with us who knew how to do that stuff.

Alcoholism continued to play a destructive role in my life and the life of my family. It seemed like love was always there until alcohol made its presence felt. Throughout my life I remember fights that came only as a result of the bitterness they had against each other that didn't come out until they started drinking. I recall one time I brought my two daughters, Tonya, who was an infant, and Yolanda, who had just started walking, to my sister Norma's house. My brothers Gino, Richard, and Philip were also there and Norma and her kids. We were partying with Gino, Mino and Dino. Then, as was par for the course, my brothers got into a fight. I snatched my kids and ran. I didn't want them around any fighting.

One day the owner of the Cave came by the building we were working on. We were surprised to see him, and he was surprised to see us because it turned out he was the super for those buildings. We hadn't known that when we moved in.

He had come by out of curiosity because he had heard something was going down, and he wanted to see what was happening. When he saw that we were not only fixing the apartments, but also maintaining the building itself and keeping the garbage out, he decided he liked the idea of having us there. We struck a deal with him and so the Casanovas became managers of the buildings and didn't have to pay rent.

Not long after that, a big party was happening at our building. I had copped some LSD, taken it and started hallucinating. I walked out of the door of the apartment building and suddenly I was in a jungle; I was hearing jungle birds squawking, animals roaring, everything. I wasn't in the city any more. It was one of the most frightening experiences of my life. I didn't know where I was or how to get back.

Then my brother Richie was with me. I don't know how I ran into him, but I was glad to see him. I had become closer to him than anyone else in my family. I told him the story, and he saw what was happening—that I was very paranoid and uptight. He got me to smoke some reefer, but that wasn't working, it wasn't bringing me down.

"How do I come down?" I asked Richie.

"It'll be cool," he said. "I'll take care of you."

He took me into a hallway somewhere and set me up with some heroin. He put it in my veins and got me off.

That was how I was introduced to heroin. Though heroin would become a major difficulty in my life, that night I was grateful to Richie. He had come through for me. He brought me down from the acid, back from the African jungle to the concrete jungle.

I was so naive that I went to Miriam's to show her.

"Look," I said, "I just got off." I showed her my arm. I was proud that I had done my first bag of dope. I was very proud of myself. I thought I was cool. That's how naive I was.

"Get out," Miriam said. "You can't stay here any more."

"What do you mean? Why not?"

"Because you're very stupid," she said.

And she was right. Later the nausea and throwing up started. From one extreme to another.

The high you get from heroin, "the nod," is fantastic, I don't care what anybody says. But in the long run, shooting drugs is a very nauseating experience. First of all you had to cook your dope. You took a long bobby pin, bent it around a coke bottle cap, tight so you could hold the bobby pin and not have to worry about holding the bottle cap when it heated up. Then you took out the plastic from inside the cap. Next you put in your drugs and the amount of water you needed. At that time we weren't into lighters; everybody used matches. You opened up a book of cardboard matches and you'd strike it. First thing, those fumes from the match would get to your nose. After a while, that smell alone made me nauseated. After a while, match fumes got to be very disgusting. To this day I associate those match fumes with heroin. Every time I struck a match in those days I was cooking heroin. That's why I only use a lighter to light my cigarettes now.

Cooking dope made another fume, curling up into my nostrils as the concoction simmered, sulfur, a smell that made my stomach turn, and I'd feel like I was going to throw up as I cooked the heroin.

The needle bothered me. Sticking needles in your arm hurts. I didn't skin-pop or shoot just in my muscles. I went intravenously, I went for my blood veins, drawing blood, the whole procedure.

Then the drug was in me and I would begin vomiting. I was always throwing up a lot during the high.

It all bothered me. But then there was the nod. The escape. Your body relaxes. It puts you into oblivion—you're not part of the troubled world.

But even now as I tell about it, I get nauseated.

I look at it this way: once I became an active alcoholic and drug addict, I wanted to be an alcoholic and a drug addict, yet it was not simply a means of escape; it was a passive suicide. With me, at first, the substances were a means of mental survival, a way of coping with my world. At some point I saw myself caught up in poverty, but without knowing a way out of it, not thinking it was possible. I wasn't happy being a member of the human race. At the time I didn't think humanity served its purpose, so I just didn't give a damn. The world had gotten to be too much for me. However, I didn't have it in me to run out in front of a bus and kill myself. I couldn't jump out a window. So I kept up my abuse of heroin and booze, knowing, maybe subconsciously *wishing*, that at any time I could die of an overdose or get so drunk that I might get run over crossing the street.

CHAPTER 9
Fork in the Road

The years of the late '60s bleed together now in my memory, and sometimes events are lost in the haze of alcohol and heroin. Sometimes I am amazed that I made it through that era alive. It took luck, the Lord and a few people along the way who could look at me and see a dignity I scarcely believed existed anymore. A dignity I seemed to be trying my best to snuff out. I had yet to recognize my worth. Only when that happened would I begin to really be able to see the value in the lives of others. It's probably a good thing I could not know how many years that process would take.

***

From using dirty needle works I got sick with hepatitis. That got me on welfare, and with the welfare money I rented an apartment with another guy. It was a fairly decent place, and as I recuperated I began to have a feeling that this was my home. However, for some reason I no longer remember, the city stopped sending me my welfare checks. The other guy didn't have any money either, so one day there was a knock on my door and it was the landlord and the sheriff.

"Mr. Casanova?"

"Yeah."

"I have here an order to evict you."

My roommate wasn't home at the time, so I sat out on the curb and watched as they carried all our furniture, all our possessions, down to the street. As I sat there next to our stuff, I watched as people started coming by to scavenge it off the sidewalk. What could I do? I had no place to take it. People took it all away, everything. I felt really bad.

***

A young lady I had met in the park had some reefer she wanted to sell. Her name is lost to me now, but I do remember she looked like a woman from Spain, a little better than pleasingly plump, with shiny, dark black hair that fell to her shoulders.

I was helping her sell the stuff on 2nd Avenue around 7th Street by Fillmore East. I was quite discreet, approaching people nice and quiet and calm, but she was yelling all over the streets. Some hippies came by driving a Volkswagen bug, flowers and all, and talked to her about buying some marijuana. Well the hippies were narcs, and they busted the both of us.

It's a three-step process in order to go upstate to prison. When you first get arrested, they take you to the Tombs, which, as the name implies, is a very dark and dungeony place. From the Tombs, you go to either Rikers Island or Sing-Sing while your hearings and trials happen and your paperwork is being processed and they try to discover where you're going to do your time. That transient place is where you do a lot of reading because it is about the only way to pass time in your cell. You'll do almost anything to get a book. From Rikers Island or Sing-Sing you go to your more permanent state or federal address to do your sentence.

The Spanish-looking young lady ended up doing time, but the bust on me didn't stick for some reason. So I was released from Rikers Island without going further. While in there, I had eaten a whole lot, so that when I came out of Rikers Island, I weighed up around 200 and change, and I'm not exactly tall. The extra weight made it very difficult for me to go up and down the stairs of New York.

I ran into some friends of friends who were speed freaks. So I started doing speed. Through becoming a speed freak I lost a lot of weight. I was always on the go, running zoom, zoom, zoom! All over the place. Later I became a fanatic of cocaine. That kept me on the move too, but it also made me very paranoid. I became a dealer of heroin. The people who were supplying me were coke freaks like me. I would get heroin to sell and use my earnings to buy coke. But cocaine was too expensive and the high didn't last, so I didn't stay on it a long time, just long enough to know it was too expensive and not worth doing.

***

An organization named Educational Alliance had an outreach center called "Contact" that helped people deal with alcoholism and drug abuse during the time of the flower child. Educational Alliance is a Jewish foundation that gives money to community organizations to help the people in the community.

Contact was on 6th Street, between 1st and 2nd Avenue. It was a regular old six-story storefront building, and Contact took up the ground floor. The main office was all the way in the back, with the center itself being the big wide open space in front. Every day people would come to the center. I used to go in there all the time for peanut butter sandwiches and coffee because that's all I could get to eat some days. Everybody else from the Village hung out there. We would sit in there playing cards or reading. I don't remember a tv—I don't think it would have lasted long.

Bob Foreman ran the Contact Center. Bob was a white dude, Jewish, about 5 feet 8 inches in height, a little heavy-set, a good all-around person. He cared. I don't think there is any other way to describe him except to say that he cared. A lot of times when people get jobs like this, they stay in the office and have no contact with the people they're working with. Bob Foreman made it a point to stay in contact with the people. He didn't sit behind a desk. He was a little bit more than a director; he was a friend. He was a friend to everybody down there.

At Contact I met a Puerto Rican fellow called Gypsy. He looked more Puerto Rican than I did, but his real name was Abraham. I can't remember his last name. I don't ever recall him doing any work. He was mostly one of the guys who just hung around. He had the gift of gab, and partly for that reason he ended up becoming one of the Casanovas. In fact, Gypsy became my brother. Not my real blood brother, but he was closer to me than even Richie was.

Gypsy and I used to go to his mother's house on East 6th Street, and sometimes we would stay there overnight. Gypsy's mother was an immigrant from Puerto Rico, like my parents had been. In fact, she looked like my mother in some ways. She didn't speak too much English, but she would always make us a humongous pot of rice and beans, and homemade bread.

When Gypsy and I didn't spend the night at his mother's, we would go with our two dogs to the East River, along the drive where there was a building like an amphitheater, but which seemed to be used at that time by the Parks Department as a big tool and equipment warehouse. We would stay there at night facing the tall Domino Sugar building that stood across the river on the Brooklyn side. We were glad to have the dogs with us because the rats there were tremendous. There was one brick bench, so we didn't have to sleep on the floor. Gypsy and I slept foot to foot on the bench, and while we slept, the dogs chased the rats.

***

On 6th Street between Avenues B and C, was another building where some of the people were paying rent, but where there were also a number of empty apartments. I started living there with a white couple. This dude and his lady lived upstairs, and I lived downstairs.

All three of us had heroin habits. One afternoon we realized we needed some money to get our drugs that day. We decided to go out and do a mug job. I had never mugged anybody up to that time.

The white dude and I walked the streets around 18th and Broadway, in the area where the money was. It was raining, but we didn't put on our rain gear. We kept that in our bags.

Outside a bank we watched a man come out counting his money. He looked like money. We walked down the street, following him. He went into a building and we went in quickly after him. In the hallway we ripped him off. We didn't have to hit him, thank God for that.

We left him in the building and as soon as we got outside we put on our rain gear so he wouldn't recognize us. We just walked down the street. Around the corner we called a cab. We had taken something like $400 off him.

At home, we changed into dry clothes; and then went out and bought our drugs. I ended up doing a lot of muggings. It seemed now the only thing I was living for was to support my heroin habit.

When I went to Washington Square or Tompkins Square, I would usually shoot some heroin first and go there to nod. The beauty was not there any more because I was never conscious enough to enjoy it. Also at that time a lot of problems had developed between the Italians and the blacks. There was a Little Italy not far from Washington Square Park, and a number of black guys had been beaten up, and a lot of Italians were getting beat up and/or shot. The atmosphere of the park was changing for the worse, yet fortune kept me from going completely down the gutter. I was about to take a first small step toward changing my life for the better.

***

One afternoon at the Contact Center, Bob Foreman came over to me. By then we were on a friendly basis.

"Come on, Cas, let's go in the office and talk," he said. In the office was a woman who I knew worked with him. I said hello to her and took a seat.

"We kind of like the way you talk in our rap sessions," Bob said. "We were wondering if you'd like to do that more often."

Bob went on to explain to me that the center was pretty busy, and they weren't always able to have a counselor present at the rap sessions, although they always wanted someone there to facilitate the discussions. So Bob asked me to be part of the volunteer staff. That made me feel good, realizing that a man like Bob Foreman thought I had potential to do social work. So I accepted, and began heading up discussions at the center on a more or less regular basis. Unfortunately, I was still living an addictive lifestyle, and that would trip me up.

***

I had started hanging with some biker types, and one day we were at the Blimpie's restaurant eating when a young lady called Rocky came in. I had seen her around, but never really paid attention to her. Rocky was a strange one. She was slim, dark-haired and white, with the mannerisms of a biker. She hung around bikers, so she talked like them, walked like them, dressed like them. I say "bikers," but in reality we were what was called "sidewalk commandos." A lot of leather and boots and attitude. Rocky was one of them, too, strong-willed to the point of being macho. Nobody would mess with her.

I had a good pair of leather gloves that I had laid on the table as we were eating. Rocky saw the gloves and picked them up and walked out of the restaurant with them. I went after her.

"You gotta be fuckin' crazy," I told her. "Give me my gloves." She gave them to me. After that we began seeing each other and ended up being girlfriend and boyfriend. Rocky came to live with me on 6th Street, where we shared the apartment downstairs from the guy I did my first mugging with.

One day I went to the West Side of the Village, just past 6th Avenue, or the Avenue of the Americas. I had a toy gun in my pocket that looked exactly like a real gun. As was usual in those days, I needed money for heroin.

After waiting and looking, I picked me out a guy. A young white dude, looked rich. On the Lower East Side you didn't have to wear a suit to have money. I went to him and stuck the toy gun in this dude's stomach.

"Let me have your money," I said.

"Help!" he shouted. "He's robbing me! Help! Help!"

So I threw the toy gun down and pulled out my knife. He shut up then.

"Okay, man, you're cool," I told him. "I'll leave you alone, but shut the fuck up or I'm gonna have to stab you."

I started backing away. He started yelling again. I shoved the knife in his face.

"One more time," I said, "and I'm gonna cut your throat."

He quit his yelling, and he went his way and I went mine, but my luck was running out. Not long after that, we were having a party one night and a dude I had been having some trouble with showed up at the door. He was my enemy and yet he had had the nerve to show his face at my door. Being in a gang, I couldn't let him get away with that. I pulled out my knife and sliced him, but I didn't kill him. I threw the knife down a grate in the street.

The police caught up with me in Tompkins Square Park. They took me back to the grate. Somebody must have witnessed me trying to get rid of the knife. They fished the knife out of there and arrested me. In 1971 I went to Comstock prison in upstate New York.

CHAPTER 10

Comstock

When I was first in Comstock penitentiary, I had to learn a new way to escape. Dope had taken over my system, so without it I was nauseated and couldn't eat. However, I didn't get the shakes like some people do when they are kicking heroin addiction, though every now and then I pounded my head against the wall because of the pain of withdrawal. Still, I didn't suffer as much as some. Like the addicted inmate I saw who pounded his head until it bled. Like the people I saw throw up and collapse in their own vomit. So I considered myself fortunate. I never was able to score any heroin in Comstock, although once I connected, I was getting reefer and alcohol. But my only real escape was my art— drawing and painting pictures. In prison that became very helpful to me. What had for so long been simply a hobby, now became a necessity. My art helped me get through prison.

The cells in Comstock were small. There was a shelf that held the mattress for a bed, a toilet, a sink and a metal mirror on the wall. I had a small table for writing and a stool. I had painted a very thin piece of paper red and put it over the light, so my cell looked red instead of white. Sometimes the guards would tell me to take it down, sometimes they'd leave me alone. At Comstock the radio was on all over the institution, and the tv, with two jacks in the wall where you hooked up your earphones. You could only listen to the tv in your cell, not watch it. Comstock is where I first heard the tv show *Sanford and Son*. I never did see it, but I remember not liking it very much because of the way Redd Foxx treated the Puerto Rican dude Julio.

In the joint I did a lot of reading. I like to read. A lot of inmates had books and we would trade them back and forth. Sometimes I'd order books from the prison library.

The Educational Alliance stuck by me while I was in prison. Bob Foreman was writing to me. He knew I liked to read and would send me books that I asked for. I read *Manchild In the*

Promised Land. I also read *The Spook Who Sat By the Door*. At the time I was in Comstock, I was mainly interested in escapism, so I read a lot of detective stories, murder mysteries and horror.

However, the serious reading I did was helpful. I wouldn't exactly say that I am self-taught because I had a lot of teaching, but I did most of my learning on my own. Prison in a way helped me become more conscious of things. Until I read his autobiography when I was at Comstock, I didn't know anything about Malcolm X. Unfortunately, I discovered Malcolm the same way I discovered Kennedy: only after he had been assassinated. That's when I first became conscious of him. I became aware of the Young Lords, Black Panthers and Black Muslims while in prison. Those organizations were at Comstock. That was a time when ethnic consciousness was becoming a political force.

I knew who were Black Panthers from people pointing them out to me. These Black Panthers were frightening to me. They were too political for me at the time. They were getting shot. I know now that the Black Panthers and the Young Lords were organizations of people trying to make valuable changes in society, but the media didn't present it that way. So I saw them as an enemy to fear rather than people to associate with. I had spent a lot of my youth in and out of institutions. I wasn't around people who were activists. Mostly the people I knew were just surviving. Yet, although I didn't realize it at the time, my surviving was leading me to activism.

At Comstock there was a factory where inmates made soap for the correctional institutions. I was the clerk in the soap shop. I did inventory and a lot of typing of records. Other inmates paid me in cigarettes to prepare legal papers for them. They would go to the law library and figure out what they needed typed up and then bring it to me. Many a shift after I did all my clerical work, I would hang out in the office, drinking coffee and listening to the radio while I typed people's appeals and other legal papers. My rate depended on the number of words, but generally I got paid a carton of cigarettes or more.

Rocky kept in touch with me and sent me pipe tobacco. I wrote her that my cell looked better than most of the cells because when you walked into my cell you wouldn't see a blank space on the wall, just wall-to-wall artwork. I painted everything and anything just to avoid looking at the cell walls and the bars. In my cell I had a lot of pictures up that I had painted, and postcards that I had made, and "Thinking of You" cards. When I had gotten to prison, I had started off doing monograms for letterheads and envelopes for the letters inmates sent their girlfriends and wives. Then I started branching out. I started painting things that I liked to see.

Most people would go out of their cells when allowed. I mostly stayed in my cell, reading or painting. As inmates passed my cell on their way to the yard or to a movie, they would stop to see what else I had painted. Guys were always coming by just to see what was new in my cell. They would come by and ask me if I could do a painting of their kid, or if I could help them make a letterhead for their girlfriend. That's how I made my money, my cigarette money. Sometimes inmates would buy paintings from me by transferring money from their prison account to mine. Although usually I would pay for my reefer and booze with cigarettes, a lot of times I paid with my artwork, too.

I did a lot of copying when I painted, but one of the first pictures I ever painted just from my imagination was a picture of an armored knight in the days of King Arthur. He had a sword, a long spear and a huge shield that stretched from his head to his feet. In the painting, the knight had just broken out of a prison cell.

It was a humongous painting for the cell, about four feet high and three and a half feet wide. While I was painting it, this one inmate kept coming by and watching me. He was white with blonde hair, and heavyset. He was an all right guy, but what I call a "Doofus" type. I don't know what he was in prison for. But as I painted the picture of the knight, this guy saw it develop. It was a pretty good picture, and eventually he told me he wanted to buy it. I sold it to him for 60 or 70 dollars, and he took it to his cell. But after a week or so, the guy came back and said he wanted to return the picture and get his money back.

"You got to be crazy," I said. "You ain't getting any money back now. You better take that picture and send it home or something."

Hundu's ex-wife Peggy, and her kids, used to come visit me sometimes. I had sent her some of my paintings on glass, and we were trying to see if we could get a business going, selling glass paintings. But that idea never did work out.

To be honest, I had reasons other than art and literature for staying in my cell so much. One reason was to avoid the tensions of the yard. This was at the time of the Attica riots. At Comstock the warden ordered lockdowns now and then during the unrest. There was always that underlying potential for Attica to happen at Comstock, so riots were always a fear of mine. Getting beat up was another fear. Another reason I stayed in my cell so much was fear of being sexually assaulted. You hear the jokes about not leaning over in the shower for the soap; well, in prison it's no joke, it's a reality. There were a lot of rapes in Comstock. I guess the guys who were perpetrating the bun rapings and were reaming guys were doing hard time, long sentences, and had not been with a woman in a long time. And the victim need not necessarily be effeminate, but just look good.

One day I was in the shower and a beefy black inmate tried to get to my ass. We got into a fight. Once he and I got through it, everybody left me alone, but being in prison remained a very scary experience. Hundreds and hundreds of men in there, murderers and rapists, and a lot of them were weightlifters. So I stayed in my cell a lot.

The stress of prison life probably accounted for my seizures returning to some extent. At that time the doctors switched my medication from pill form to liquid. Because they were experimenting with dosages, they accidentally gave me too much and overdosed me. For a time I sank into the old pattern again where I wouldn't eat and never got out of bed. One day I finally collapsed, and the guards came to take me to the hospital. As they walked me down the hall, an inmate on each side holding me up, I began to have drugged visions of Matteawan. I started to panic, thinking I was there again, visualizing Matteawan.

"Calm down," one of the inmates told me. "It'll be all right, it's not so bad, you'll be okay, you're going to be okay."

If it had not been for that inmate talking to me and walking me to the hospital, I might have snapped. As it was, my condition was so bad, they had to transfer me from the prison hospital to a civilian hospital, where doctors did a spinal tap on me and treated me for about a month.

While I was recuperating at the civilian hospital, I was told that my sister Pauline had died. I had barely known her, but the authorities allowed me to get out long enough to go see her at the funeral parlor.

They gave me a minute alone with her even though I didn't really want it. I didn't know what I was doing in that funeral parlor. I had barely known her. I wasn't doing all that hot myself. But I have always been curious.

The police took the chains off me. You could barely hear the church music they had playing in the room. I walked over to the coffin. I never really gave death too much of a thought, but now I looked down at this dead woman Pauline, who had been my sister. What had been her life? I wondered.

Tears filled my eyes. I was thinking of the peace she had now, a peace I had wanted myself at times, but was afraid to take. The peace that seemed better than the life I and so many I knew were living.

I kissed her and then told the guards to take me back.

***

Gradually I became more self-assured and confident. In prison they limited the amount of hair you were allowed to grow on your face, but when I got back to Comstock I grew a beard, partly because it was harder to shave in prison and partly because it seemed like it was always cold weather, and a beard keeps you warmer. I didn't like shaving that much anyway. I also started wearing my afro in the era of Angela Davis, when she was in the news. I kind of liked my 'fro.

The Black Muslims were always having meetings. Out of curiosity I went to a meeting. I guess I was always on the lookout for some type of religion. I listened for a while to what they were saying, and then I had some questions, so I raised my hand. But the Muslim leaders ignored me; they would not give me an opportunity to question anything. At the end, a Muslim brother said he was glad I had come, and he was looking forward to seeing me again.

"I ain't coming back to this," I told him. "How am I supposed to know what the hell you're talking about if you won't answer my questions?"

I started playing sandlot football with some of the other inmates. We played without gear and had a good time for a while. About that time it became fashionable to have football teams in prisons and the warden decided we should have organized teams and some real games. They came up with equipment for us, helmets and shoulder pads and so on. So the guys who had been playing already continued playing together. We called ourselves the "Ebo Assassins." So again I was an "Assassin." Once the sport became serious and organized, we had to practice and jog a lot.

Comstock's football field was in the big open exercise yard. Concrete walls that doubled as handball courts surrounded the yard, with guard towers on each corner. In the center of this was the area we used as our field. It was more dirt than grass.

I played fullback or running back. The games were ferocious. Comstock was a very rough prison and had the roughest football I've ever seen—worse than the Burt Reynolds movie *The Longest Yard*. When you're in prison you make a lot of enemies, yet you're not allowed to get physical, or you go to detention or solitary, so you use that when you play football. So a lot of the guys weren't out there to catch a football. They were working out all their revenge kicks during these so-called games. They played to hurt. The warden gave us pads and all that stuff, but none of it did a damn bit of good when a guy got you in a headlock and started gouging and punching away on your face.

During a game I got a little sprain in my neck. I came out of the game to the sidelines. Now there was this dude out there playing, a good-looking young guy, a light-skinned brother. It so happened that he was going with the best-looking homosexual in the institution. So a lot of guys hated his guts because of jealousy. They were playing to hurt that day, to get him out of the way, so somebody else could deal with his boyfriend. As I watched from the sidelines, they achieved their goal. He ended up in the hospital as a result. I said "no more football for me."

***

Bob Foreman of Contact and Educational Alliance had continued staying in touch with me by letter. Eventually Bob wrote and asked me if I'd be a counselor, run the groups. I felt honored as I read the letter. I also felt surprised that somebody wanted me to do that. Bob Foreman had seen something in me that I didn't know was there. His noticing my potential let *me* know that I had potential, that I *could* do something. He's the one who saw this in me, this caring in the heart. That I actually had a job to look forward to that would pay me to help people, that felt good.

It was all part of my old dream of becoming a social worker. In the orphanage they had never asked "Why did you do this?" It was always "You did this!" Bam! and you were punished. There was no "why?" or caring, or understanding that I felt bad about being the youngest one of eleven kids in an orphanage and without a mother or father. If you are going to be a social worker, you are supposed to get involved in knowing what is making a person hurt, what makes them feel the way they do, and then you try to work with the person on the problem. I knew I could do that.

Bob said in the letter that if I wanted, he would talk to the parole board. I wanted. So Bob went to bat for me with the parole board. I had not been a disruptive inmate. I went to school, I did my job, I painted. So I had a good reputation. When I got paroled, it was mainly because I had a job waiting with Educational Alliance.

I had written Rocky with the good news. We arranged to meet at the Blimpie's on 7th Street and 2nd Avenue. When I got out of Comstock I got high and started drinking to celebrate. I made it to Blimpie's and Rocky showed up. We went to her apartment. When I got there I realized she was sharing the place with another dude.

I took a shower and then Rocky and I made love.

"I can't stay here," I said afterwards. "Not while you're living with another man."

"What did you expect?" she said.

I split. I had liked her and the fact that she had paid attention to me all the while I was in the joint and sent me tobacco for my pipe. I had thought there were some possibilities for us. But apparently there weren't.

CHAPTER 11

Rise and Fall

When I began working in Educational Alliance's Contact program as a paraprofessional drug and alcohol counselor, I was clean from heroin and had been throughout my stay in Comstock. The Village had decayed since I had been away, particularly on the Lower East Side. In the '60s there had always been reefer and there had always been coke and even heroin, but in that Bohemian era people had stayed relatively mellow.

Then things started getting rough. People from Jersey and Long Island began coming down to the Village to get their drugs. Though Washington Square at that time was not a tourist trap, it was beginning to be. It became like "Go West, Young Man, go West!" That's the way it was for the middle class in the suburban areas. Go west to Washington Square. After a while it became an epidemic. They just kept coming. And they often came specifically for the drugs.

I'm not condoning any kind of drug, but you have to consider the type of drug. There are some distinctions. Reefer, or marijuana, was more of a laid-back drug. You smoked that or ate that and you were still able to enjoy life and sit back or play music or read or paint or rap. It was that kind of flower-power, John Lennon- or Beatles-type thing. It was just a relaxed atmosphere.

But now there was only heroin! For some reason or another, it became the thing to do. Never had it been as prominent or as dominating as it was when I returned from prison, and I saw it feeding the Village's deterioration.

I moved to the Lower East Side because I knew more people there. Though the heaviest part of drugs and heroin was on the Lower East Side, Tompkins Square Park was a little bit more down-to-earth than Washington Square. Tompkins Square was ten and a half acres of park with trees, surrounded by an old neighborhood whose brownstone and brick buildings with metal fire escapes were full of life. Generally you didn't go over to Tompkins Square Park unless you lived in that area, and you walked your dog, or you played with your kids, or you were homeless and stayed in the park. The people there were trying to survive, not just entertain themselves. Several of the neighborhood bars made a pit in the middle of the grass where they would cook, and we used to eat barbecued pig while sitting on the benches in the shade of the trees. I hooked up with Gypsy again, and we would still sometimes go to his mother's to get our rice and beans.

As part of my parole, I was talking to psychiatrists. I told them I did not think my seizures were totally real, that in the beginning they had been an act, a way to get out my anger. One of the doctors told me it was a good idea to think about getting off medication if I didn't really need it. So I began weaning myself off the epilepsy drugs, and my seizures did not return.

I was working for the main office of Educational Alliance, down on East Broadway. We were on the top floor. The daycare center was also on that floor, and on the roof.

First thing in the morning I would come into the office, put on some coffee, check my messages and phone calls, and then start typing up my report of the previous day's activities. When we needed a new secretary, I conducted the interviews with the applicants. Another part of my job was to go out in the streets and parks and talk with people, let them know about Contact, that we were there and trying to help. I had some clients that came in to see me there, but that office location had "Federal Federal Federal, Federal Government" written all over it, so a lot of the people I needed to be helping would not come near the building. Educational Alliance did in fact receive some Federal funding, and people in the streets develop a very suspicious attitude toward social worker institutions in general, particularly ones associated with the Feds. Besides, social workers are usually a pain in the butt.

Unfortunately, I spent most of my time in the office dealing with administrative tasks instead of working with the people we were intending to assist. As I grew frustrated, I began to get a more rounded perspective. I found that there were some social workers who had the same ideals I had, who were doing whatever they could to help. Usually, to become a social worker in the first place you have to start out with the ideal of helping people, to be one of the ones who helps make things better in the world.

But then you get caught up in the bureaucracy. You get told:

"You're not supposed to do this."

"You're not supposed to do that."

"You can't help this way."

"You can't help that way."

So your ideals are quickly shoved aside and there is a tendency to become very cynical, very uptight as you start conforming to the establishment. Unless you're a rebel.

In the meantime, my brother Philip was still working hard, and had more or less become the patriarch of the family. He let my brothers and sisters know that our father, who must have been in his late 50s or early 60s by then, just wasn't making it. Pops wanted to go back to Puerto Rico. My family, especially my brother Philip, decided that the best thing to do was to send him back home. So Philip got my brothers and sisters together to buy him a ticket. Philip made the arrangements.

The last time I saw my father was at Philip's house a few days before he went back to Puerto Rico. Pops just sat there. He didn't know English, and most of us knew little or no Spanish, so he wasn't doing too much talking. But he smiled a lot. He knew he was going to Puerto Rico. He was a *jíbaro*, and he was returning to the hills. I think he had a feeling or premonition that he was dying or getting ready to die.

***

Gypsy had a friend named Sharon Fuller who came around one day to Tompkins Square Park, where the Casanovas were hanging out. Sharon was a fine-looking white woman, taller than me. The first time I met her, she had her long brownish-blonde hair tucked up under a hat. Over the next few days I got to know Sharon from her hanging out with us. She was going with some dude at the time, and she didn't want to be with him anymore. In fact, she had joined the Army, taking the delayed entry. When I met her, she had a little less than three months before she had to report for training. Every time I saw Sharon, she would "cry on my shoulder" about her breakup with this other dude. But that wasn't all we talked about. Sharon liked Gypsy's dog, scruffing its ears while we talked about everything we could think of. I learned that Sharon grew up in Boulder, Colorado. Her personality had been shaped by being an only child, and all that entailed with over-protectiveness from her parents. Yet she was very independent.

When we talked, Sharon would laugh a lot. I hoped it was at my attempts of humor. One day I pulled her hat off, letting her long hair tumble free over her shoulders and back.

"Why did you do that?" she asked, smiling as I kept her from grabbing her hat back.

"You're a beautiful woman. I want to see your hair."

It became a teasing game between us, and we would wrestle as I tried to get her to show her long, fine hair, and she tried to get her hat. I enjoyed her evasiveness, but I made up my mind that I wanted her. Being pretty much a straightforward person, I let her know.

"Cas, " she said. "I like you, but I'm not ready. I don't want to be with another man yet. "

Now I am very persistent, but I got the message and stopped messing with her.

A few days later I was sitting on a bench in the park with some people smoking a joint. Along came Sharon.

"Come on, Cas," she said. "Let's go."

"Where to?"

"To get something to eat and a hotel room for the night."

So we had danced around our desire for a while, but I believe that it was with both of us knowing the outcome, knowing we would come together.

We lived in a place on 6th Street between B and C. Sharon helped me feel good about life. I was very protective of her. I have never liked perfume, and one of the things I loved about Sharon was that she was always clean and fresh. To me, Sharon was beautiful, and I loved the length of her body. She had a passion for life, but also an easy way about her. She was a loving, caring person, not just to me, but also to other people, to cats, dogs, anything with feelings. She would cry about movies, paintings and music. Sharon and I had many happy times in those two months.

I was continuing my work as a counselor, and Sharon would sit in our discussion circles and take part. In order to deal with people not wanting to come to a big office, the people at Educational Alliance opened an extension of the Contact program at 14th and 3rd Avenue, an area with a "Ho-Stro," a lot of pimps working tricks with their prostitutes.

We took an old laundromat and turned it into an office and a center, getting people off the streets to help us take out the old washers and dryers and pull out most of the plumbing. We put in a drop-ceiling and fluorescent lighting.

At that location we succeeded in getting people off the street and into counseling or detoxification programs. Word got around the streets that I was working there and wasn't doing drugs anymore. Most of the clients knew what I was about, that I had been down there with them and was not going to lay a sermon on them.

A lot of people came into the office simply because they knew they could get coffee and a peanut butter and jelly sandwich. That never stopped. They would come in there for that, and in that way I could talk with them and get them into conversations. Some of the people who came in were for real. They really wanted help. We offered drug and alcohol counseling. Or if somebody needed assistance with AFDC or welfare, we were there to help.

Contact had work crews. People would come off the streets and get rehabbed off drugs and/or alcohol. Then they would get on-the-job training renovating buildings that Educational Alliance was working on. We had field-managers, work crew bosses, who would go into buildings and teach our clients how to do carpentry and plumbing. That training was another of the services Contact provided.

As our clients got detoxed, if they wanted to continue their education they would receive a stipend as they went to school. Part of my counseling job was to help them get into school. Once I got them into the school they would get another counselor. Sometimes a former client of mine would still come by to see me because we had become not just counselor and client, but friends.

Every now and then somebody would say thank you. Rarely, but one young woman stands out. One day this blonde-haired young woman with a kid had come into the 14th Street office crying. She was crying because she needed help, but could not get through the usual bureaucracies. We were able to get her some kind of assistance. Weeks later she dropped by the office again. This time she had a smile.

"I wanted to say 'hi'," she said. "I'm doing all right now and I just wanted to thank you guys."

You don't do social work for the thanks, but it helps when people do appreciate what you are trying to do. It helps you keep on with the day-to-day grind. And her thanks at that time helped me feel that at last I was starting to realize my old dream of being a social worker, helping people in need make a better life for themselves.

***

About every two weeks, I would go down to the parole office at 4th Street and 8th Avenue. I would report in, sit down for an hour and then walk out. I was essentially punching a clock when I went in there. I used to get my epilepsy medication through the parole office, but once I dropped that, they were doing nothing to assist me in any way.

In fact, if anything, they were doing just the opposite.

I don't remember my parole officer's name. When it came to authority in those days, I didn't pay attention to names, I paid attention to what they did.

One day my parole officer came into the Contact center, his coat wide open, so everybody could see his gun on his side.

Though I had some people in there with me at the time, this parole officer came right into my office. He threw his manila folder on the table so everybody could see my records laying all over.

"We have some paperwork to take care of, Casanova." He turned to the people in the room and said something like "It's okay. I'm his parole officer."

This happened more than once. The man was not concerned with me, just concerned with his own power and keeping records. He was one ballbuster.

I told Bob Foreman about the situation and he was very supportive. I even talked to the parole officer's immediate supervisor, but it did no good. Nothing changed.

The call came while I was at my job. Someone phoned to tell me that my brother Richie had overdosed on heroin over on 6th or 7th Street.

Richie was already dead by the time I got to the hospital. It hit me hard. Richie was closer to me than anybody else in my family. They would not let me see him I was so distraught. Finally they had to give me a shot to sedate me, to calm me down.

***

Sharon and I were sitting in East River Park having a picnic on my birthday in June.

"I think I'm going to hitchhike out west," she said out of the blue.

"Why do you want to do that?" I asked.

"I want to see my hometown one more time before I go into the Army."

There were just a few weeks left before she had to report for duty.

"I'm leaving," she said. "If you don't come, I'm going by myself."

I did not necessarily want to leave Contact, to leave my job, but I really liked Sharon. She had my nose open. The fact that I was still hurting from Richie's death may also have influenced my decision. I was not ready to lose another person I was close to.

"All right," I finally said. "If you want me to go with you, let's go to the liquor store."

We went to the liquor store and bought four bottles of wine. We drank it all. I got drunk enough to decide I was going with her. Hell, I was fed up with the parole office anyway.

We got Gypsy to take care of the house and the dogs; then we hitchhiked to New Jersey through the tunnel. To tell the truth, I thought once we got to New Jersey, nobody would pick us up and that would be the end of the trip. Here I was with a big old Afro and Sharon a blonde white woman. So nobody was going to pick us up, right?

Of course, as soon as we got let off in New Jersey, a Volkswagen van pulled up. I didn't even have time to change my mind about going. In the van were a couple of Jewish brothers, with long curly hair, and they gave us a ride all the way to Ohio. We made it to Boulder, and we camped in a park. The next day was sunny, and Sharon took me to a lake near where she had grown up. We sat with our feet in the water, looking up at the mountains. Later I met Sharon's mother and aunt. They were not too happy about me being with Sharon, but they gave us money for a room.

Soon after we got back from that trip, Sharon had to report to Fort Ben Harrison, in Indianapolis, Indiana. She went out there and I followed a month later on a bus. I got on welfare until I could get on my feet. I moved into an apartment in a big huge hotel. I think it was $180 for a one-bedroom apartment. The man who ran the building hired me to work maintenance and to do security for the building at night. For that I got the apartment, plus pay. So I called the welfare department and told them I no longer needed public assistance because I had found a job.

You could get lost in that hotel if you didn't know where you were going. Part of the building was being repaired and renovated. One of my jobs in the daytime was to get rid of the rubbish and debris from the construction. In the nighttime I was the security guard. Sharon was living on base and when she could, she would come visit me.

On December 27, 1976, I married Sharon Fay Fuller at a ceremony on the army base. She wore a culottes pants suit, and I had on a Seventies-style, Botany 500 three-piece burgundy suit with flared pants.

Now officially I was still on parole, which meant legally I should not have left New York. Sharon and I talked to a lawyer back in New York to see about the process of squashing any warrant out for me and to see about making it okay for me to be in Indianapolis. He said he might be able to help us.

Meanwhile Sharon got orders that sent her to Germany. She and I felt it was a possibility for me to join her in Germany if our lawyer got the parole situation worked out and helped me get a passport.

As we kissed and hugged right before she left, I had no idea that it was for the last time. She flew to Germany in January, 1977.

I would not see her again.

Now when I had gone to Indiana, I had never hidden my name or anything. That meant my name was on the payroll at the hotel where I lived and worked. I was washing windows at the hotel when they came.

All of the sudden I felt two guns in my ribs, one on each side.

"FBI," the man said.

I guess we didn't follow through quickly enough on my parole situation.

"Don't move. You're under arrest."

So I didn't move. They were two white FBI agents. Authority figures in suits. They handcuffed me and took me to jail. I waived extradition, so they flew me back to New York on a commercial jet. That was the first time I had ever been on a plane. The agents took the handcuffs off me once we were on board the plane. They even let me have a drink.

When we got to New York I was processed, and they put me in the Tombs. That night I had to sleep on the floor because the bunk beds were filled.

Next day I went to court. When I saw my court-appointed legal aid lawyer I could hardly believe it. He was wearing a burgundy Botany 500 three-piece suit with flared pants, just like the one I had on. We were a sight.

The court slapped me with more time for parole violation. From the Tombs they sent me to Greenhaven, a maximum security correctional facility. There I worked in the factory making license plates. After a while I got a better job, sewing women's underwear. We made bras and panties. It was a cool job; of all the prison jobs, it paid the most and there were fringe benefits such as good sandwiches, sodas and cake.

I wrote to Sharon in Germany and explained what had happened. She wrote me back that she had become a marksman, and she sent me a coat and some money. I used to try to remember Sharon's voice, hear the passion for life that it held. I would look at her words on the paper and think, *her hand wrote these*. Sharon's letters were helping me make it. She was my connection to the outer world.

One thing you have in prison is time to think. What I thought about was that all my life I had been in and out of prison. I was tired of this life I was living. I thought about the people I had been helping before I went off to Indiana. As difficult as it had been at times, I had gotten satisfaction from working at Contact. Once again in my life I was realizing that was a direction where I had potential.

They had counseling at Greenhaven, and I let them know I wanted to get my G.E.D. I had been a model prisoner at Greenhaven, so the authorities eventually okayed a transfer for me to Otisville Correctional Center, a B-minimum security institution.

Electric fences surrounded the compound at Otisville rather than high, hard walls. At one time Otisville had been a training school for boys, a semi-orphanage. I believe I may have even briefly spent some time there as a teenager. If you ran away from an orphanage, they put you in a training school. The next step from there was prison. But for me Otisville was now a step in the right direction. It marked the birth of my higher education.

At Otisville I lived in one of the cottage buildings that were left from the days when prison-bound boys had stopped off there. Inmates were housed dormitory style in a big room, with partitions for some privacy. You had a bed, you had a desk, you had lamps, you had bookshelves. I wrote some poetry, I raised some flowers. Each cottage had a kitchen, so if you didn't want to eat at the regular cafeteria, you could go to the commissary and buy what you wanted and cook your own food.

Eventually I realized that Sharon's letters had not been lost in the mail. She had stopped answering my letters. I kept writing my wife, but got no reply. Nothing.

My days consisted mostly of studying and jogging, jogging and studying. I was also doing paintings on glass. From that I got the idea of making patterns for glass paintings. To make a pattern I would draw a picture from my imagination, then put it onto tracing paper. That tracing paper was the pattern. A person could take that and put a rectangle of glass on top of the tracing paper, trace the image and then paint it. I got more money from the patterns than I did for the glass paintings, usually ten cartons of cigarettes for a pattern. The price was high because you could take a single pattern and make a lot of pictures from it.

The correctional officers liked my work, and I was on fairly good terms with most of them. They were always looking for ways to make the cottage look better because there was a competition in the facility for who had the best-looking cottage. So when I asked if I could paint a couple of murals inside on the walls of the cottages, the C.O.s agreed. They even got me the colors of house paint I asked for. I painted one mural of the Puerto Rican-American baseball hero Roberto Clemente, and I did one of the Statue of Liberty.

Then one day I got a letter from an Army officer named White. He was a chaplain's assistant and he wrote me that he knew Sharon was not answering my letters. Apparently I was sending so much mail he felt I ought to get an answer. He tried to get Sharon back together with me, but nothing came of it. My wife and I lost each other. She never wrote again. This is the real deal: when a person goes to prison in the middle of a relationship, most relationships end. It hurt, but I had expected it.

After a while, I stopped writing Sharon and was writing to White and his family. His grandmother used to make blankets and sent me one in prison. We became close through the mail.

When I got my G.E.D. there was no graduation ceremony. There was nothing fancy in prison. They just gave me the paper in the classroom and shook my hand. But for me it was a milestone. Maybe I could make something out of myself after all.

I enrolled in college courses that were offered in the prison through the Orange County Community College. I studied horticulture for ten months, so I learned how to grow vegetables.

White wrote me that Sharon had gotten kicked out of the Army. In a way I was not surprised. She was always rebellious, and in the end she could not conform to Army rules and regulations. She could not go along with all the Army procedure, so they gave her the boot and sent her back to the United States.

In the meantime, White had gotten orders to be transferred to a post in Whitewater, Wisconsin. He had a house there with an apartment in the basement. Now White knew I was coming up for parole. He offered that when he got to Wisconsin and I got paroled, I could live in his basement apartment while going to college.

I asked White to check out the college there and find out what kind of social welfare studies they had. It just so happened that the University of Wisconsin had a good program in that field. So I wrote two letters: one to the parole board and one to the dean of the School of Social Welfare at the University of Wisconsin.

In the letter to the parole board I explained my past and that I wanted to change my life around, that I had earned my G.E.D. and that I was enrolled in the Orange County Community College. I went on to explain the opportunity of Assistant Chaplain White's offer, and said that I wanted to move out to Wisconsin to continue college in hopes of becoming a professional social worker.

I sent a letter to the dean explaining who I was, where I was, and what had led to my being in prison. I said I wanted to become a student at his college.

The dean wrote back, accepting me. He also wrote a letter to the parole office telling them that I had been accepted into the University of Wisconsin. White wrote to the parole office telling them I could stay at his house. On top of that, several of the C.O.s at Otisville wrote letters to the parole office on my behalf. Before I knew it, I had been paroled to Wisconsin.

CHAPTER 12

New Chances, Old Patterns

From New York I took the train to Wisconsin, and in Chicago they lost my damn luggage.

White and his wife picked me up at the station in Madison. It was really an enthusiastic greeting they gave me. We were happy to see each other after so many letters. Glad to finally meet. .

"Do you go by Ronald or Ronnie?" one of them asked.

·"Call me Cas," I told them. "My friends do."

They drove me to their home. By the time we got there, we were pretty tired, so we just went to sleep.

When I walked onto the modern-looking campus of the University of Wisconsin at Whitewater, in 1981, the feeling of freedom was almost overwhelming. I was excited. Nobody in my family had ever gone to college before. Maybe that alone should have told me I wouldn't be able to go and finish.

I had been in prison for several years, and I came out very horny, which led me to make a mistake. I had been hearing stories about the free-spirited women at colleges, and I believed those tales more than I should have. So instead of approaching the coeds in my usual calm, collected way, I came on far too strong and obvious. Frighteningly so.

I didn't get anywhere that way.

I enrolled in an art class, hoping they could teach me something, but the class was too constricting, too boring, too confining.

"In order for you to do a picture of a human being," the teacher said, "you've got to start with circles."

What the hell did I want to start with a circle for?

"You start with the circle, then you put in the nose, then you put in the eyes."

I guess you could learn a certain amount of balance out if it, but to me it was a waste of time. I was already able to draw without all the circles.

Being on parole in Wisconsin was all right because these people were a little bit more human than they were back in New York. I mean they paid more attention to you and they didn't interfere with your life. The parole officers would call you when they were coming to see you and all our meetings were not necessarily at my house or their office. Sometimes the meetings were in restaurants. They would treat you to dinner. Compared to New York, Wisconsin was a different atmosphere altogether.

Although I had financial grants, I also had to work to pay for part of the courses. Through the college, as part of an "on the job training" course, I got a job as a psychiatric attendant at the Elkhorn Psychiatric Center in Elkhorn, Wisconsin, 30 miles away. To commute to my job I would need transportation, so I got my driver's license, and, with money from some of my financial loans, I bought my first car.

Being a psychiatric attendant was a different position for me. After all, at one time I had been the patient. When I began working at Elkhorn, they knew I had been in Matteawan. They knew everything about me; I didn't hide anything. In fact, they considered it a valuable life experience for the work I was doing. Who else could better understand a person in that predicament than a person that had been there himself?

In fact, I had no idea what I was getting into. All I knew was that I needed a job and I liked working with people. It was not until a training session that I realized I would have to be doing things to patients that had been done to me.

At this psychiatric hospital they had residents who were kicking alcohol or drug addictions. People would come in having the D.T.s. Other, more permanent residents, had problems that did not have to do with drugs. So a number of us new employees had to be at a training session on how to put a person in restraints.

Knowing my experience at being in a straitjacket, they used me as the guinea-pig in the demonstration. While they were putting the jacket on me, visions of Matteawan State Hospital came back to me, so I was very uptight. But I lay still in the straitjacket as an experiment for myself, and fortunately, after a while I was able to overcome my fear.

My routine at Elkhorn was to come in, check the logbook, read the logbook on each resident, see how they had been that night, the day before, and see if there was anything new I should know about them. Then I would go around checking the blood pressure and temperature of the residents, as well as helping them clean up if it was needed. For one old man I used to have to get in a bathing suit to take him in and give him a shower. I would hold him up so he wouldn't fall.

At group rap sessions which I led, we mostly shared experiences. Though I was no longer doing heroin or cocaine, my being able to talk with the patients about reasons why *I* had been into drugs helped them feel easier about discussing their own drug abuses.

Once I got settled into my routine of school and work and had some money, I thanked the Whites and moved out of their house and onto the campus. I preferred the independence. I even got a bicycle for getting around campus.

Unfortunately, even as a counselor at Elkhorn I was still into alcohol, drinking heavily. I had to go to work with a hangover so often that I ended up switching my shift from the morning to the graveyard shift because the patients would all be sleeping when I came on, and all I had to do was monitor them and do my homework from college.

One night at about one or two in the morning, the police brought in an agitated woman. They brought her up to the second floor, which was the security floor. The ground floor residents had their own rooms and could move about more or less freely. The second floor had cells specifically for restraining people.

We took her to one of the cells, which had a bed and a grated window. She started pounding her head against the grated window, so we decided we had to put her in restraints. The thought of me doing that to somebody was pretty weird. But she kept ramming her head, which was damaging her face, hurting her. So I came to the realization that sometimes for some people such a measure was necessary.

We put her in the bed in a straitsheet. It was a necessity to put her in the straitsheet. It was necessary for her to lie in the bed; otherwise she would cut up her face. At this institution restraint was done in as humane a way as possible. Straitjackets and straitsheets at Coxsackie and Matteawan were more as punishment than a help.

But I remembered those belts. Being strapped down affected her and it affected me. I remember sitting at the door through the graveyard shift hearing her hollering.

"Help me! Help me! Get me out of this! I'm okay, I'm okay! Take me out!"

My instinct was to get her out of the straitsheet, but my reality kept me from doing it.

Incidents like this had me saying "I don't need this. I'll just go to college." On the other hand, after a bad day at college I would say "I don't need this. I'll just work as a psychiatric attendant." Fortunately, I got myself a job that was a lot more rewarding—as a juvenile counselor at the Elkhorn Juvenile Center. There I got to work with kids between the ages of ten and 17 as a house parent and counselor. I lived on my job there for three days and then I was off three days. I led group sessions with these young people to help them work out problems and solutions. I was not only the house parent and counselor, I was also a father, a brother.

That job was good for me because it was the first job in my life where I not only felt satisfaction, but also really enjoyed the work. That job was very important because it was a chance for me to offer those kids the kind of interested guidance that the people at the orphanage never gave me. I'm not saying that their caring would have changed my life, but maybe it would have. Maybe I would have seen something different than what I saw as I was growing up. Maybe I would have seen more than gangs and substance abuse and living in abandoned buildings and sleeping in hallways and parks. Maybe if an adult counselor had taken some kind of interest in me when I was young, I might have been able to avoid years of uncertainty and hardship. I might have accepted my being adopted. A whole lot of things might have changed.

***

Twenty years prior to my time in Elkhorn, Wisconsin, there had been a curfew on black people there. You had to be in the house by eight o'clock. No black people had been allowed on the streets after that hour. Even by the early 1980s, I was pretty much the only black person visible in the town. It was easy for me, though, because I was working with the kids. Most of the kids reacted favorably toward me, so as far as I was concerned, the town was all right.

My parole officer was also parole officer to a lot of my adult clients and to some of my kid clients. So he and I were to some extent equals, both professionals. I would go to the court with kids, and my parole officer would be there representing the kid— or me.

One night at the psychiatric hospital I was giving the old man a shower when his doctor came in. The doctor took a towel from the floor, wound it up and started slapping the old man with it, this old man who could hardly talk beyond a kind of blubbering. I had no idea why the doctor did that. I didn't know what it was about, but I knew it wasn't right. I pushed the doctor away.

"You got to stop that shit!" I said.

I pushed the doctor out the door. He went to the office and made a complaint against me. I got called to the office. I went in there knowing I was fired. Whose word were they going to take, a doctor's that they had been paying for years, or mine? I ended up losing my job, but it was worth it. Stopping that doctor from abusing that old man was worth the job to me. Besides, at the time I had the job as a juvenile counselor to fall back on.

Then President Reagan made all those budget cuts. Since I was the last one hired, I was the first one fired. When I tried to apply for different work in the same field, I believe the old prejudices under the surface of the community came out because I never was able to get more work there. I found myself unemployed all over again, which was a violation of my conditions for parole.

I'll be honest with you: when I lost my job counseling the children, I became a lush, to the point where I didn't give a damn about what was happening. I didn't have a job, and I was not able to take care of my rent. White and I had gotten along very well, and had I gone to him and explained my situation, we probably would have been able to work something out so I could keep the apartment. But at that time I was beyond reason, so I did not pay attention to what might have been arranged with him.

Wisconsin was full of snow that winter. It was even colder than New York City. Tired of the freezing weather, I hitchhiked down to Florida with another guy who lived in the same hotel where I had been staying. I didn't care that it was a violation of my parole. Hell, I was already in violation for not having a job. We figured Florida would be sunny and warm.

The oranges were frozen on the trees when we got to the Sunshine State. If my toes and fingers hadn't been hurting from the cold, it might even have seemed funny. I would have said I was out of the frying pan into the fire.

The first night we spent in the precinct jail—not because we were arrested, but because the local authorities gave us a place to sleep out of the cold. The other guy stayed on in the jail a few days, but I had a dislike for cells. I borrowed his camping gear and went out to sleep in the orange fields. The next morning I picked him up, and we went to look for work. Fortunately, the freeze had not been too hard and most of the oranges had survived.

If you wanted to pick oranges, you had to show up at five in the morning. They would take a busload of us out to where they had us picking that day. There were a lot of migrant workers. The guy I had come to Florida with ended up going to work for Tropicana, while I began working for another company, and that was the last I saw of him.

We had some black dudes who were the foremen. You were given a tub or barrel that could hold ten bushels of oranges. Then they would give you a bag and a hook and you'd climb up a ladder into the tree and fill the bag, climb down and dump it into the barrel. Up and down, up and down. I was making good money—$10 a barrel, $80 to $90 a day. Unfortunately, there was no decent place to live anywhere around the groves.

I was not generally liked because I was not part of the orange pickers' system. In their system they had camps for the orange pickers. I heard stories from workers who stayed in the camps about the conditions there and the way the bosses treated the workers about their money. The bosses and the police were in cahoots. If the bosses didn't like a worker, they would call the police, who would then come out and arrest that person and make him move on. Some of the workers hardly ever got fully paid for the work they did. Instead they would be given alcohol by the gallon.

Not wanting to be in the camps, I found a family to stay with who were drinkers, alcoholics like myself. So it was convenient; we understood each other; the atmosphere was cool. At the end of the day, on my way to the bar or the liquor store I would walk past the orange pickers' camps. You would see the people and their families sitting outside the insubstantial shanties the growers had them in. The workers would be sitting on the stoops of these shanties drinking.

The situation of a laborer picking oranges was deplorable. Though you had to be at the orchard at five o'clock in the morning, you got nothing to eat or drink until five o'clock in the afternoon, which made for a very exhausting day. It was profitable, I was making good money, but it was very exhausting.

One day the lady of the house where I was staying suddenly got religion. Suddenly she decided alcohol was to be banned from the house. No more smoking was allowed either. No alcohol and no smoking! For those reasons alone I never would have made it there. Besides, I wasn't ready for religion at the time, so I left their house to find another place to stay.

I ended up living at the labor camp after all. The workers were dirt poor and uneducated Jamaicans, whites, Hispanics and African-Americans. Most of these laborers were alcoholics, a fact which the owners took advantage of. They convinced or just told these alcohol addicts to accept being paid in liquor or wine. In fact, if these unfortunate workers got any money, they would get something like 20 dollars for two or three weeks' work. The rest of their pay came in alcohol and cigarettes. I had left the religious family because I was drinking myself, but I knew I could not stay in the labor camp, either. Eventually I would have gotten killed because I would not have accepted the treatment by the bosses or the conditions these laborers kept themselves in.

Instead, I kept asking around, and somebody finally told me of a guy who had a place outside the camp that could be rented.

When I got there, I was less than enthusiastic. What it looked like was that they had taken huge equipment crates from a ship at the docks, set them on the ground and then cut a window and a door out of each one. A number of these containers stood in a row. This is what they rented to workers who didn't want to stay in the labor camp. That's what I was living in, complete with rats and mice. After work, exhausted and not knowing anybody, and the only place to go back to being that crate, I hung out at bars and played pool and drank and drank and drank.

One morning after about two months, I got fed up with the way the workers lived. I got fed up with the antisocial atmosphere—I was from New York, and around the orange fields of Florida they didn't care for New Yorkers. I realized I would rather do it differently. Even after all that work, I did not have enough money to get back to New York, so I fell back on my youth tactic again: I turned myself in to the authorities. I turned myself in to the police in Florida, who sent me to the parole office in Wisconsin, and from there they brought me back to New York. I told the authorities that I no longer wanted parole.

"Look, man, I've had enough," I said. "I want to max out. This is not going to work, always going in and out. I am not going to pay you guys any attention. You are not paying any attention to me. You don't care what's happening, so let's stop playing games. Let me go back to prison and finish out my time so I can be done with you."

They granted me my wish, and I returned to prison in Queens as a parole violator. Originally my sentence had been for three years. In the end I had violated parole so many times, which meant added time, that I did not get done serving time for the crime I committed in 1971 until 1985.

This time in prison I sold paintings and some Christmas cards I made. I also had about a thousand dollars back pay from my job in Wisconsin. So when I came out, I had about two thousand and change.

When I walked out of prison a so-called free man, I had all the good intentions in the world. By then I had lost track of everybody I knew. I wanted to get back in touch with them. I looked up Miriam and saw my daughters. I felt that my life could get back on track.

What I wanted, after time in prison, was women and the so-called "good life," but I worried that if I had a lot of money in my pocket I would abuse it, so I wanted to find a place and pay four or five months of rent up front. But no place in the city that I went would accept monthly rates. I soon realized my situation wasn't working. I was disgusted with the idea that the only places I could find where I could pay rent by the month were up on 42nd Street and 8th Avenue, which was out of my financial range. The places I knew only did things by the day. They would not accept money any other way. So there I was, all this money in my pocket, at a room that cost $20 to $27 a night.

Depressed, I tried to be slick. I bought a radio for $85. I bought clothes. I bought this and that, the money was going fast, but always in the back of my mind I felt that if push came to shove I could sell that stuff and get whatever I wanted.

I ended up going on a drinking binge. During my binge I met an East European woman named Barbara. She was Yugoslavian or Ukrainian, and she also spoke French. By the time I got down to the Village three or four days later, I was broke. I sold my radio for $20. I sold all my clothes.

In Tompkins Square Park I met a Puerto Rican Indian with red hair, who said his name was Red Wolf. He had a brother named Brown Wolf. Red Wolf was a skilled carpenter, so once he got a good job, he could usually hang onto it for a while. But he was young, so like me he chased women and drank. We didn't keep any of our jobs too long.

We lived for a while in various abandoned buildings together, and pretty soon I went back to shooting heroin.

***

I was lying around sick from lack of drugs. There were none available to me.

A white dude who used to come to the Lower East Side to get off came in where we were staying. The noise he made woke me up out of my sick sleep.

I saw that he had shot up right there and was getting high, but when I asked him, he said there was none for me. But he wanted to talk.

I lay there listening to him running off his mouth.

"Listen, man," I said. "I'm sick. Can you be cool? Be quiet?"

But he just kept yacking and yacking and yacking. He kept it up and up and up, irritating and irritating and irritating me, and I just stabbed him.

That shows how drug abuse can twist you. Except when I have been sick from needing heroin, I have always tried to avoid violence. In this case I wasn't even particularly angry with the dude. I just wanted him to shut up. Fortunately, he didn't die, and, fortunately, I was never arrested for that.

One day I ran into Barbara again, the East European lady, and I told her my situation. She took me in, and I started living with her in an abandoned building on Avenue B between 4th and 5th Street. Barbara was always getting money, I never found out how. But I do know we had a lot of cocaine. She always had money for a good supply of coke.

After a while even that got old, and I realized I had to do something different. Eventually we broke up and I found myself taking a bus up to a shelter for men in Chester, New York, called Camp La Guardia.

CHAPTER 13
A Bowl of Soup and a Prayer

During the first year I was at the La Guardia shelter, I quit doing hard drugs and worked as a meal-ticket puncher. I also painted a lot of murals. I made money painting pictures on t-shirts and painting greeting cards. My customers were my friends, the fellow residents of the shelter. I did that for about a year and the staff got to know me well.

The following year they gave me a job as an aide and it worked out pretty well. In those days I used to get off work and go downstairs to paint. Everything was cool. I loved it out there in that area, near Goshen, the Catskills, Sugarloaf, Middletown. Near Sugarloaf was the orphanage Pius Twelve where I had lived for a while as a youth.

My plan was to rent a storefront in Middletown. It came with an apartment in the back, all for $380 a month. While still keeping my job at the institution, I planned to open up an art store, doing my art on my days off. If everything worked out right, I would have Miriam and our daughters Yolanda and Tonya move in with me.

Despite my personal goals, I didn't forget the people. All the people who were my clients, who were residents of the shelter, were people from the streets. They were my friends. I wasn't about to stop my relationship with them. Even when I became staff, I would sell my art to them for a lower price because they did not have much money. I spent more time with the residents or painting than I would spend with the staff. To me that was preferable because all the staff would do is go out and get drunk. It was not that I was intending to be antisocial, it was just that I was attempting to improve my life. I was no longer into partying all the time. But I guess that infuriated the staff.

It started with petty things. For example, the staff got angry with me for the way I dressed when I came to work. I still had my Afro and full beard. I dressed comfortably. I don't dress for anybody else, I dress for me. They could not accept that. They called me a "revolutionist" and "antisocial."

Friction with the staff grew worse. Somebody started spreading a rumor that I had finked out to the administration that one of the cooks was selling reefer to the residents. To be honest, I don't remember if he was or not. If he was, I was probably buying it myself, so I wouldn't have been telling anybody about it. But this rumor, being spread, I believe, by someone on the La Guardia staff, was threatening my well-being and my kids' well-being.

"If we ever catch you in a bar," one of the cook's friends told me, "We're going to kill you. We might even get your kids, too."

Since I was unfortunately still into alcohol, they did catch me one night in the bar. They beat me up, and after that I had to walk around with a cane for a while because in that beating I got a big gash in my toe.

I could not deal with the pressure and jealousies. I had no intention of staying there to get beaten. Probably if I had not been drinking I would have stayed at that job. But I *was* drinking, so the booze, plus the money from the job in my pocket, told me to say the hell with it. One morning I woke up with $80 in my pocket and a hangover. I needed a drink. I had had enough of the La Guardia shelter. I bought some wine and a bus ticket to New York City.

Back in the Village, I learned that Barbara, the East European woman I had lived with for a while, was dead. Her boyfriend had beat a man for his cocaine. The guy whose cocaine had been stolen came back with a gun in order to kill Barbara's boyfriend.

The apartment in the abandoned building where Barbara was living did not have a secure door. Anybody could go in and out. The guy with the gun went in.

He saw a shape in the bed. Thinking it was Barbara's boyfriend, the guy fired his gun. Turned out it was Barbara, asleep in her own bed. The shot killed her.

***

The shelter at Wards Island shelter is a depressing place that looks like a maze to run rats through. Whenever I got on line to eat at Wards Island, I was awfully careful not to bump anybody because if I did I might get a knife in my side. I was awfully careful that I sat where there was enough light so I could be careful not to eat a roach while I was eating my dinner. Taking a shower there was as dangerous as when I was in prison. People get raped in shelter showers. After getting some of my stuff stolen, I came up with three locks to put on my locker. I slept with one eye open and my knife in my hand. I tied my shoes to the bed.

To my knowledge there is no training required to become a security officer in the shelter system. All you got to do is need a job. That means drug addicts, alcoholics, people of depravity are hired to do the security of the homeless people. That does not work.

Social Service Department workers, though well-intentioned in the beginning, become frustrated eventually because of the limits on what they are able to do, or what their administration allows them to do. When they become frustrated they become angry at the people they are supposed to be helping. They become clock-punchers. All they want to do is get that paycheck. So their effectiveness is gone.

I'm not going to give all of them even that benefit of a doubt, however, because some of them never did give a damn. Some of them started the job with the attitude of just getting their money and going home. So the job they are supposed to be doing, training people, or trying to get them to training, is being ignored.

What you end up with are institutions like Wards Island, full of people who are ready to die or are going there to die. Like those graveyards for elephants, where they go all over the world just to get to this one spot to die. And you get the vicious ones with nothing to lose, who will kill you for your shoes or your ass.

One night while I was staying at Wards Island, a guy who was sleeping got stabbed in the chest for his SSI money. After that, I figured it was safer to go back to the streets.

***

Down between 5th and 6th Street off Avenue C in the Lower East Side of the Village I lived for a while at a camp in a vacant lot that we called "Shanty Town." Homeless people had congregated there and put up tents or shelters out of cardboard and wood. I have done a painting called "Shanty Town" that shows a lady and her ovens. The story behind that is that there was an old woman living in Shanty Town, a German or Yugoslavian, who liked to bake bread and strudel on a regular basis, so one day we decided to build her an oven. We took a couple of new garbage cans from outside of some building and washed them out. Then we set them on their sides next to each other on some bricks and made holes in the bottom so the air could circulate. She made some good bread in those ovens!

In the painting I pictured Shanty Town in the shadow of a large six- or seven-story Habitat For Humanity building. A number of us in Shanty Town tried to get into the HFH cooperative to get an apartment, which would have meant we would get to take part in the rehabilitation of the building. That was cool with us, we liked the idea of fixing the building. It was what a lot of us had been doing already when we lived in abandoned buildings.

But we were not acceptable as far as Habitat For Humanity was concerned because we had either no income or else no steady income. The fact is, it is very hard to hold a job without having a building in which to live, although many homeless people do work some sort of paying job. It's hard to stay clean, and sleeping on the ground takes its toll on your body.

That rejection irked us and caused a lot of antagonism between Habitat For Humanity and the people of Shanty Town. Ironically, a number of people who work with HFH in different places have since told me that one of the reasons they became involved with HFH was they wanted to help homeless people get housing. I try to say all this as diplomatically as possible, because regardless of how I feel personally, Habitat For Humanity *is* doing some good for some people, and that's the important thing.

***

Every time an episode of my adult life was over, it was back to Tompkins Square Park until I got on my feet. This time was no different. From Shanty Town I eventually went and stayed in Tompkins Square Park again. In the winter time, the Parks Department would trim the trees and bring truckloads of wood to us for the fire. They even brought food for my dog. Some Christians calling themselves "Disciples for Christ," from the Bowery Mission, used to come to Tompkins Square Park and talk to us, but they did not convert me at the time.

In the immediate area of the park were a number of bars that I used to frequent. A number of the neighborhood bars stayed in competition with one another and in the summer played softball. On the corner of 7th and Avenue A was a hippie bar. The Alcatraz, on the corner of 8th Street and Avenue A, had once been a pizza joint and bar, but in the '80s they turned it into a yuppie bar. The Frog Pond was on 9th Street between Avenue A and 1st. You had to go down four steps to get into this joint, which was a big open bar with a pool table in back. I used to hang out there a lot with my brothers once upon a time.

Some nights I even went back to my old stomping grounds around Washington Square. One night I was checking things out at the Blue Note, drinking. My table was right in front of the stage. Lionel Hampton was right in front of me. He was getting ready to start playing.

"I want to shake your hand," I said to him. "I just want to feel your hand."

He wouldn't shake my hand.

"Man," I said, "how come you don't want to shake my hand? I been admiring you or your music all my life. By accident you're here and I'm here and all I want to do is shake your hand. I don't want your money. I don't want anything but to listen to your music. And shake your hand."

Finally, after about a half hour of my being there, running my mouth, they got tired of my opinion and took a break before the show even started.

The bodyguard came over. I figured maybe he was going to beat me up and throw me out.

"Come on," he said. "Lionel would like to shake your hand."

So I got to meet him. I guess a lot of people want to shake his hand.

In the Reagan era I mostly went to a Polish bar called the Cherry Tavern, on 6th Street, across from the park. It had a pool table and served hamburgers. You mainly saw Polish people hanging out in there, older generation Polish. A lot of the homeless who were living in the park were homeless Polish immigrants. They had a relationship with the bar owner, and he would give them food there. I went there basically because it *wasn't* a yuppie bar or a hippie bar; it was what I call a hometown bar. One of the dudes there, Ed Rutter, had come over from Poland in the late 1950s. Eddie had gray hair and a friendly smile. He was a puttering kind of old dude you wanted to put your arm around protectively. When I would get some money somehow, I liked sharing my bottle with Eddie. We drank a lot of vodka together.

***

Though La Guardia had not worked out, by sometime around 1986 I knew that I needed to try something different. Living in the streets is tough enough. To be a drug abuser and live in the streets you have to do things to get your drugs, you have to hang out with certain people to get your drugs, you have to say and/ or do things you won't normally do because you need that drink or you need that drug. When you're a drug addict, you put your life in the hands of the dealer. When you're addicted to any kind of drugs, including alcohol, you're not yourself, you have no control over yourself. You are addicted. Your whole life is completely turned over to the drug and whoever is in control of that drug, to the alcohol and who's got the alcohol. Somebody you know walks into the park with a bottle of booze, suddenly he's more your friend than he's ever been before. Once that bottle is empty, then you find some other friend.

One day I was just weary with the whole trip. I made up my mind that I didn't want to live that way anymore.

I didn't like the associations. ,

I didn't like the smell of alcohol.

I didn't like the nausea of heroin.

Living in the middle of it, I didn't give a damn, but once I had detoxed during those three years in prison, once I was reading again, once I had gotten my G.E.D., my mind was already changing and could not give up my ambition to better my life and help others better theirs. For years I had been trying to detox and rehab from drugs, but every time I got out of detox, I went right back to the bottle or some kind of drug. Everything else I had tried had not worked, so that day I made up my *mind* to go into the Bowery Mission, knowing that I would not like the rules and regulations. I made up my *mind* that I was going to follow their rules and regulations, to put up with those rules and regulations in order for me to survive. I knew it was going to be strict. Whatever they said, I was going to do, as long as it helped me kick drugs. I knew that I was going to have to become a Christian in order to get the services that I was looking for. So I said good-bye to the lady I was with at the time, and I went into the Bowery Mission with the intention of laying up and getting myself together. This time I said, "Fuck it, let me go to God and see what happens."

To my dismay, only two or three days after I went into the Bowery Mission, the Disciples put me in charge of twenty-some-odd residents. They made me the housekeeper. That meant getting these guys who worked underneath me to do what I said. We had to feed over 300 people three meals a day. We had to maintain the cleanliness of the house. We had to make sure that the people who came in for showers and clothing got showers and clothing. Now the bad part about that was I had not gone in the Bowery Mission to be in charge of other people. The good part, the important part, was that the experience once again showed me I could be a leader.

When I became a member of the Bowery Mission staff, it meant I got my own room in the mission and had a tv. I began painting again. I got a relationship going with some kids out on a Mennonite farm in Pennsylvania. I would send them paintings I had done.

The Bowery Mission always had a security guard at the door. To leave, you had to get a day pass, and to get a day pass you had to be recommended by the staff. Then the director of the Bowery Mission would decide whether or not to issue you a pass.

Once they gave me permission to go out, I looked up the lady I had been with before I went in to the mission, and we began seeing each other again. I also started going to Alcoholics Anonymous and Narcotics Anonymous. I think those programs work for some people and not for others. I think they are very good programs for people who are contemplating stopping drug and alcohol abuse. At A.A. and N.A. they can see that there are other people of like mind. They are able to share their experiences and their reasons for wanting to stop. All people who are thinking about recovery should go to at least a month or two of meetings, if not more.

To me, however, A.A. and N.A. got boring after a while. The same conversations time after time. What I saw happening in A.A. and N.A. was that you got a social group that had nothing else in common other than their fight against drugs and alcohol. Our world is much larger than that. Whether we want to or not, we have to deal with other people outside of A.A. and N.A., and in a way those organizations hinder that because they don't want you to socialize with people who are drinkers or who do drugs. That does not cut it in my line of work. I come in contact with people who drink and drug on a daily basis. Not everybody becomes an alcoholic just because there is alcohol. Sometimes it's because she feels she has no life worth staying sober for. Sometimes it's because his job got taken away from him. Figure out why this man or that woman became an alcoholic. Listen and learn all the reasons why people have lost their homes.

You take any drug—cocaine, alcohol, marijuana, heroin—if you can afford it, you are not considered "an addict." If you cannot afford it, you're an addict, a menace to society. You've got executives that spend two hours every day at lunch drinking, some of them doing coke. They have the convenience of doing their illegal drugs in their home, of detoxing in very expensive luxury hospitals. They have the money to support their habit, so they are not considered addicts.

I don't like dope. I've lost family members to heroin, but point blank, if I was a dope fiend and I had a million dollars, I would be applauded for seeking counseling instead of being chastised or arrested. Rich people have rights poor people don't get.

The Bowery Mission had a truck, and we would go out once a week and give out food, soup and bread. When the Disciples of Christ went out there and fed people, they also fed them their Gospel tracts and preached Jesus Christ. As far as I was concerned, there should be more to it. It's all right to preach the Lord, if that is what you believe. But once the Disciples of Christ had left, I saw people still hurting, people who still had to deal with their immediate problems, their physical problems. And homeless people often have nobody to talk to. Though spreading the word of the Lord and/or recovery was cool, I felt that we needed to talk *with* the people, not just *at* them. I felt we had to become more a part of their lives than just a bowl of soup and a prayer.

These were my own people we were feeding. In the old days I used to get high with them. We had warmed ourselves over fires together for years. In fact, a lot of the people in the park were the same people I had been doing everything with since 1965. The thing that made me uncomfortable now was that each night after I would see these people and talk to them and give them food, I was going home to the mission, to a nice warm shower and bed, while they were doing without.

I asked the authorities at the Mission if they would allow me to expand our feeding program to include Sunday because Sunday is the roughest day for homeless people. Sundays are bad for homeless people all over the United States. People are in church or taking the day off; they're not out there feeding the hungry.

I convinced the Bowery Mission to let me take two pushcarts full of food and clothing and give it out in the streets of the Lower East Side. First thing in the morning I would go over to the A.A. location where I had been a member. Early in the morning a lot of people that were homeless were making their journey to Tompkins Square Park or to their destination for making money. I would stand outside the A.A. building alone or with an assistant, handing out food and clothing from the carts— blocks of cheese, bread, and sandwich spreads, a lot of gloves and hats. Whatever the mission could get. And always I would talk to these people, get to know them as individuals, not just a mass of humanity that we fed once a week and forgot, not just a faceless crowd that we helped in order to save our own souls.

Unfortunately, when organizations fed people in the Lower East Side, they only went to Tompkins Square, and not all the homeless were living in Tompkins Square. So I rolled my pushcarts down 2nd Avenue, Avenue B, and Avenue D, where people were living in the abandoned apartments, and I went to Shanty Town. What I was learning was that it seemed more people were becoming homeless. The park was getting more crowded. People have always slept in Tompkins Square Park, but not to the point that it was becoming. Tompkins Square wasn't always a homeless convention. Soon I was asking the Mennonites if they could build me some wooden wagons for carting more food around.

The extra feeding day I had initiated made the Bowery Mission and its efforts look good. I was getting things done. I even became part of the front door security. They also were sending me out to a church to wash dishes, and in this way I was able to earn additional income.

Now Mennonites were good supporters of the Bowery Mission. The Disciples' plan was for me to graduate from the Bowery Mission and then move to a Mennonite farm somewhere in Connecticut or Pennsylvania and continue in their Christian atmosphere out there. But that was not my agenda. That was not me. That was just going from a city institution to a country institution. So when I eventually graduated from the Disciples of

Christ, they gave me a certificate, but I chose not to go to the farm. I thought that they would help me find a job and housing in New York City.

I had graduated, yet they kept me on at the mission at the same tasks. Two years down the line and they still had me doing the same things for them. I had grown, but they allowed no room for growth outside their narrow confines. The problem was this: once you become staff, you have to shift the way you act and behave because you have increased responsibilities. If you live on the premises, that makes your job a 24-hour-a-day job. You can't really unwind. You can't have your privacy.

Their restriction hurt in another way as well. In growing, you are supposed to be able to take on other responsibilities, such as the responsibility of having your own apartment and paying the rent. That should have been part of my growth. I needed to relearn how to pay utility bills, how to pay rent, how to budget so much money to buy food and so much to buy clothes. If your organization is trying to rehabilitate a person who has lived outside the mainstream of society, you have to teach not only Christianity, but also economics; you have to teach how to live within this great community we have. These things are necessary in anybody's growth as a person.

In the end, the Bowery Mission made another mistake with me, one that made up my mind. The crisis came when I got venereal disease from my lady friend. Naturally I had to get it taken care of, so I told the people in the mission office so I could arrange for treatment. However, when they found out I had V.D., it quickly became public knowledge within the institution. They berated me tremendously. They restricted me to the mission building, and they took away my jobs. They took away my paint brushes and my paints. They would not let me paint. They knew painting was my outlet, they knew by taking that away they would really be hurting me. That was their punishment for me. I have to admit, that was my catalyst for leaving the mission.

Had they allowed me to get an apartment outside the mission and still work there, things might have turned out differently. Had they reprimanded me differently, I might have stayed at the mission, because I had become a Christian there, not just in word; I had become a believer. Although I understood the need for reprimanding me, the extremes they went to eliminated my desire to work with them, to be part of them. I realized that being a Bowery Mission-brand Christian had nothing to do with being Casanova.

***

In my experience, all institutions tend to want you to remain dependent on them. That's the welfare system, that's the AFDC, that's Christianity. It is great to go out and feed people, but it is more important to help people learn to feed themselves. It's like that old saying that if you *give* a man a fish, he will have food to eat that day and that day only; *teach* him to fish and he'll be able to get food for himself and have something to eat for the rest of his life. Moreover, he can teach somebody else how to fish.

I cannot stress this enough. I won't ever stop emphasizing it, because this country has built a population of dependents, people who depend on someone else for their lives. As long as you depend on someone else, you are in their control. You are not your own person if you are on Aid to Families with Dependent Children all the time, or on the dole from the church. If we have a system of AFDC that sets us up to be dependent on AFDC for the rest of our lives, then we are not our own masters. We cannot make decisions based on our own beliefs; we have to make our decisions by the guidelines dictated by AFDC, by the government, by the churches, by the people who then control our lives.

If a person is on AFDC on a temporary basis and is being trained to become self-sufficient, then that's another story. That is the way the system should ideally work. If somebody has a car with an engine that guzzles gas, they don't take a sledgehammer to the engine. The answer is not to destroy these programs, but to tune them up.

CHAPTER 14

Tent City

There are many things I haven't touched yet in my story, and many people that need to be in it. I have forgotten some of the events, some of the names and some of the dates. But I do know that on August 6, 1988, at two in the morning, I was standing in Tompkins Square Park near the entrance on Avenue B, across the street from a bar and a liquor store, holding a Bible in my hands, watching a riot between police and people in the park.

I always seemed to come back to Tompkins Square Park. That night I stood watching it all, watching over some of the homeless people who wanted no part of the clash and who were trying to sleep on benches behind the band shell. Right then I didn't even care if I was part of the world. At that time I was experiencing inner turmoil. I don't remember exactly, but I believe I was either contemplating leaving the Bowery Mission or had just left it.

A writer named Sarah Ferguson, who lived in the neighborhood, asked me that night why this group of homeless was outside the circle of violence.

"We just want to be left alone," I told her.

The police had told us to stay where we were in the park, and we did, so we weren't caught in the beatings. It felt like we were in a bubble that the raging violence couldn't touch. Later I painted a picture of that night which I titled "Shadow of Protection."

In the end, a lot of people got beat up in that action. One hundred and twenty-one complaints of police brutality got filed, although not one of the officers was ever convicted or punished, mainly because the court system would not find police brutality had occurred unless fellow officers said it had. And they were not talking.

Rather than put myself through the Bowery Mission program any longer, I withdrew. Hurting, disappointed in my life and the world, I went out of control, I returned to my old ways of drinking and wildness, living in abandoned buildings and in Tompkins Square Park again. Once again alcohol was in control of me, not the other way around, like I sometimes believed. Though I did not commit any crimes or do needle drugs during that period, I was wild, reacting against the strictness and the unfairness of the Mission toward me.

After I left the Bowery Mission, I went back to Shanty Town for a little while, but by that time it was ruled by a homeless gentleman who was controlling people in the camp through alcohol, through drugs. With him it was all about power, but power just for him. That was not my cup of tea, so I went back to living in Tompkins Square Park.

I'll give credit to a Christian crew out of Jersey. I forget the name of the organization, but they used to come down there to Tompkins Square Park and try to talk religion to us, and they always brought us food. The Christians from Jersey would come down every Saturday to sing their Gospel songs, pass out their tracts and feed hundreds of people. They served the best food, so a lot of homeless from Queens and the Bronx came down on Saturdays to eat. Though the feeding was good, it brought all kinds of people, and not all the homeless were very friendly. Sometimes they were very angry, sometimes they would steal, sometimes there would be a fight.

Because of my recent experience at the Bowery Mission, I myself was feeling anger toward Christians at that time. In the beginning when the Christians from Jersey would come, I used to tell them "Please, leave me alone. I'm sick," or "I need a drink," or "I want to get high."

They were smart, however. They learned not to keep shoving their religion down our throats. They did not stop coming and showing their concern for us just because we refused to be listening to their Christianity. What convinced me of their sincerity is that they came back *despite* our refusal, because of their humanistic ideals, still feeding and clothing and listening to us.

For a time I moved in with some squatters at a building on 9th Street between B and C. While I was there, somebody from the Bowery Mission tracked me down because they had something for me which came as a surprise: a good-sized wooden cross. All the time I was at the Bowery Mission I had been after the Mennonites to build me some wagons for hauling food around the streets to help feed people, and here instead they sent a cross. But I guess I must have smiled when I saw that cross because it had been put together for me by the Mennonite kids as a class project, and I had a fondness for those kids. As it happened, one of the squatters in the building was a black-haired Mennonite minister named Frank, who had a blonde wife and baby, so I donated the cross for the room in our building we had set up half as a kitchen, half as a meditation room.

That winter it got very cold, even for New York City. One night about the middle of December, 1988, my Polish brother Ed Rutter went to sleep on a park bench in Tompkins Square Park. Even in the winter, Eddie wouldn't go in a city-run shelter because he was afraid of getting hurt or robbed there. That night he had an overcoat, two blankets and a bottle to keep him warm. Another homeless man, Eliot Lopez, helped Eddie over to a bench next to where Lopez had built a fire in one of the park's metal trash cans. During the night, a police officer kicked the trash can over.

"No fires allowed in the park," the policeman said.

And the mercury just kept falling. It got down to five degrees that night.

By morning, Eddie had frozen to death. Lopez said Eddie's hand was reaching out to the scattered, cold ashes where the fire had been. Later when I heard what had happened, it made me angry, but scared, too. I thought of my own plight. I was almost 44 years old and without a secure place to live. I could end up like Eddie. But for the time being, all I did was drink until I forgot to be scared.

Unfortunately, at the squatters' building we had problems sometimes with the Puerto Rican brothers and sisters in the neighborhood because they considered squatters to be hippies, and they did not like the idea of all these hippies moving into their block. So most of the neighbors there did not like us. They were the Latino rich; they were only into their cars and didn't think about the problems of people with no place to live. Partly because of that animosity, I quit living there and returned to the park.

***

It seems to me that it was around my birthday in 1989 when I ran across my old friend Red Wolf. I was sitting on a bench in Tompkins Square Park and he came by. We had not seen each other in ages.

"Hey, man, what's up?" he asked.

"Ain't nothin' to it," I said. "I left the Bowery Mission a while back, and right now I need a place to stay."

Red Wolf was on his way out of the city, but he pulled a tent out of his knapsack and gave it to me. I pitched the tent in Tompkins Square Park close to 9th Street and Avenue A.

Next day, Red Wolf was back. He ended up not leaving town, so we shared his tent. We were there about a day and a half when a friend of ours, a fellow named Spider, pitched a tent next to us. Next thing I knew, my good friend Gypsy showed up and set his tent up as well. Within that week we must have had anywhere from five to ten different tents in this one area of the park, and a number of the people in them had been part of the Casanovas. I felt a sense of security being with people I knew, a comradeship.

All kinds of people came to the park whether they lived there or not: African Americans, old Polish people and Ukrainians, Cubans, long-haired hippies and spike-haired punk rockers, Puerto Ricans playing *jíbaro* music, skin-heads in steel-toed army boots, Jamaican rastas with dreadlocks. People walked their dogs while skate-boarders shot past concentrating chess players and heavy metal bands, and Reeboks were squeaking as pick-up teams played basketball while mothers walked their infants in strollers. But something different was happening this time. People who were coming to sleep in the park began to act aware of themselves as a community. I felt happy because it reminded me of the Village in the old days.

People just kept coming. The police themselves, all over New York, began telling homeless people in the subways and doorways of the Bronx, Brooklyn and Queens to go down to Tompkins Square Park. We had an influx of people coming in, pitching tents and building shacks. The park became a sanctuary. I guess the cops and the neighborhood liked it that way because while we were in the park we were not sleeping in their doorways. We were not blocking any businesses. At the time we did not realize that we would soon have to fight to live in the park. We did not know that we would have to fight to survive. And the police had helped to set up the scenario.

But June 1989 was fantastic. We were a festive combination of squatters, anarchists, activists and mostly just homeless people. Some people slept in the band shell, some people slept beneath the flat roof of the brick pavilion that was between the rest-rooms. We had a lot of homemade lean-to type tents made out of clear plastic stretched over wooden frames. They were about the size of pup tents. Refrigerator-box cardboard walls for some, store-bought tents for others. Tents pitched side by side on the hard-packed dirt underneath the park trees near park benches. People slept covered by blanket and sheets, or some had sleeping bags. We were getting a lot of clothes donations, which we hung up on fences for anybody who needed them and could use them. Beside each one of the tents we had campfires, and there was one communal campfire where we fed any people who were hungry. People in the neighborhood would go out and buy or collect food and bring it for our kitchen. People began to get the word that we were feeding the homeless and anybody was welcome.

I had experienced people living in the streets since I was young, a youth living in hallways. The general plight of the homeless did not really affect me back then; I only worried about myself. But by that summer of 1989, things had changed very drastically from the way they had been. I had never seen so many homeless people.

We had a veteran living in the park with us, another drinker, who we called Old Man John. Old Man John was disabled mentally; he couldn't live with his family, and his sisters couldn't take him—he couldn't live with anybody. In fact, he was a thorn in my side because he was a very aggravating person.

Old Man John was a coffee fanatic. He made sure we had coffee. If there wasn't coffee at the crack of dawn, I was the first person he would come to.

"Cas! Where's the coffee? Where's the coffee? Where's the coffee?"

I guess I had the patience of Job in those days to keep from kicking his ass. But he did not want to live in an institution, and I understood that. So I would get up and take the coffee pot somebody had donated and start boiling the water on the fire. We strained our coffee the best we could.

Old Man John also wrote poetry of a sort. He would jot down sentences, fragments of thought. A woman from the neighborhood used to put out a paper printed in Jersey called *Voices From the Street*. She somehow got John to write out one of his poems and she edited it down and printed it in her paper. Unfortunately, I lost my copy in one of the police raids that were to come.

Soon we had a lot of churches supporting us. One day some people we knew from Long Island brought a van full of food from a gourmet store. We had something like 18 boxes of groceries. We bagged them individually and passed the bags out to people who came by and needed the food.

Everybody and anybody could eat with us. At first we would be cooking on fires outside the tents. We did not have a stove. Then the Parks Department warned us no fires were allowed in the park, so when we finished cooking a meal, we put out the fire. So for a while the authorities left us alone. Eventually, however, they started messing with that, again saying no fires in the park. They brought in the Police Department and the Fire Department, trying to get our camp fires in the park extinguished. But that plan backfired. As it turned out, the police and firefighters went all over the park checking these fires. The

Police Department said there was nothing wrong with them. They were safe fires. The Fire Department also said they were safe fires.

Not happy at all with this result, the Parks Department went to court about it. This time it didn't go our way.

"Put them out," the court ruled. So we moved our cooking inside of a tent where we made ourselves a big stove out of bricks. Pretty soon we lucked out and got us a cook, a black dude by the name of Artie Wilson. He first came to the park because some of his friends had come to Tompkins Square from different institutional shelters. When we saw that Artie could cook, we got to know Artie very well. He became our official cook. Artie liked cooking for the people who came.

"People are here for various reasons," I remember Artie saying. "How you wind up in the park, you don't want to remember, but you *are* here, so we have to deal with it from there."

On that brick stove, Artie prepared food three to four times a day and fed several hundred people at each meal, and did a very good job of it. Our regular meal times were morning, afternoon and maybe about five o'clock in the evening. The neighborhood anarchists helped with the food. They worked out of a bookstore called Sabotage, which closed at four in the afternoon. Afterwards, they would come to the park and drop off chickens and vegetables. The anarchists liked to wear dark clothes, a lot of black, and they smoked cigarettes continuously. Frank, a Latino anarchist, dressed all in black and wore a beret. He had a narrow face and whiskers on his chin. Frank was very intense.

"We're facing a fascist police order in this city," Frank said one time, "that is out to attack and kill blacks and Latinos especially, but really is indiscriminate in terms of poor people in general."

In a big pot Artie would cook the chicken and vegetables the anarchists brought. Later at night the squatters would come by with more food and so we would eat again. The late crowd. We would pretty much be feeding people throughout the night because people would come at various times.

Neighborhood people would come down with their instruments and play music. One night a guy brought his portable xylophone and played while we sat smoking reefer and drinking beer and talking. On every bench you could see people sitting conversing, politicizing They were all comfortable here. It was a beautiful atmosphere.

I noticed a tall, slim woman talking with some people. I went over and introduced myself. She said her name was Karen Margolis, and she was an activist. Back in the 1950s, when she was only eight years old, she had gone on a CORE (Congress of Racial Equality) Freedom Ride. Later she worked against U.S. involvement in Vietnam, and in the '80s she opposed U.S. intervention in Central America. Until recently Karen had taught school in New York.

I expressed my interest in getting to know her. Well, that night she still left with the married couple she had come with, but in the days to come she became one of the neighborhood people who would come around bringing food.

Early in the morning Karen would be one of the first supporters to come to the park. She would come wake me, always bringing me something to eat. She was a lot of fun to wake up to. In the freshness of the morning Karen and I would sit and drink coffee and talk, and as the summer days passed, I learned about her. Karen had lived for a year on the Upper West Side of Manhattan with a dude she said "turned into the fiancé from hell." Karen told me that after she had gotten pregnant, her fiancé had gotten physically and mentally abusive. So Karen left him and spent a few months with a friend. Eventually she took the shelter route, moving into a shelter and going on welfare. She was 39 at the time.

In those days, Mayor Koch had a program for pregnant women whereby Karen was able to get into a low-income tenant co-op in the East Village. While Karen was living there, she had her son, and she named him Ethan.

"The name means 'strong'," she told me. "It's such a beautiful name."

I looked at Karen, this tall, willowy woman and thought that *she* was strong, *she* was beautiful.

"I'd like to meet Ethan," I said.

She then told me Ethan was in Kansas City, Missouri, with her parents, and that she was going to get him soon. I questioned Karen some more and learned that New York Hospital had told her that Ethan, two years old then, might be autistic. She tried to get him help through Medicaid, but the help didn't come. Her parents were well-to-do, and they had promised the best in help for Ethan, but only if Ethan stayed with them for a short while. So Karen took Ethan to stay with her folks. She had stayed in constant contact with her parents and had been assured by them that Ethan was progressing very well and that he was probably not autistic. But they told Karen that as yet Ethan was not quite ready to return home to her.

Our community grew, and we soon gave it the name of "Tent City." Things were happening fast. Tent City did not happen as a planned organization. There was no revolution, no movement there. It started as a place where people came because they needed a place to stay. We had no place to stay, so we went to the park and pitched a tent. It was people of like mind, comfortable with each other, sharing their space in the park. Tent City was open to anyone and everyone who rejected the city's so-called solutions to homelessness. We had a slogan: "No Housing, No Peace." Now that did not mean that we wanted a violent confrontation with the authorities. That meant we were not going to allow ourselves to be quietly put out of sight and mind in jails or dangerous shelters. That is no solution, that is burial.

Some of the squatters and anarchists and other activists from the neighborhood who were already in the antipoverty movement started talking to us about how to deal with the authorities. There were several groups and they all had plans and ideas. I would just pick out which one sounded the best to me and make suggestions along those lines to the Tent City residents. Usually they agreed.

Something was happening in Tompkins Square Park. All our lives we had accepted poverty as a way of life, whatever the reason. People had accepted welfare as a way of life. Now we were doing things for ourselves. Outside the entrance to the park we set up a table with information about Tent City, poverty, homelessness, and about social services people could get and how they could go about getting those services. We began educating people about the politics of poverty. During the day, while most people from our park community would go looking for work or do their hustle to bring some money in, I would sit there in the camp and paint. That was *my* hustle. I would keep an eye on peoples' clothes and property while doing my art.

I would stretch a t-shirt over a section of cardboard and slant it off my knees as I sat up against a tree painting. Then we would sell them at the table we had set up. That summer I painted and sold a lot of t-shirts showing scenes from Tent City and Tompkins Square Park.

***

Since I had been living in the area off and on since the mid-'60s, I had a lot of friends in the street, a lot of people who knew me. Sometimes they and the more curious people from the neighborhood would come by the park to find out what Tent City was about.

"Why are you living in the park?" they would ask me.

First of all, I would explain, most of us in the park were single people, and we could not afford to rent. If you were to rent a room in Manhattan, you would be paying something like $200 a week. First of all, if you could even find a room in that low a price range, the place would be roach-infested and filthy. You were lucky if you got a window. You were lucky if nobody broke into your room.

Let's say you are working and getting paid the minimum wage of 1996. You cannot even afford that rent. Do the math. For the sake of discussion, let's say you're getting paid one and a half times the minimum wage; hell, round it off to $6.50 an hour. You might be able to make rent, if taxes don't take too much. But then where do you get the money to eat? What happens if you get sick? If you have kids, what about child care? How do you get your laundry taken care of? What about transportation? Utilities? And on and on and on and on. The minimum wage needs to be tripled.

"Why don't you homeless go into the shelters?" some people would come by and ask me.

"Have you ever been to a shelter?" I would answer. "Have you ever been to the shelter on Wards Island? Go to Wards Island," I would tell such people. "Then take a walk through Tompkins Square Park to see the difference."

People in Tompkins Square had their problems, but they also kept their own kind of dignity, which you will not find among the fearful inmates of a shelter. The homeless of Tompkins Square remained individuals, refusing to become the beaten-down penitents that too many of the shelters want, demand, and make.

Kids did not live with us much at the park, although kids would come down there to visit a parent who was living in the park. Some of these kids came with their grandparents or some other relative.

Despite the fact that a lot of the shelters are terrible, there are reasons some people go there, even though they may not want to. Being homeless is hard on couples. If you really love a person, you don't want them sleeping on the ground and worrying about where they are going to eat. A homeless family living on the streets has an added problem: the welfare system or the courts will take away the kids if they catch up with that family. So if there is a homeless family that does not want to go into a shelter, they have to dodge the law so they can keep their kids with them. Some of the family people I have met in the streets are responsible parents. For example, they try to stay in one area so the kids can go to school, and if the kids get sick they take them to a clinic or hospital. But it is much more difficult to stay out of the shelter system if you have children or a loved one with you. Some families who do go into the shelter system don't want to, but they do it for the sake of their kids.

***

One of the biggest problems we experienced at Tent City was that the Parks Department would lock the public rest-rooms every day at 4 p.m. That made things difficult. At that time, counting Tent City and the other folks who were not part of our camp, you had anywhere from 300 to 325 people living in the park, including some women and children, and no bathroom after four o'clock. Of course that meant that you would get a bad smell in some areas. We preferred the rest-room to using the trees and the grass. We did not want to go to the bathroom outside, but we were left with no choice.

Late that month, the police told us to move to the other side of the park. We told them we did not want to move. Finally, Deputy Inspector Michael Julian, of the 9th Precinct, came in person. Julian was tall, slim, and fairly good looking. He had come into power under the banner of Bush's "kinder, gentler" phrase. But he was very condescending. He came over to us and told us we had to move to the Avenue B side of Tompkins Square Park.

"We'll leave you guys alone in this park if you go down to Avenue B and pitch your tents," he told us.

I said, "Hey, you gotta be crazy."

I told him we refused to go because that side of the park was drug-infested. That was where the people hung out who did the drugs, and we did not want to be bothered with that. We did not want anything to do with hard drugs. Imagine a situation with over 300 people living in the park at one time, and a little bit more than half were doing needle drugs. There were also people from the neighborhood who came to the park to buy needle drugs. In every section of the park except ours, they were dealing heroin and cocaine. We had created our own security force in Tent City, and we would kick out people who were doing heroin or coke.

Besides the hard drug situation, we had strategic reasons for not wanting to be bunched together into one crowd with everybody who was living in the park. Not all the people living in the park got along with each other. We had an ongoing feud with the punk rockers who lived in another part of the park. More importantly, though, we were aware that a park curfew law was going into effect starting July 5th. We were aware that the parks department police were going to come and get us.

"There is no way you are going to put us in one bundle, one crowd of people and make it easy for you to come and get us out of this park," we told Julian. "We don't intend to make it easy for you, and we have no intention of leaving."

So we stayed where we were and Julian and the city officials stayed where they were—for the time being. Their stated reason for wanting us out of the park was bogus. They said they were concerned about the drug problems in the park. Drugs had been rampant in the park for years and the police ignored it. Now suddenly they were concerned.

One part of the problem was that since the police were sending any and all homeless people to the park, drugs in the park naturally increased. But the truth of the matter is, if it weren't for the fact that Tent City existed in Tompkins Square Park, they would not have done anything about the drugs. Once we started making noise about poverty and homelessness, the cops started putting it in the paper and in the neighborhood that the homeless people in the park were all drug addicts. They also said later for the *New York Times* that we had been living there for only a week, as if that lie could justify what they eventually did.

On Wednesday, the fifth of July, 1989, we waited.

Police were gathering, but nothing overt was happening yet. Over at Washington Square Park, a lot of skinheads had been burning American flags, demonstrating against anybody living in Tompkins Square Park. Then they left Washington Square Park, marching to Tompkins Square Park. They came into the park raising hell, trying to scare all of us out.

I was sitting in front of my tent with Red Wolf. We were just sitting there on one side of the benches, the skinheads and their crowd on the other side of the benches. As long as the skinheads stayed on their side of the benches and their side of the fences and didn't come to our tents, we were going to leave it alone. But Red Wolf and I sat ready with our pieces of pipe. Instead of trying to calm down these skinheads, or walk them out, the cops just watched.

We passed the word around that the skinheads were coming. If there was not a unity among all the homeless people in the park, there were a lot of people who were scared, but not ready to lose their tents to the skinheads. It was bad enough we were going to get taken by the cops, but we were not going to let anybody else do it. Everybody started coming out from their tents, and even the punk rockers came over carrying sticks and pipes. They were with us.

We were ready to do business.

The skinheads were being surrounded, then. They were not only confronted by the homeless residents of the park, but also confronted by the activists and people from the neighborhood who were coming to our aid. That's when the cops started dispersing the crowd. As it turned out, most of the skinheads, seeing the crowd of homeless people with clubs and bats, realized they were not going to be able to do what they wanted so they backed off. So we had a rest that day.

At nine that evening the police force came.

More than 250 police in riot gear with long billy clubs advanced on the park, with about a dozen Parks Department police. Helmeted police on horses. Helicopters loudly chopping overhead. The police told all non-homeless people to leave the park. But by that time we had almost 200 supporters from the area.

At 9:30 three green Parks Department garbage trucks rumbled into the park. The line of police pushed us back, while the Parks Department workers came in tearing and ransacking, knocking down our handmade shelters with sledgehammers and axes and throwing food, clothes, and IDs into the garbage trucks.

The cops were already hip to the idea that Tent City contained the noise makers and the ones that were going to give them the problem, so they cleared out all the other shacks and tents in the park before they came to the Tent City area. This was Inspector Julian's "kinder, gentler" way—the same as all the rest: dragging off homeless people.

"Out of the park and into the street!" people were chanting. "No police state!"

This was my first time being involved in anything this heavy. As I watched, I was scared, but I was angry too. I had no intention of leaving because my blood was in that neighborhood. One of my daughters had been born on Ludlow Street nearby. My Polish friend had died on a bench there, frozen to death. All my life I had tried to escape New York and make a life. I had worked in New Jersey, Wisconsin and Florida. But by the night the cops came in, I was at the point where I didn't want to go anywhere else anymore. I no longer wanted to escape New York. This time I would not stand apart from what was happening.

When the cops were coming to tear down all the tents, Red Wolf and I stayed, as did some of the punk rockers and some concerned citizens from Jersey who were willing to stay there and maybe get their heads beat in. I decided I was going to sit there by my tent, and they would have to pick me up and take me away. An inspector or captain kept coming up to me.

"Take your stuff and leave," he would say.

"I'm not going to leave," I kept telling him.

At last he said, "If pretty soon you don't do it, we're going to have to come in and people are going to get hurt."

That was good psychology because I did not want any blood on my hands, especially of people we were trying to help. I did not want anybody to get hurt. So I told the guys to come on and we split.

One of our Tent City residents, a black man named Keith Thompson, was sitting on the ground crying, with one arm over his suitcase and his other clutching a garbage bag of his belongings. Armed police stood guard with their arms crossed or hands on their guns, making sure that no one stopped the Parks Department workers from trashing the belongings of the homeless. I watched as real litter got left in the park while the Parks Department workers threw everything some of us had—including ID, medication, and clothing—into the mouths of those big green trash trucks.

That is the moment I became an activist, when I saw the destruction. I realized that the government or powers-that-be could do that at any given time. Now it became personal.

As it turned out, we ended up going out onto Avenue A and 7th Street that night. That's where the real demonstration started taking place.

CHAPTER 15

Up from the Wounded Streets

That night, after the cops kicked us out of Tompkins Square Park, we gravitated toward 7th Street and Avenue A, the site of the bloody confrontation that people in the neighborhood were having with the police. The cops barricaded all park entrances and made sure their forces were numerous enough that nobody could get back into the park.

In response, over 400 neighborhood supporters, housing activists, squatters, and homeless proceeded to block the streets so that no cars were getting through all night long. The intersection at A and 7th was filled with people. More than 30 plainclothes officers were helping to arrest people. We ended up starting a bonfire in the middle of the block between 7th and 8th Street on Avenue A. Somebody set an American flag on fire. Firecrackers were set off under cars. Some people threw bottles and eggs at the police. Thirty-one people were arrested and others got beat up by the police or the skinheads. It seemed as if the cops did not care who they hit. They were indiscriminate. People came out of buildings, who knows, maybe just to try to get to the store, and they were attacked by police. It was a very bloody incident.

A fire truck pulled up. The firemen came with the intention of using the fire hose on us, but at first they didn't do anything. They just stood there and watched. By that time we had been there almost eight hours. Eventually Inspector Julian decided it was time to stop the fire and get the people out of the street. So they put out our bonfire, and we started another one.

Finally the authorities decided they had had enough of us being in the streets, so they let us back into the park. Everybody who still had any of their stuff brought it back in. But the police had destroyed most of the tents.

When they tore down our tents that night, I realized for the first time just how much they really didn't give a damn about me.

When they tore down my tent they were tearing down part of my heart. They took out everything, my clothes, my identification. If I had not held onto my birth certificate, I would have had no ID. When they took away people's ID, then those people in effect became homeless criminals. Because when they take that away, even though you might not realize it at the time, your identity is gone. Go look for a job without an ID. If you don't have ID when you apply for work today, they tell you to go get a green card. I was born and raised in the United States, but do you know how hard it is to get a green card with two federal arrests?

The cops came back about four o'clock the next morning. By that time the only people they had to confront were the people staying in the park, not the supporters from the neighborhood, who had gone home. When they came this time it was myself, Red Wolf, Spider, and a few others. They came in and ushered us out of the park. Then they tore down everything. It started raining the next day.

The cops and Parks Department had destroyed our tents, but neighborhood people brought materials for us to rebuild. We had a unity going with the neighborhood to where we had a backup of supplies. I have been told that during the Depression in the 1930s residents of this same neighborhood used to defy evictions by helping people carry their belongings back into apartments after evictions. This time they started going to the hardware stores and buying heavy-duty plastic, wood, and hammers for us.

Miriam Friedlander, a city council member, made a big public statement July 6th, complaining that the community had not been consulted about the raid and demanding that the city replace the possessions of the homeless that had been destroyed. She also called for them "to immediately rehab all city-owned buildings in the Lower East Side for low-income housing, and...cease harassment of the homeless." That sounded good for the moment, but that's the last I ever heard of that demand of hers.

The same day as the Friedlander statement, the New York Supreme Court ruled that the city could not prevent real estate speculators from demolishing or converting SROs—single-room occupancy housing—into condominiums. Although that type of hotel shelter is not my favorite, the ruling showed the attitude of too many of the powers-that-be toward the homeless. Even Mayor Koch was quoted in the *New York Times* as saying that the ruling was a "devastating blow" to the effort to keep homelessness from spreading.

An example of this problem of gentrification was the Christadora House, a 16-story settlement house building in the Tompkins Square area which had once been used as a city welfare office and then kept empty for a long time, until it was yuppiefied, renovated into expensive condominiums for rich people.

At 1:30 in the afternoon that Saturday, which was July 8th, people marched past the Christadora House carrying a banner "HOUSING—NOT CONDOS." That was more laid-back than it had been in the spring, when the anarchists heaved cinder blocks through the Art Deco entrance as they shouted "Die, yuppie scum!"

Police patrol cars, paddy wagons and green garbage trucks lined 10th Street between Avenues A and B. The people marched on to the Ninth Precinct station on 5th Street to protest the raid on the Tompkins Square Park homeless. They carried a banner that had "NO CURFEW, NO EVICTIONS" painted on it, and posters that said "STOP WAREHOUSING APARTMENTS."

At the park, about 200 homeless and our neighborhood supporters held hands and linked arms around the new shelters we had built. A big painted banner strung up between two trees said "NO HOUSING, NO PEACE/SQUATTERS RIGHTS NOW." When six o'clock rolled around, about 70 cops in riot gear, along with Parks Department workers, who we called "Green Meanies" because of their green uniforms and general attitude, ripped apart our plastic tents. And again we put them back up. At 8:45 that night the cops swept through the park and cut down six tents. One person got arrested for playing a radio without a license. Interestingly enough, I got the feeling that some of the police did not like being part of pushing people out of the park.

We hung on to our place in the park. Somebody came up with the idea to evict Henry J. Stern, the Parks Commissioner from his home. It was the consensus among the various groups: yeah, let's do it. So I designed and painted a t-shirt for the occasion, and it was presented to Stern outside his office as he was coming down the stairs.

On July 12th, we marched to the home of Henry J. Stern, who lived at 510 East 84th Street, and placed an eviction notice on his door. About a hundred police blocked off the street between York Avenue and East End Avenue. We marched on to Gracie Mansion, which is where the mayor of New York always lives. At Mayor Koch's the police tried to get us surrounded, but we broke away, split up and scattered, with police after us. We knew the back alleys and thereby mostly eluded them, regrouping to march past the United Nations on our way back to Tompkins Square.

That night we celebrated in Tompkins Square Park, enjoying music and food, while a few police officers kept an eye on us. Somebody offered them a taste of some donated cavjar on crackers and stuffed mushrooms, but they declined to eat with us.

Without exaggerating, I would say we were raided ten to twelve times that season. We could expect the cops any time, but usually when they did come it was when the people in the neighborhood were asleep or at work. Sometimes the authorities would leave the rest of the homeless in the park alone, coming specifically to Tent City to harass us.

"Why do you come to us?" I asked one of the Parks Department workers.

"Because we were told to come to you guys first," he said.

Each time the cops came for us, the neighborhood came back stronger after the cops left. The neighborhood people were becoming more involved. Food would come in and clothing would come in. From our table in the park we sold "Tent City" buttons, passed out flyers and collected food, clothing and medical supplies for the homeless in the park.

We had a lot of community support on the Lower East Side, organizations such as Emmaus Haus for women, run by Father

David Kirk; Homeward Bound; St. Augustine Church down near Grant; Trinity Church, downtown between Avenues B and C, which had been feeding homeless people for years; and a church called Graffiti Church, on 7th Street, which was another organization that had consistently fed the homeless. There was also Diane, a lady who for three or four years had been coming out to the park feeding people on Saturdays, Mondays, and Wednesdays. She had an abundance of food and connections. I had first met Diane several years earlier, before I had joined the Bowery Mission. It was snowing that Thanksgiving. She came down to the park with a busload of food—Thanksgiving dinners. She just brought it to us in the park and set it out. We had Thanksgiving Dinner for three days.

These groups of people and others like the squatters and the anarchists, as well as people who just lived in the area, came through for us. They were for real. Every time we ran out of equipment, they brought in more equipment for us to rebuild. The police would tear down, we would build up; they'd tear down, we'd build up. Tear 'em down, build 'em up. People were going to the hardware store all day long. The hardware store got rich that summer.

Not everybody who was homeless and in the park was in agreement on how to deal with our situation. Our side of the park held the activists. The rest of the park wanted nothing to do with us because we were making too much political noise. They felt like we were destroying their harmony with what they had in the park. In reality, they had next to nothing, but they did not want to lose even that little bit.

I understood how they felt. I myself had been one of the people who was, if not content, afraid to make any changes, afraid to make any noise, content to be on that bench because I could see no other place to go. Afraid to lose that spot.

**

After we had been raided about the second or third time in July, we received a visit from some people from Philadelphia who came specifically to meet us. They told us of something called a "National Survival Summit" that was coming up in Philadelphia. One of the people who talked to us was Leona Smith, a dignified black lady, a former homeless person and the president of an organization called the National Union of the Homeless. We were told that she and another homeless person named Chris Sprowd had started the Union of the Homeless themselves, and that 90 percent of the board was made up of homeless or once-homeless people. The Union had a shelter run by homeless people.

These facts made some difference to me. While I still did not like shelters, the fact that these folks had homeless people in control of it was a different story altogether.

A brother named Willie Baptist, wearing a baseball cap, also talked with us. Willie was a very articulate dude. He called himself a "political educator" and said he was also a member of the Union of the Homeless, and of another organization called Up and Out of Poverty.

All that afternoon we talked and talked and talked about the homeless situation and the differences from the way it had been in years past. Talked about if anything had changed in the past few years about homeless people.

"Nothing has changed," I said.

"That's not true," somebody else said. "Think about it. There were homeless people before and a lot of them fought their situation, but you didn't have the struggle then the way you have it now."

I realized that was true. In 1989 one-bedroom apartments in the neighborhood, on Avenue A, were commonly costing $1,200 a month. Prices kept going up. Even the Cherry Tavern, the down-to-earth Polish bar I used to frequent, had started going yuppie, trying to appeal to the rich. (The Cherry Tavern would end up closing down anyway.) The consensus of our talk with these folks from Philadelphia was that there were more people who were homeless, but there were also more people involved with the homeless struggle than there had ever been before. That much progress had happened.

For Leona and the others to come talk with us was a reinforcement of our resolve. Before they came, we thought we were alone in our fight. All we knew was that we were hurting, we were fighting to survive. Now it seemed that there were other people who were fighting the same fight.

We had a Tent City meeting to discuss the so-called summit. One of our people, a fellow named Justice Robles, felt it was a good idea.

"Our government," he said, "would rather see us under the ground than lying on top of the ground. They would rather have us buried underneath Tompkins Square than sleeping on top of it."

Somebody mentioned my name as a candidate for attending the Philadelphia conference.

"I don't want to leave the park," I said. I still thought my plight was only in Tompkins Square Park. That was where the immediate battle was, where people were going to jail.

"Cas, we want you to speak for the homeless living in the park," somebody said. At that time I still did not fully understand my position, but Karen Margolis and a majority of the Tent City homeless finally convinced me that it might be a good idea for me to go and represent them, to speak for the homeless of Tent City. There was something in the air and Tent City wanted to be part of it.

I still wasn't very happy as the contingency from Tent City traveled to the survival summit in a van driven by David Green and Shigemi, who were with an organization called Homeward Bound, one of the sponsors of the event. But now I was curious. Leona had told me that there were going to be Indians—Native Americans—at this meeting, as well as coal miners and other organizations fighting against poverty. My curiosity, more than anything, got me to the summit.

I went with two other homeless people from the park, Justice Robles and a black woman named Darleen Bryant, who liked her nickname of "Mama." That night the organizers put us up, along with other summit participants, in nice student quarters at St.

Joseph's College in Philadelphia, two to a room. It was decent, and that impressed me.

The next day, the three-day conference, organized by the National Welfare Rights Union and the National Union of the Homeless, began in the auditorium at St. Joseph's College. I do not think I can truly put into words the emotions I felt when I walked in there to that conference and saw all those people. The vitality of the struggle against poverty struck me. This was the first time I had ever seen so many people, and such a variety of people, together for the same purpose of doing something about their plight themselves. I couldn't help but get caught up in the enthusiasm. About 50 people from 30 to 40 states showed up, representing people from various races, young and old, from all walks of life, all different organizations, not only the Union of the Homeless and Welfare Rights, but also others such as Up and Out of Poverty. You had the American Indian Movement and coal miners concerned about black lung and welfare rights activists and kids against drugs. Maybe more women than men.

Then, when people started getting up and talking, it was as if *I* was speaking. It was phenomenal to see other people's struggles, hear their fights and ideas and get inspired at this unity. Nearly everyone who stood up and spoke touched me and my life and the life that we were living in New York. It was as if we were all living the same life, but in different places. It almost freaked me out. It sure woke me up. It was the best thing that could have happened to me.

I liked the name of the group from Minneapolis, which was called Up and Out of Poverty, and was led by a woman named Cheri Honkala. I thought that was a good banner to be under because this issue of poverty encompassed all the other issues we were dealing with.

Then I heard Leona Smith speak. She was wearing a black-collared t-shirt and a dress. I found her to be a forceful, earnest speaker, and she emphasized her points with her index finger. I could see the emotion in her talk and realized that she was a person who deeply cared about other people. She herself had experienced being homeless in the streets. She was a very strong go-getter, vibrant not only in organizing, but also in getting out and talking to the politicians. But it was more than that—she was not just a talker; she had been to jail for what she believes in.

I learned that Union of the Homeless also had a school where they taught political science as it pertained to their lives and the future of their kids. They had a program called Dignity Housing. They would take people out of shelters and put them in a house. The only obligation for the people in the house was for them to go to school, learn a trade, and/or get a job. And they had to put time back into the Dignity Housing Program—put back some of what they got.

All things considered, Union of the Homeless impressed me quite a bit. They were changing the situation. Instead of "advocates" being in control, the homeless themselves were gaining control of their own destinies.

After Leona spoke, a heavyset black sister in glasses, wearing a yellow baseball cap and a red sweatshirt, led the group in a cheer:

"What are we going to do?" she asked.

"Fight!"

Tent City made an agreement with Leona Smith and Union of the Homeless to have our own homeless convention in Washington, D.C., and take part in a "CD" or civil disobedience in Washington on the sixth of October, the day before a big nationwide protest rally against homelessness. We were intent on taking over the HUD building.

On about the third day of the summit I finally got to speak. I was bearded, with a moderate Afro, wearing a black t-shirt with a few buttons up near the neck. Justice and Darleen and I introduced the fact that Tompkins Square Park Tent City intended to build tents out of American flags. As I spoke I rapped my hand with a rolled-up agenda, explaining how we thought if we used the American flag as a symbol of protection, that would prevent the cops from destroying our tents.

The response to our plan at the summit was tremendous, it impressed me. People were jumping out of their chairs and clapping hands and cheering. Our announcement went over so grand and gloriously that I thought, oh well, it looks like I'm in this for a while.

What enthused me the most about the Summit was the reinforcement of the realization that if I wanted to get my life straightened out, I could not depend on anyone else to do it for me.

We were doing for ourselves in Tompkins Square Park. There were no real alternatives. All we knew was that we needed housing and we needed jobs, but we had no idea of how to get them. By then we were thinking in terms of organizing politically, but we did not know exactly how to go about it. And before going to the summit I thought we were alone in these troubles. My job for the homeless of Tompkins Square Park had been to go to the Survival Summit and find out what was happening with other people like us. What the Summit did for me was to give me more courage, knowing that Tent City was not alone, that things were happening all over the country, and there were people all over doing the same things we were doing. So it kind of built me up. I started waking up my consciousness.

On Saturday, July 22, 1989, the day that the flags were scheduled to go up in Tent City, we were still at the summit. I wanted to get back to New York so bad that I put pressure on Darleen and Justice.

"Come on, let's go," I said. Darleen and I ended up leaving Justice at the conference.

We came back into Tent City with just enough daylight to see our tent made out of American flags. A rope had been strung between two trees, and then four flags—big flags, about seven or eight feet by four or five feet—had been attached to the rope side by side, the blue fields of stars up near the rope and the red and white stripes angling out, fastened to the ground. A gathering of people were sitting on the ground beneath the shelter of this tent. A couple of other people were walking around holding a banner somebody had painted: "KOCH VS HOMELESS." The area was beautiful. We even had an art festival going. People were there in the park with their art. People were eating and it was a festive day. People were everywhere. It seemed like the Fourth of July, like our own independence day.

When it started getting dark, the Parks Department came and told us we would have to break down the structures. Of course, we were not about to take them down. So the Green Meanies backed off for the night.

In the warm, humid dawn 20 cops in riot gear formed a line standing shoulder to shoulder, facing our line of homeless. Behind the cops a dozen or so Green Meanies waited.

For the moment I almost believed they would respect the symbolic refuge we were claiming by using the flags.

Then the cops moved in, fighting us, tearing down all the flags. There was a tug-of-war between the police and us for the flags. Though we gave them a struggle, by 7 a.m. the helmeted cops had folded up our flags and taken them away.

I had come back from the Summit politicized, which now influenced my strategizing. On July 25th we got a flyer typed up. A well-educated black man named Thomas was our press man, our computer whiz, our brain. Thomas had parents he could have moved in with, but he stayed downtown, he stayed working with us in the streets. Although he liked computers, he preferred to work in a socially conscious atmosphere. He worked with us and he worked with the Tenants Association.

Thomas put out our flyers, printed our newsletters and did our press releases. In the July 25th flyer we noted that, "We now are organizing, educating, and feeding one another without institutions to guide us to: drugs, alcohol, TB, AIDS, and Criminal Ways of Thinking." It was signed by me as chief representative, a dude named James Naphier as chief of security, and Chris Henry as Public Relations for what we called C.H.S., or "Creating Housing Somewhere."

Our lawyer found out that the police had taken our flags to somewhere in Long Island. I guess they were figuring we had neither the money nor the support to go all the way out there and get the flags back. Fortunately, we had a receipt for them. We got a ride out to Long Island from a lawyer friend of Chris Henry and his lady, Barbara Henry. Chris was one of the founders of Tent City and a member of the Tent City board of directors. Barbara was our secretary. We went with a couple of supporters who had given up the money for the flags in the first place, and we got the flags back on July 31st.

The day we got the flags back, we put up the flag tent again. Since the parks department had still refused to agree to our proposal to keep the bathrooms open on a 24-hour basis and were still officially outlawing any temporary structures in the park, we also proceeded to build another eight shelters.

The police and the Parks Department left us alone at first, probably because we had such a big turnout of supporters. We were told that we had until 6 a.m. before the authorities would come in.

But this time the attack came just before midnight. Most of our supporters and the curious had drifted away as 40 to 60 police in riot gear came against us, along with about 40 Green Meanies and a couple of dozen maintenance people. This time they threw all the flags except one in a garbage truck, along with all our food and clothes and property. That showed us how much the flag meant as a symbol of protection.

The last flag we managed to get away from them. We had a tug-of-war, yanked it over the fence and got away with it.

Nearly a week later, on the night of August 6, 1989, a year after that first big police riot, the homeless of Tompkins Square Park were again forced out of the park. We were told by Inspector Julian and some of his task force that around four o'clock or five o'clock in the morning they would be coming in to take everything again. So we were on vigil, waiting.

At the brick, flat-roofed pavilion between the rest-rooms, people were sleeping. A Green Meanie came over and politely said, "We're getting ready to clean up this area. Could you get all your personal belongings, please?"

They had more than one team of Parks Department workers. One guy from the Parks Department talked with me. He was a heavyset young white dude.

"We're going to clean the entire park, section by section, starting here," he said.

"What about the tents?" I asked. I was a little bit hoarse that morning. I had a butterfly bandage on my right cheek from the previous encounter with the authorities.

"You'll just have to take them down while we do the cleanup," he said. "We're not looking to confiscate. What we're asking is that everything be physically moved off the benches because we're going to clean the park."

"You're saying that we have to take everything outside the park?" I asked.

"If you take it outside of the park, that's even better while we do the cleanup. We've got a 40-man crew here simply to clean the park."

"Why can't we just pick everything up," I asked, "put them on the benches and get it out of your way?"

"Because we're going to clean around the benches, in the benches, down the benches. Everything's going to get cleaned."

My friends and I talked over what to do.

"They want us out of the park," somebody said.

"We could stop traffic," Chris said.

"All right," somebody else agreed. I turned to the Green Meanies a little ways off from us.

"You're not going to like what we do," I said. "We'll take it out, but you're not going to like it."

We went around informing the other residents of the park of the situation and what we intended. We started gathering what little we had in the way of possessions.

"What's most important?" a guy asked. "The food or the blankets?"

"The food."

It was August. In the winter the answer would have been different.

"Food," I said, "because right now we're going to be sleeping on the street."

Ultimately we held on to all that we could and tried to keep the Green Meanies from trashing the rest. When we saw them filling their garbage trucks with our belongings, tossing them into the backs of those trucks, we could not help getting agitated and provoked, and calling them names.

I went up and grabbed a metal cabinet out of the back of the garbage truck. At first they tried to stop me, but then the black

Parks Department man wearing glasses and a blue t-shirt stopped them.

"All right," he said. "Is it yours? Take it out of here."

So we moved out of the park early that morning, but we put whatever bedding we managed to salvage out right in the street, blocking traffic. People just lay down in the street on their pads. I myself was sitting in the middle of the street on Avenue A on my spread-out sleeping bag near a Parks Department dump truck. One of the homeless had put up a sign "THIS IS OUR LAND." Somebody else had made a sign that said:

NO
• NIGHT-STICKING
• GLASS THROWING
• BEAT-UPS, BY
ANYONE!

I was mad. I started drinking beer and got even angrier. I was standing in the street with a bullhorn in one hand and a brown-bagged quart in the other.

"No housing, no peace!" I shouted. "It don't make no difference what anybody says. Just remember what we're here for. Fuck what anybody else says! We're here to get homes, food, clothing...."

Not my most persuasive speaking engagement, but I was feeling frustrated. Still, no traffic was getting by, so I was not the only frustrated one.

That night people kept demonstrating. There was singing and lots of yelling. Cops chased down demonstrators and broke up the protest.

"It's over," one cop kept saying. "It's over. It's over."

People were videotaping the proceedings, and at a paddy wagon one plainclothes cop can be seen growling at the cameraman in Nith LaCroix's video *First Anniversary Tompkins Square Riot Demonstration*.

"Take a walk, asshole," he says.

Next morning thc sergeant of police came to us in his crisp, white, short-sleeved shirt. It went like this:

"You're welcome in the park," he said.

"They told us to get out," we said.

"Your complaint was you were asked to leave the park," said the sergeant. "Now you're invited back into the park, so I wish you would just vacate the street, so the people can get back to work."

"But we were told to vacate the park."

"Okay," he said. "You're welcome back into the park. Right now you're obstructing traffic. You're welcome to go back in the park right now, all right? You're welcome to go back in and keep your stuff."

That's the way it went. We were stubborn. We had still more battles with the cops, fighting with them almost continuously the rest of the summer and into the autumn. But we were still in the park.

CHAPTER 16

The New Exodus March

WBAI, a community radio station in New York, had Tent City on
the air quite a bit. Being on the radio helped us get the word out
to more people about what was happening at the park and how
we were working to change conditions for the impoverished. In
September of 1989 people started coming down to the park
telling us about a big march that was going to be happening in
a few weeks. They told us Mitch Snyder's Community for
Creative Non-Violence (CCNV) and the National Coalition for
the Homeless had got a lot of money to do a "Housing Now!"
march from Boston to Washington, D.C. The idea was to bring
to the public's attention the severity of the problem of
homelessness and to raise support for dramatic increases in low-
income housing.

Then David Green and Shigemi of Homeward Bound
contacted us about the march meetings being held at the union
hall for the Hospital and Health Care Employees Union Local
1199, which was a place where people often gathered to have
meetings to organize on various issues. As part of the meeting,
a big dinner was planned for the homeless to help prepare them
for the march. People had gotten to know Tent City, so we were
asked to run a workshop.

So Tent City went to the meeting and set up a table with
literature telling people what we were about. The people in
charge of the meeting put on a big, dynamite dinner of different
varieties of ethnic foods, and after dinner a show with some
name-brand entertainers. It was all free, so a couple of hundred
homeless people came. These were people who, like ourselves,
were disgusted by the shelter system, fed up with other people
advocating for them, and enthusiastic about getting organized to
make changes.

Filled with good food, people listened when the Housing
Now! and CCNV people began talking about how they had the

funds and the means to support people on the march to Washington. Comfortably digesting a rich meal, the homeless believed these organizations when they began promising that they would provide food for the marchers, arrange accommodations each night, have a medical van driving along with the marchers all the way to Washington, and even provide rain gear and shoes. Among the homeless there that night I saw a lot of enthusiasm for this march and for being in the fight to get out of poverty and out of the streets. In those days it still amazed me to find so many homeless aware that it was time for them to do something about their own plight. It made me more attuned to the fight. Listening to the homeless speak had me feeling optimistic.

However, I was leery of how the march was being set up. While the Survival Summit in July had been made up mostly of grassroots organizations, the 1199 meeting in September was conceived and run by more of what I call the "establishment organizers." Even though groups like Tent City and the National Union of the Homeless were there participating, the Coalition for the Homeless, CCNV, and an advocacy group called the National Low-Income Housing Coalition dominated the proceedings. These organizations needed homeless people in order to make their march work.

"We have got to be the ones to make changes for ourselves," I said when it was my turn to speak. "The time has come to stop letting other people talk for us. Nobody can tell you your problems better than you. Nobody but me can tell you why I am homeless or why I need this or if I need this. I don't want no Mitch Snyder from the Community for Creative Non-Violence speaking for me. I don't want Housing Now! or Coalition for the Homeless or any of these people speaking for me. Because they can't. They don't know anything about me."

I could see a lot of homeless people nodding their heads in agreement. You could hear them respond to the idea of being their own advocates. We did not care about any organization called Housing Now!, only the fact that if there was any reason to march, it was for "housing now!" It was this response of the homeless that convinced Tent City to commit to going along on the march. We were ready and willing to take the risk.

If I had offended the sponsors of this feed, or shocked them, they played it cool and hung back on the fringes. They had got the people to this meeting, they had met the quota of homeless they needed if their march was going to work.

However, Tent City was becoming a symbol of the broader homeless situation. With this in mind, prior to the march on Washington we took part of our camp to the United Nations Plaza to bring into public and maybe international focus the point that homelessness is not just Tompkins Square Park, it's not just New York City, and it is not a problem you can solve by outlawing camps or by cramming people into rat-infested, tuberculosis-ridden shelters. You cannot solve the condition by sweeping parks and throwing everyone out or arresting them. Somebody in Tent City came up with the slogan "Tompkins Square Everywhere," which was both pointing out the widespread crisis of homelessness and poverty, and also calling for the homeless everywhere to resist being disposed of.

At the U.N. Plaza, a group of Chinese people had set up a camp to protest the military violence at Tiananmen Square. Usually camp demonstrations are not allowed at the U.N. Plaza, but the Chinese students had been given permission. Portable toilets had even been set up for them. The Chinese were cool; they supported us in our struggle and let us set up by them. We set up tables distributing our literature and selling t-shirts I had painted.

Karen Margolis was there with us. All summer she had been supporting us a lot, even though she didn't live in the park. By this time, Karen had gone to Kansas City, Missouri for the second time to bring her son back to New York. But she told me that when she reached her parents' house, she had been met by a process server with a thick bunch of papers stating that Karen's parents had been appointed co-guardians and co-conservators of Ethan, and that as such they retained custody of him pending any further court order. Karen went to several lawyers, but couldn't get anybody to represent her because she had no money. One woman lawyer told her that her parents had tricked her.

"Let me take a look at the papers," I told her.

Karen got me the papers, and I showed them to some of my friends at Welfare Rights and at the Anti-Hunger Coalition. I wrote letters and my friends wrote letters to Legal Aid in Kansas City. Eventually Legal Aid sent Karen a list of attorneys in Kansas City. Soon the case was accepted by a lawyer, and Karen was able to begin legal proceedings on behalf of her son.

Meanwhile, we had managed to stay at the U.N. Plaza about a week or so without any authorities bothering us. Then the police and Parks Department must have figured out who we were because one day they came up to the U.N. Plaza and started harassing us. Although the Chinese people were allowed to camp there, the police started enforcing the 1:30 a.m. curfew on us. They chased us out that night, telling us we were not allowed to sleep there at night. They even told us we could not use the porta-potties that had been set up for the Chinese protesters.

Well, when you got to go, you got to go. One thing led to another and seven of us got arrested and taken to jail for trying to go to the bathroom in porta-potties.

***

By September of 1989 the squatters' movement and Tent City were tight. We had done a number of actions together. Our squatter friends were very good at what they did, which was locating usable abandoned buildings. John, the spearhead of the squatters, came to Tompkins Square with his lady to talk with me and the people of Tent City. They told us they were planning to occupy the old Public School 105, which had been abandoned for five to ten years. Addicts were now using it as a shooting gallery. The squats planned on cleaning it out and inviting homeless people in there.

Tent City held a few meetings on the issue, talked about it and decided it sounded like a workable idea. Tent City would join them when we got back from the march to Washington.

Meanwhile, the rest-room situation at Tompkins Square continued to be a problem. More office buildings in the area were locking their rest-rooms, and more restaurants, even fast-food establishments, would not allow someone who appeared homeless to use the rest-rooms. People with homes take going to the bathroom for granted. Put yourself in the position of the homeless person—not having a place to go in has a very strong effect on a person's dignity. So the public rest-room in the park was a very important issue. We needed it open past four in the afternoon. Otherwise, you got the health problem of people using the park itself for a bathroom.

We finally came up with a plan of chaining ourselves to the fixtures and the doors in the rest-room. But we also had another agenda, and that was to get to Washington on the march, so I didn't want anybody going to jail at this late point. Since we needed as many people on the march as we could get, we needed a strategy to keep the bathrooms open, but one that would also keep us out of jail.

I figured the police did not really want a major confrontation over the rest-rooms. I took it upon myself to let the information about our plan of chaining up to the rest-room leak to one of the homeless people we knew was dealing with the police. It worked: the authorities got wind of our plan.

Next morning around five or six o'clock, a couple of Parks Department men came to my tent and woke me up. They called me out to the side.

"How can we help?" they asked. "How can we work this out?"

I was pleased. They had decided to negotiate.

Tent City ended up getting the bathroom open 24 hours a day. In fact, Tent City was put in charge of the rest-rooms; we had the responsibility to monitor and secure the facility ourselves. We proceeded to clean the rest-rooms and get rid of anybody who was shooting drugs in there. We put together our own first aid setup and established rape prevention security. We even helped the police get rid of the drug addicts in certain areas of the park.

Meanwhile, some Parks Department employees got fired because they refused to do everything they were told to do about getting us out of the park. Others quit because they didn't like what they were told to do.

Maybe it was a small victory, but with it people got to see that, wow, we were not just running our mouths, we *were* getting something done. People were able to see that if we stuck together, there were possibilities of making progress. From that little bit of bathroom victory, all the homeless of the park were drawn closer together.

So it was that when we joined the Housing Now! march, it was as a united band of people who said, "We are going to Washington and we are going to be heard and we are going to be the ones talking. We are not going to let somebody else talk for us." As I have said, I was not going on the march because of the organization called Housing Now! I was marching because of the words themselves, "Housing Now!," because that was what we needed. I joined the march in order for homeless people to speak for themselves to the people running the government.

When the day came, only a handful of us from Tent City and Tompkins Square Park made the march. Karen came along. Thomas, the computer whiz of Tent City, came too. There was Chris Henry, his wife Barbara, Artie, Stanley, myself, and Terry Taylor, also known as "The Minister of Madness." Terry was a tall, slim, dark-skinned wild dude. He was angry and stayed drunk a lot. He was angry about the conditions of living in the park and about poverty. Last, but not least, there was Old Man John, who had bad feet.

Also on the march came representatives of Emmaus House and the United Homeless Organization (UHO), as well as people from the various homeless shelters. It's a sad truth, but a lot of them probably lost their bed space in the shelters and weren't able to get back into them. But they felt it was that important for them to get out there and speak for themselves. A lot of women living in shelters came on the march with us.

We started out from the U.N. Plaza at seven o'clock in the morning, around the middle of September, 1989. We wore these yellow and white hats that said "New Exodus" on them. Our Chinese friends gave us a gift of money for the march out of their collection. The woman, the mother, pulled $60 for Tent City out of their pot of donations. That got us started.

From the first step I was scared because I knew the power of the government. If they wanted to, they could stop us very easily. They had proved that a long time ago with Hooverville, when they ran tanks and cavalry through the tents of the veterans and their families. To this day I'm not sure why the authorities did not stop us with force. Maybe they felt we did not have enough power to bother with, or more likely they were counting on the establishment homeless organizations to keep everybody in line.

The day was cloudy and a little cool. None of the people from Housing Now! or CCNV or Coalition for the Homeless did any walking. They were staff. Only the homeless walked. Hurricane Hugo was blowing in, but we were not too worried because the Housing Now! people had promised they would provide rain gear. As it began raining, they began passing out the so-called "rain gear"—black plastic garbage bags. And they did not even have enough of those to go around. I took out the wine I had brought along and began drinking.

We walked in the rain across Manhattan to the river. At that point Karen Margolis left us to keep an appointment with her lawyer about to make arrangements about her son. When we began boarding the Staten Island Ferry, Mitch Snyder arrived in a car and took a look at us all getting on the boat. I shook his hand, but I felt that he was avoiding me. It was probably just as well. He was too friendly now with the establishment to suit me, and I did not think there was enough input from the homeless about how the march was going to go. We did not see eye to eye, and had we got to talking, I would have probably told him what I was thinking about the wonderful rain gear. With the media there, however, any argument would only have served to detract from the march.

Snyder took the ferry over with us, but he was gone soon after that. As we marched across Staten Island, I thought back about my time there and wondered if any of the nuns or priests were watching the marchers, and what they would think if they knew what I was involved in.

The State Police met us when we reached the Jersey bridge. As a pedestrian you had to go up a spiral stair to get onto the bridge. Our intention was to march down the middle of the road, blocking traffic, thereby making more people aware of our march and our cause.

The Jersey state troopers had a different idea. They were waiting for us at the base of that stair and ordered us go single file and only on the sidewalk of the bridge. When word was passed back to me that the police would not let us cross the way we wanted, I barged to the front. I was drunk, so I wasn't in control. I was angry and started cussing out one of the State Troopers.

"You can't stop us!" I raged.

The officer pulled out his pistol and stuck it right at my nose.

"I ought to blow your head off," he growled.

Have you ever seen a cartoon where all of a sudden the cartoon character gets so scared that all the color drains out of him and he turns white? That's the way the alcohol went out of me as I stared down the barrel of that officer's magnum.

The policeman would not or could not shoot because there were too many people. And his boss told him to back down.

We did it their way. It took us a long time, almost an hour, to get everybody across the bridge single file, using only the sidewalk. The wind began blowing the rain harder. Hurricane Hugo was at his best. As we walked, I watched the other marchers, struggling through the messy gray weather toward a dream of a better life. Troubled by my behavior with the officer, I did some heavy thinking.

When I first got involved in organizing that summer, I had a very selfish motivation: I wanted to *live*. *I* wanted to get off the street, *I* wanted to eat, *I* wanted decent clothing. I want that really understood: I went at this to save *my* life. I had no real concern for other people. (Maybe I did, but because I was in so much pain from my own life, I couldn't admit anybody else's pain.) Though I had been to the summit and other meetings with other groups, until the march I didn't have a real conception of a movement of a larger community of people working together to help each other. But I had been noticing that as I fought for the things I needed, I coincidentally ended up helping other people get the same things. The people of Tent City had psyched me into believing that I was a leader. In the little bit of time between the Survival Summit and the march, I had learned that people *did* listen to what I had to say.

Walking in the rain, I realized that if I was going to be an effective leader, I had better get smart and not be doing stunts like drinking a lot of wine and needlessly antagonizing the police. You can run your mouth all you want, but when you are actually out there, facing the enemy, that's a heavier thing.

Looking back at the more than 200 people beginning this march so hopefully, including a number of pregnant women, I realized that I cared. I knew we could be charged by the police at any time. We were going out there against Washington, the Establishment. Back when I was eight years old, I had made up my mind to become a social worker, a better one than they had in the orphanage. More than just the handful of Tent City homeless had been banking on what I did in that moment facing the policeman's gun. In that moment I felt the weight of those hundreds of lives. Never before had I had the push to become truly socially conscious, a community-minded person.

This was my opportunity. Our opportunity.

I threw away my booze. From that point on I have not had a drink of alcohol, nor have I done illegal drugs. That moment facing the bullet I truly recognized and accepted my responsibility as an activist for homeless people. Prior to that, whenever I stopped drinking or drugging, I had nothing to exchange for my alcoholism or drug addiction. There was nothing there, no substance. So I always went back to my old ways. When I started realizing my art, I started realizing I had a voice, that there was more to me than just getting high. But it took looking down that gun barrel, it took becoming part of the movement rising up and out of poverty to give me a substance.

Karen rejoined us when we got to the Jersey side, and the march stopped the first night at a gymnasium. The Housing Now! people had their offices upstairs, a nice big office area and a big meeting room, while downstairs we marchers had to vie for space on the floor to sleep. We had long, long waits to use the bathroom and shower.

I couldn't believe it. The same things we were angry about in the shelter system, we were experiencing on the march.

This fact did not go over well with the New York people, who were acting somewhat wild as compared to the tame people that the march organizers were used to from the shelters in Washington, DC. So one of the guys who was part of the leadership from CCNV and Housing Now! on the march gave us a speech. He was a big, fat, tall, light-skinned black man named Lonnie. I guess he thought he really had to put a hold on the people, tell them every little detail of how to behave, as if we had no sense. But we had walked all day long, partly through a tropical storm, and his attitude made us angry. I don't remember the words to the first part of his speech, but I remember those words did not go over well.

Terry stood up and shouted back to the guy "I am a man!" in a loud, strong, baritone voice that echoed through the gym.

I recall more clearly the next part of Lonnie's speech. He said something to this effect:

"I see there are women here. What we have to do is share and share alike. We have to make sure there's enough woman to go around for everybody. We should make sure that we all have our piece of woman."

"That's the most degrading thing I've heard in my entire life," Karen said to me.

Happily, Bob Brand, Jim Fike and a Miss Wells, all from the Welfare Rights group, showed up at the gym in a big school bus full of food and rain gear. That was fortunate because the remnants of Hurricane Hugo rained on us for several days more.

In Trenton we stayed at a Presbyterian church. A rally was held on our behalf, but in fact, the homeless people were not really a part of it, as all those who talked that day were politicians or establishment organizers.

A lot of people on the march did not care for the way we were being told what and how we were to do things and where we were to march. At least 24 groups were represented on the march, among them the shelter homeless, the panhandling homeless, Tent City, and welfare organizations. A number of unaffiliated homeless people and supporters who simply wanted to be part of the movement eventually wound up marching with whatever group they felt comfortable with. Tent City got a lot of them.

As a result of the growing discontent of the marchers, Housing Now! and CCNV started having regular meetings with representatives from the various groups on the march to decide which routes to take and what needed to be taken care of. At one of these meetings we decided that any rallies we held in the towns would be organized collectively. But that didn't really happen. The march did become more of a joint effort, though the majority of the time we still ended up going the way Housing Now! wanted us to go. But at least we established a foothold in these very private meetings that the leaders of CCNV and Housing Now! were holding. That way we found out things a lot quicker, and sometimes found out things they did not want us to know.

On Friday, September 22nd, our "leaders" took us to Wolf School in Eastwick, south of Philadelphia, to stay for two nights. Now the school officials evidently had no idea we were coming in the first place. A Mr. Ed Schwartz and company kicked us out the next morning, saying that some of our people had lice. What did they expect from people who had been homeless and marching on the roads and sleeping in the woods? When we asked if he could help us find an alternative place to stay, he said we had to find our own. They just kicked us out and left us to fend for ourselves.

It had been our understanding that Housing Now! had received a lot of donations for this march. Yet the rain gear they promised us turned out to be big black garbage bags we were supposed to wear, and the Housing Now! meals were not anything like the banquet they fed us at that meeting back in September. Meals on the march consisted for the most part of peanut butter and jelly or baloney sandwiches day after day.

Shoes they had promised and shoes they gave us—old worn-down shoes. We had people with sore, bloodied feet who could barely walk. Old Man John in particular was hurting. We had already had a few medical emergencies, yet the promised mobile medical team never appeared.

It got to the point where I was approached by one of my guys from Tent City.

"We don't need these people," he said. "We can get to Washington ourselves."

I phoned Leona Smith, president of the National Union of the Homeless, to let her know what was going down and told her Tent City was going to Washington whether anybody helped us or not.

"Fuck Housing Now!!" I told her. "We're tired of these folks. We can't deal with them. We can get to Washington on our own, do our *own* march."

"Cas, you've got to hang with the people," Leona told me. "When you get to Washington, you've got to be there with all the people you started out with from New York."

Leona and the Union of the Homeless came to the rescue, letting the Tent City marchers stay at Dignity Housing in Philadelphia. So I was able to convince Tent City to hang on and keep with the big group. If we split up then, we would have lost track of our intent. We had left New York together and we were supposed to get to Washington together. By hook or by crook.

The next day after booting homeless people out of the school, the hypocrites of Philadelphia had the nerve to put on a big public display of so-called support for the homeless. They had a group of dignitaries up on a stage platform, including Ed Schwartz, the man who had put us out of the school. These people were taking turns speaking about wonderful wonderful things they were doing. Unfortunately for them, they also had me on that platform, and they had me speak.

"What the hell are we doing praising this dude?" I asked the audience, pointing at Schwartz. "He just threw you out on the streets!"

The dignitaries sat dumbfounded, while the audience roared its agreement.

Union of the Homeless gave Tent City $300 for the march. Now Thomas was like our quartermaster on the march. He took care of the cigarettes. I took care of the money, however, because though Thomas was cool, he was under the influence of his buddies, such as Old Man John, who was an instigating type. If Thomas had held the money and they had talked to him about buying some booze, eventually they would have conned him into getting some. So I held onto the money and made sure it was spent for things we had to have to make it through the march.

By that time we needed a break to regroup, so when Leona handed us that money we decided that Tent City and the marchers hanging with us would go have a good breakfast the next day. The next morning about 17 of us went to a restaurant and had a humongous breakfast. We sat down at several tables and we ate, we talked, we were family. When we were done, we bought a few cartons of cigarettes and got back on the road. There we had good news: Lonnie, the dude who had made the derogatory speech at the gym that first night, got fired by the higher-ups. In reality, they had no choice—the man had continued to aggravate people, so that everybody was ready to kick his butt. I was so happy when we got word of his firing. We marched on to Chester, just outside of Philadelphia. Fortunately, the town of Chester came to our rescue and treated us well.

We marched on, down along Interstate Highway 95.

We needed medical services all along the way, but did not have them. One person got hit by a car. Others had seizures and asthma attacks. A woman began having pains in her chest and couldn't breathe. The man in charge did not believe anything was wrong with her, so he kept having her walk instead of ride. When she finally passed out, the people ganged up on him, and we came close to having a riot. The man almost got himself lynched.

Despite the fact that the promised medical support still failed to materialize, the determination of the people to get to Washington was phenomenal. Old Man John's feet were in bad shape, but you could not stop him from marching. It was too important for him. He had to go.

A number of people detoxed on the march; I was one of them. When you are kicking alcohol or drugs, something inside your body is coming out, an internalized pain. When you are withdrawing, sometimes it is almost like an epileptic seizure. You are foaming and getting out the poisons. Every day I was on the road, walking, walking, walking, walking, sweating the alcohol out. The sun helped.

Things got so bad regarding living arrangements for the marchers that a Housing Now! man came to the Tent City group. He was a heavyset white dude with long brown hair in a pony tail. He asked us if we would teach the rest of the marchers bivouac; in other words, how to live and cook in the streets or in the woods. Yet when we had first started the march, they had told us they were going to be the ones to find us places to sleep out of the weather. Here they were admitting they were not able to fulfill that duty.

We were willing to do the teaching, but one day not long after we left Philadelphia, an organization out of Berkeley, called Seeds of Peace, showed up with a couple of buses. They had heard about the march and decided to become part of it. Seeds of Peace was a tremendously helpful group. If it had not been for them, we would really have been in a lot of trouble. One bus carried medical supplies and a lot of our gear, and the other carried food. They brought four or five portable toilets. They did the best they could with regard to supplying marchers with first aid and medical services. Seeds of Peace volunteers also went ahead of us into some of the towns and found accommodations for us. Had it not been for them, in a lot of the towns we would not have had a place to sleep.

After the march I heard from the Seeds of Peace folks who dealt with the marchers' medical needs that five women had miscarriages along the way. Most of the hospitals along the march did not want anything to do with homeless people. In the minds of so many people, too many people, we were already proven guilty of various crimes just by the fact that we were homeless people. Each woman who miscarried had the option to return to New York. That was made available by Housing Now! But these women all continued the march. I think in all, only four people went back to New York before the march was completed.

Somehow Old Man John got hold of his disability check while on the march. Evidently, we passed near a town where his sister lived. He went to see her and came back with several fifths of vodka and whisky, which he began passing around to the Tent City guys. There I was kicking, and the rest of them were drinking up a storm. But I guess Old Man John's feet didn't hurt as much then. Though tempted like hell, I resisted taking a drink.

One of our purposes on that march was to go through the hearts of cities and towns and talk to and recruit other poor people and supporters and take them with us on the march, similar to Martin Luther King's march, similar to the WWI veterans' Bonus March on Washington. Every place we went we were supposed to pick up more and more people. Our goal was to focus the attention of the media and the citizens on the plight of the homeless by filling the streets, getting arrested, and attracting more and more marchers. Although the media were waiting for us to come through the cities, in most cases we did not march through the centers of towns. Instead, the Housing Now! organizers collaborated with the police and detoured us to the outskirts of towns, as if we were ashamed of what we were doing. As a result, we did not make the splash we were supposed to make. By detouring us, they made sure that some cities did not even know we had been there, and thus a lot of local and national media coverage that should have come was lost.

Sarah Ferguson was with us, covering the march for the *Village Voice*. I knew her already from talking to her in Tompkins Square Park, and I knew she had written a good article about the police riots in 1988 for a magazine called *Mother Jones*. However, a lot of the marchers did not like her around; they were suspicious of her because she was media. Sometimes people like her who are good-hearted, nevertheless don't understand homeless people, and so they say the wrong things without meaning to. Sometimes the questions Sarah asked made people angry. I kept thinking "Nobody understands her." She came to me one time.

"Oh, man, why does everybody hate me?" she asked. "How come they don't like me? Why don't they want me here?"

I tried to explain things to her, but rather than coach her, I felt I had to let her experience the march. Those of us from Tent City who were familiar with her convinced the other marchers to leave her alone, to let her be with us, because the issue was getting the news of the march covered. As I said, because of Housing Now! constantly detouring us, the other newspapers and tv stations were many times not able to find us. As it turned out, however, the article that finally got printed in the *Village Voice*, written by James Ridgeway along with Sarah Ferguson, while favorable to the homeless, told nothing about our struggles on the march itself.

In some towns that we did go through, we experienced hostility, what I would call "shunning," when even just one or two of us would go into a store to buy a soda or some food. Sometimes people yelled at us as we marched past. It was not a racial issue either. Even when walking through black neighborhoods, black people would shout "Homeless people go away!" It was a class issue.

Near Edgewood, the march controllers planned to put us up at a U.S. Army base. Here I must give credit to Karen because in the beginning I was all for going to the gymnasium on the base. But as we started onto the base, Karen refused to go.

"Come on, Karen," I said. "What's wrong?"

"I'm not going in there."

"Why not?"

"Because I don't want to go to prison, and as far as I'm concerned, that's what this base is for us."

If I had paid attention, I would have figured that out myself. Instead, I got on one of the buses, and they started driving us to the base gym. Karen stayed out front, outside the gates.

It was not until we were driving through the base that I saw the setup, all the armed soldiers in the area. Then when we got to the gym and I saw where we would be sleeping, the overcrowding, hundreds of people stepping over each other, the possibility of fights, I realized what was happening.

If anything happened, we were trapped.

"I've decided I'm not going to stay here," I told the people from Tent City. I explained my reasons. "Anybody else that doesn't want to stay here, come with me. We'll find someplace else to crash."

A Boston crew that was on the march also decided to leave with us. So we got back on the bus and left. We told the march coordinators where we were headed, so they could pick us up the next morning.

Outside the army base we met up with Karen and walked to a picnic area. We figured to pitch our tents and camp there. Then the local police showed up.

"If you folks don't leave this park, we're going to have to arrest you," they said.

"Well, you're going to have to arrest us, then," I said. "Because we're not going anywhere."

"Maybe we can find a farmer who'll let us camp on his land." It was one of the white boys from Boston.

He and his girlfriend went to a farm a good distance off the march route, down the road from the picnic grounds, and convinced a man to let us sleep in his hay field. So we didn't go to jail that day.

We hiked out to the farm and pitched our tents in a hay field. By then Karen and I were staying together in one of the tents by ourselves. It felt like a regular camping trip. We got to know the Boston guys a little that night. We would not stay together with them during the rest of the march, but this episode we shared gave us a good feeling.

Later, after everyone was sleeping, I looked outside our tent and saw the big full moon. To me this was better than being cooped up in another damn gymnasium. Out here we didn't have to worry about anybody stepping on us. Out here it was quiet and calm, except for the crickets and grasshoppers.

Next day, had it not been for the Tent City crew who did stay in the gym, the leaders of the march would have left us behind.

Larry McGill especially wanted to take off without us. McGill was involved with the shelter system homeless. He ran an organization whose existence mostly came out of panhandling. Neither he nor the other leaders wanted to come get us, but the other marchers forced them to. They sent a van to come get us and take us to the place where we were starting the march that day.

By that point in the march, about 30 other people had decided to march with Tent City. People were leaving their organizations and marching with us. Among them was one man with a huge snake and another who brought a pit bull on the march.

Along the road to Washington, the reception of the people who *were* expecting us was tremendous. By September 26, we ended up in Wilmington, Delaware. It was so inspiring. The mayor was there, and the dude from the district league. No matter how many times I spoke at press meetings, I always spoke about how it was time for the homeless to talk. No matter where I went in Wilmington, I found people there already feeling this prior to my saying it. The town named September 26 as National Homeless Day in memory of this day. After all the misery of the march, this told us that people were still hearing us and still listening.

The following Sunday we made it to Baltimore, where the homeless organizations, homeless people, welfare mothers, and other well-wishers met us at the college gymnasium where we were staying. They brought us rain ponchos, and they brought sandwiches they had stayed up all night and day making, enough for all of the marchers to have two sandwiches apiece. They also brought plenty of soda.

Now this was the kind of support we had expected from the leaders of the march. It came instead from the people. I saw that if we could tap that same level of commitment and concern that these people in Baltimore were using to help us, if we could harness that same kind of enthusiasm and energy for the overall movement up and out of poverty, we would be winners. It can be done by poor people. Our energy, our ingenuity, our experiences, our survival instincts are the resources that are going to get us over.

After three hard weeks on the road, we made it to Washington. We were very hyped up because even though we had detoured all the way through the march, we still got to Washington. We arrived in the suburbs of the District of Columbia with about 260 to 275 people. We should have had anywhere from a thousand to two thousand people with us. Still, we were lucky.

That was a heavy day. When you first think of doing something like that, and you can't see to the end and then you finally get there...I felt very honored having had the privilege of marching from New York alongside the people I marched with.

On reaching the District of Columbia, we were given quarters in a big, tall, brand new office building. Since on the march I was the representative and speaker for the National Union of the Homeless and Tent City, I was told of a briefing with the Exodus March staff that was going to be held at the CCNV building in Washington. I went to this meeting with Willie Baptist, whom I had originally met at the Survival Summit back in July. He and I were the only two people from the march who attended the meeting. Karen came with us as we were driven into town.

The building that Mitch Snyder had gotten from President Reagan with a hunger strike and had turned into a shelter was humongous. Karen had come along because she was interested in seeing the building. Way before she knew me, she had been part of the effort to get CCNV that building. She wanted to see for herself what it was like.

It was a big, light-colored office building with lots of windows. Only four blocks from the United States Capitol Building, it was even more degrading than the shelters we had in New York. Twelve hundred people lived in there. All we got to see was the downstairs. It was clean, but overcrowded. People were sleeping in hallways. There was alcohol, there were drugs. At the time Karen was looking around, the actors Jon Voight and Martin Sheen were visiting down in the basement office. Both those guys were close to Mitch Snyder. Later Sheen played the role of Mitch Snyder in a made-for-tv movie.

The Housing Now! and CCNV people had pizza and beer for us at the meeting. The fact that in their shelter they provided alcohol for us told me how sensitive they were about the alcoholism among the homeless. As the meeting started, Willie and I brought up how poorly they had provided what they had promised.

"If you had gotten everything that we promised you on that march," one of their representatives said, "you would not have gotten to Washington mad."

I was stunned.

"You gotta be crazy," I said. "We were on the march because we were mad. You had nothing to do with us getting to Washington."

I wanted to slap him upside the head. I wanted to knock him out. I am serious. That man's words told me that there really never was any intention to give us the proper gear and supplies. Even though I had suspected it, it shocked me that they would so casually admit they had been lying to us all along. No matter what, honesty would have been the best policy. Had they told us the truth ahead of time, we could have decided for ourselves whether or not we wanted to rough it that much. Had they been straight with us, it might have made us more comrades or brothers and sisters. How could they possibly figure that we had to be made miserable (and drained to the point of exhaustion) by the conditions of the march in order to display our anger?

What got us to Washington in the first place was our own real anger, our hatred of the system, not something tricked out of us by scheming advocates. At that moment I detested Housing Now! and the people who ran that march.

Tired, I went outside the building and sat at one of the picnic tables to smoke a cigarette.

Across the street I could see police gathered. They were there to prevent the homeless from getting in the park.

As I sat at the table, rats started coming up to me in broad daylight like your cat comes up to you wanting a snack or to be patted. I saw more rats than I care to remember.

Willie, Karen and I went back out to the office building in the suburbs where we were staying that first night. CCNV contacted the marchers there, saying that everybody was going to ride in the next day on the bus. That was a mistake. The purpose of the march was to dramatize homeless people's determination, and putting us all on buses would detract from that. Again I felt like they were undermining our efforts.

"Keep your fucking buses," I said. "We walked all the way from New York. We have no intention of riding a bus into Washington."

What we ended up doing was telling the kids and old people who wanted to, and those who could not make it, to go ahead and get on the bus. Karen looked at Old Man John, Old Man John looked at Karen. We all knew his feet were killing him. He didn't care. He was going with us all the way.

The next day, we marched in.

Because Washington, D.C. is the capital city of the United States, I expected it to be the best-looking city in the world. But it's just like day and night. Go to one part, it's fantastic, it's beautiful: the Capitol Building, the Jefferson Memorial, the reflecting pools, the lights. But then you go to another part of town, nearby, and you see the walls falling down, you see buildings burnt down, boarded up, people sleeping on sidewalks, at bus stops. I had not realized that poverty and homelessness were so prominent in Washington, the capital of the biggest democracy in the world. It overwhelmed me.

Donna Brazile, who was in charge of the Housing Now! part of the march, and the other controllers of the march, had first wanted us to stay at CCNV, but after the conditions we saw, we had no intention of staying there. Tent City and part of the Exodus crew intended to meet up with Leona Smith and the Union of the Homeless and have our own convention. So Donna Brazile and Mitch Snyder and the other march organizers told us they had made arrangements for us to use a campground where we could have our meetings and do our own thing. They led us to believe that we were going to get us a decent place for our Union of the Homeless convention.

We would have preferred to camp right in Lafayette Park, where the veterans of Hooverville camped, where Martin Luther King went, where all the big parades and marches and camps happened. In actuality, they put us out in the boondocks on the far side of the RFK Stadium parking lot, in the woods, where nobody would see us. Yet the whole point was to be seen and to be heard by people who normally would not look at us nor listen to us.

I felt we had been conned, and that fired my intention to follow through on the Union's original plan and take over the HUD building the day before the big rally. Leona, however, told me we were going to play it cool because a meeting had been arranged with the Secretary of the Department of Housing and Urban Development, Jack Kemp. Our meeting was scheduled for Friday, October the 6th, at the main HUD office. They said they would allow us half an hour.

Out where the Union of the Homeless, Tent City, Up and Out of Poverty, Welfare Rights and other grassroots organizations were bivouacked, the march organizers had big tents for everyone to congregate in. Tent City went off to the side, and we built our own separate area. There was a white shack out there that we believed, and which I believe to this day, housed the undercover cops who were keeping track of us. That's where the drugs and alcohol in the camp came from.

Friday came. The HUD building was a big curved federal office building. The words "Department of Housing and Urban Development" were in stainless steel letters on a big tall separate slab of concrete out front. Not the most compassionate-looking architecture. Some of us carried a banner that said "STOP THE WAR ON THE POOR AND HOMELESS OF THE WORLD." The heavyset sister I had first seen at the Survival Summit was leading the cheers again.

"What do we want?" she asked.

"HOUSING!"

"When do we want it?"

"NOW!"

Leona Smith was up front, the sun shining on her. She had on a cream-colored pants suit, with the sleeves shoved up to her elbows, and a dark, patterned blouse. She put her hand up to shield the sun from her eyes.

"Casanova, from Tent City," she called. "Casanova, come on through, brother. We're half an hour late, but that's okay. They've been keeping us waiting for far too long. We'll let them wait on us now."

I came on through the crowd to stand with Leona. I wore jeans and a heavy plaid lumberjack shirt. Leona raised her right hand as she talked to the people.

"We're going to go in, we're going to meet with Jack Kemp. We're going to present Jack Kemp with our resolutions that came from you, and the rest will be up to them."

With a gentle fist raised, she ended her talk. Hand in hand we walked to the entrance of the HUD building, hundreds of our supporters following us to the door chanting.

"We're going to take houses!"

"All night long!"

The riot guards let me, Leona, Alicia from Dignity Housing, a guy from Texas, and one guy from California into the HUD building. We waved back at our friends, smiling, because it was invigorating to have all those supporters, but as we went in past the police, some of them African-American, with their riot gear, visored helmets, and dark sunglasses, I felt scared and worried.

They locked the doors behind us.

They took us upstairs into a large, secluded meeting room. As we sat down around a very big conference table, I was very very upset, I was very very uptight, I was very very agitated because of the position we were being put into. Had the meeting been arranged in a more visible, open area, maybe I would have felt more comfortable. But we were in their territory, and they were heavily armed.

Jack Kemp introduced himself. I already had an impression of Jack Kemp before I went up there, and in those days I wasn't pulling my punches.

"The times for beating around the bush are all over," I said. "I don't trust you. And I don't like you, understand? You guys are in charge of people's lives, but as far as I am concerned, you politicians are a corrupt crew. I'm an artist and I'm getting ready to do a painting of you. I have a vision of you as a very nice thief, good-looking but weak."

I got to admit, Kemp kept his cool. He hoped to change my opinion. He talked a little bit about his football career, and I talked about my homeless career and Tent City. It went around the table, everybody introducing themselves and their issues. Barry Zigas was there. He was the one of the top march coordinators and president of the advocacy group called the National Low-Income Housing Coalition. Robert Hayes, the guy who ran the Coalition for the Homeless in Washington, was also there.

Gradually, as Kemp started talking and we started talking, we began to get a little more comfortable. Everybody expressed their opinions about the situation of homelessness and poverty, and how they felt about it, in detail and very graphically. I talked about the reasons people had brought the fighting to the capital, namely, the sorry conditions in the shelter system, the availability of houses all over the U.S. that are vacant and boarded up.

Kemp had a friendly manner. He listened to us, and then he started saying the things that we wanted to hear.

"We're going to start a program called Project Hope," he said, "so we can get homeless people into housing."

He then told us about a three-phase program of helping people move from short-term, or transitional housing to permanent housing. He said 10 per cent of HUD housing would go to the homeless, to be rehabbed by and for the homeless.

Halfway through the negotiations, a call came from downstairs saying that the homeless were trying to chain themselves to the doors and break the doors down. The people were restless. They had not marched for three weeks to just stand around and do nothing. Leona made a decision to go down and talk to our supporters and cool them off a little because we felt that we were accomplishing something up here.

From the moment she walked out that door, I was worried all over again. The moment she left our sight and she was not with us, I felt that the authorities could snatch her at any time—while she was going down there, or on her way back upstairs from talking. That kind of threat was there from the beginning of the march, all the way. There was always the possibility of the establishment arresting us. Personally I believed we were not going to accomplish anything if we tried to do it all at meetings or all in the streets. A combination of both was necessary. But I was praying that nobody downstairs did anything to get shot.

Finally Leona came back, having convinced our people outside to give us a chance to see what we could get done with HUD. I felt relief.

Gradually, as the negotiations continued, I was getting to like Mr. Jack Kemp. We talked about the program where for one dollar you can buy a building. I thought that was a good idea because anybody can come up with a dollar. Even I would panhandle under that condition. But the implications of what you are getting into are not announced when they say "A Dollar A Building!" When you buy that building, we realized later, you have to rehab it within a certain amount of time or lose it. *U.S. News and World Report* estimated that it takes $65,000 to $70,000 to gut and rehab one apartment in a vacant building.

At last Mr. Kemp handed us a piece of paper with his commitments and promises. I felt it was like a treaty. Kemp's letter committed HUD and the George Bush Administration to "make available" to the homeless 10 per cent of the government-owned, single-family "affordable" houses, or about 5,000 houses, in 1990.

Next, the letter committed the administration to seek to "reorient our voucher and certificate programs to assist those most in need to become self-sufficient" and to "review specific proposals to expand the Dignity Housing model and to try to adapt such new housing initiatives as Operation Bootstrap to make this possible."

I liked the idea of helping people become self-sufficient. The government gives out AFDC, they give out welfare, but with that money they pay out they don't accomplish anything that lasts. Sure, you can give somebody their rent money, let them pay their rent and buy their food, but if that's all you're doing, then you're not really doing anything. There has to be training involved, and an interest in the individual, not just paperwork.

Kemp also made a promise that "representatives of HUD and representatives of homeless and low-income people will meet in October to begin to review specific proposals to use HUD funding and property to help the homeless."

Not mentioned in the letter were Kemp's implications that these meetings would happen on a regular basis and that HUD was going to pay us money as consultants at these meetings, as well as arrange for us to have transportation and housing during these trips to Washington. It only seemed right. We homeless and grassroots organizations did not have the kind of money to be making several trips a year to Washington, no matter how important it was. By definition we were poor, so traveling expenses were hard to come by. Government money is our money anyhow. Even the homeless pay taxes when they buy a bottle of wine or a pack of cigarettes. We have been paying taxes all our lives; our families have been paying taxes.

The key point was that none of the meetings, which would take place at least once a year, were supposed to take place without homeless people being represented. I would soon learn that Kemp's idea of homeless representation was different from my own.

Kemp's letter also stated that the Bush Administration "will propose changes in the use of CDBG funds so that they will be used to fight poverty, increase self-sufficiency and opportunity in low-income communities and expand and preserve affordable, decent housing for low-income people."

Tent City was the only organization there that did not ask for government funding. I was in agreement with Malcolm X, who said, "I'm for whatever gets results. I don't go for any organization...that has to compromise with the power structure and has to rely on certain elements within the power structure for their financing, which puts them in a position to be influenced and controlled all over again by the power structure itself." That was my whole gripe with the march organizers.

But Tent City did not go to Washington with a selfish attitude. We were there in support of the other organizations who had people with families and children and who needed government-funded housing. The families that were part of this movement went for the grants because they needed them. The only thing Tent City actually asked the government was to give up some of the abandoned buildings they owned in the name of the American people. We who marched to Washington were American people.

Who could disagree with this statement: "We must turn the abandoned homes throughout our cities and towns into decent, affordable homes for the homeless and low-income people..."? The only problem was that the Secretary of HUD added "I pledge to work directly and aggressively with state and local governments to make this happen." We asked Secretary Kemp, why don't you let *us* rehab those buildings ourselves? In fact, one of the things that Kemp told us he would do was hire the homeless to rehab housing owned by the government and then let them move in. Technical services and advice would come from Washington. Unfortunately, he didn't put that in the letter in as much detail as he said it to us.

"I pledge," Secretary Kemp wrote in the letter, "to work directly with individuals and groups throughout the country to assure that HUD's programs, properties and funds are used to expand opportunities for low-income people and help make decent, affordable housing a reality for all and to make it possible for all homeless men, women and their children and their families to live in a decent home."

Amen.

Our scheduled 30-minute meeting ended up as a three-hour meeting, plus lunch. When all was said and done, we came downstairs with this letter of commitment, and I felt real proud. All of us who had been at that meeting felt that we had accomplished what we came for. This was something we could take home to our people. We wanted to believe what was said in that paper, and so we did believe it. We wanted to believe in Kemp's letter. I stood on a brick planter and read the letter to everybody who had waited, while other people were getting copies made.

But out of all these people, one woman from California, named Dorothy, was not happy with the letter. She pulled me to one side.

"You know, that letter don't really mean anything," she said. "It don't mean shit."

I should have paid attention to her.

***

While we had been at HUD, a rumor was apparently going around camp that somebody had found some kind of paper telling how much money CCNV and Housing Now! had, and about how much we had been lied to and conned. Feeling duped, a lot of the people from the New Exodus March went over to the CCNV. The Exodus people were voicing their opinions on this, trying to get in to talk to Mr. Mitch Snyder himself. It got to the point where CCNV called out their own security. A riot broke out. A couple of Exodus women got injured and went to the hospital.

***

The following day, Saturday, October 7th, we marched into Washington for the main event. It felt good to be there, to see all the people getting together to confront homelessness and poverty. I understand that while we had been marching down from the north, another group had also been marching from the south; they had started from Atlanta. Besides Tent City, a lot of organizations were represented that day, such as the Urban League, the YMCA, the United States Conference of Mayors, Greenpeace, SANE, the Gray Panthers, striking Eastern Airlines pilots, the AFL-CIO, the U.S. Catholic Conference, PTA members, and the National Organization for Women. *People* magazine reported that there were 40,000 people gathered in Washington the day of the rally.

The *Village Voice* estimated at least 100,000. Housing Now! said it was more like 150,000.

The sun was out and there was enough wind so that the banners of "BUILD HOUSES NOT BOMBS," "EVERY HUMAN BEING DESERVES A HOME," and "HOMELESS, NOT HELPLESS" rippled and flapped as we headed east on Constitution Avenue toward the bright white Capitol Building.

"No housing, no peace!" people were chanting.

Again the cops wanted us to stay on the sidewalks, but this time we walked through the streets. Our multitudes took up the streets. A spirited young African-American sister linked her arms with other marchers who linked their arms.

"Let's take it in," she shouted, "'Cause we're fired up! Let's bring it in!"

"We ain't takin' it no more!" her companions shouted. "'Cause we're fired up!"

When we got to the rally, the reception was tremendous.

"There's Tent City!"

"Tent City!"

"Tent City!"

"Tent City!"

"No housing, no peace!"

At the rally site, a lot of tourists came mainly to see the stars. In fact, Housing Now! had put on a $150 a ticket dinner to raise money for themselves. The way they got people to pay this was to advertise that they would have 250 movie and tv stars at the dinner. So that is why I say I felt a lot of the non-homeless in the audience were primarily interested in seeing celebrities rather than helping homeless people. Jesse Jackson and Coretta Scott King were there, and Sugar Ray Leonard. I saw Mrs. King and wanted to go speak to her, but it felt like she was part of all the show business. They also had Geraldo Rivera and all these movie stars and people introduced by movie stars, talking about the homeless fight.

I wondered how the hell somebody with a million-dollar house could talk about being a homeless person? They didn't know what we needed.

The actors and stars were well-intentioned, but they were misinformed. They thought they were helping us. They weren't doing anything for us. The money was going to Housing Now!, which meant CCNV.

"If it hadn't been for Mitch Snyder and God," one speaker said, "the march wouldn't have been, it wouldn't have existed."

Even before we got to Washington, many of us realized that Housing Now! and CCNV were using us. We waited for the opportunity to have our say. But as the parade of celebrities continued, we realized they had no intention of letting us speak.

Well, we had marched all the way to Washington, not to listen to movie star politicians, but to speak out ourselves, to make it plain that homeless people and people of poverty were taking their own initiative.

The Anti-Hunger Coalition, led by Serena Martin, Diane Johnson and Diane Bernard, began pushing their way to the front. The women didn't think about all the whys and why-nots. All they said was "They're not going to let us talk. Fuck it, let's take it in. We need houses, we need homes, we need food." They led, and I followed.

In the background you could hear the homeless people.

"The homeless have no tvs. Let the homeless speak! Tv later, housing now!"

A lot of the Tent City crew, other marchers, and the Welfare Rights group were bellied up against the wooden picket security fence that was about 20 feet out front of the stage.

"Let the homeless speak!" they shouted. "Poverty pimps! Homeless people can speak for themselves!"

The security men behind the fence wearing blue shirts, white caps, and slacks were looking nervous. Organizers on the stage were looking down at us, shaking their heads and wagging their fingers.

Leona had made it backstage. Karen and I were at the gate that led to the stage. I saw Coretta King back there.

"They ought to let us go through the gate," Karen said. "That's why we're here, to speak."

Karen wanted me to go onto the stage. I was ready to just let it go, but a security dude, a big dark-skinned brother, started getting rough with her, started pushing her. So I got over there quick and angry and let that brother know who we were and why we were there.

Serena and the women of the Anti-Hunger Coalition were watching the confrontation I was having with security. The mood had already gotten ugly. The potential for a riot had already existed because the organizers were not allowing the marchers to get up and speak. We had not walked all the way to Washington to shut up and watch and listen to someone else. And now the security guys were compounding the crowd's anger by pushing Karen around. Fortunately, someone behind the stage knew who I was and told the man to let me in.

"We want Leona!" the crowd shouted.

Had they not let Leona Smith speak, I believe we would have torn down that fence and the stage. As it was, Leona was escorted to the lectern to cheers.

"What do we want?" she said.

"HOUSING!"

"When do we want it?"

"NOW!"

Leona looked out over all those faces.

"The struggle is not over, my brothers and sisters," she said. "Until every single homeless man, woman, and child in America have a right to decent, affordable housing, and a right to a decent quality of life. It does not stop. It does not stop."

They cheered her because they knew she was one of them and spoke what they felt. They finally convinced the organizers that I should get up there and speak too. As the pretty white woman introduced me, I felt nervous. To some extent I was overwhelmed by looking out and seeing thousands and thousands of people. It was the most people I had ever faced. But I looked for and saw the yellow and white New Exodus hats, and then I wasn't speaking to the movie stars or the tv stars or the tourists. I appreciated all the other people being there, but they could have no concept of what the homeless who had made that march were feeling, why we were there. I wasn't talking to them; I was speaking to the people who actually walked the New Exodus March.

"Hey," I said. "We made it, huh? We finally made it. I also want you to remember that no matter what anybody says, you guys have got to pat yourselves on the back. Realize what you have done. You walked all these miles. You went through all these trials and tribulations. So you can be heard. You made this rally. You made everything that is happening this day happen. If it were not for you, there wouldn't be a movement. Don't let these advocates make you feel that they have done anything because if it weren't for you there would be no advocates.

"I'm here to say that we, the homeless of New York, can no longer let other people or the so-called higher powers talk for us. We, the homeless, the people living below the poverty level, must talk for ourselves. It is our duty, it's our job, to go back and keep this fight going, no matter what anybody tells you. Keep it going!"

I never have and still don't consider myself a *victim* of society, except in the sense that I believe there is oppression of the poor. Let me amend that: I consider that I was a victim as long as I accepted my condition, my plight. None of us was accepting our plight that day. Standing up there seeing all those thousands and thousands of people who had come together, I felt that we were not going to come out on the bottom of the totem pole this time.

CHAPTER 17

The ABCs of Politics

As I have said, I never had any intentions of becoming a political activist. I had been a pacifist all my life in that I had accepted the government-supported segregation of the homeless and poor people. But once the avenue of activism became clear, there has been no stopping me.

My life experience leads me to get intense in the struggle. I get really upset, not only with the poverty pimps, but also with the homeless people who don't realize that they need to act. We, the homeless and formerly homeless, have to be the ones who run the shelters, the homes, the soup kitchens, the welfare—anything that deals with people in need. But this will be a struggle because there is no way the poverty pimps are going to give up the shelter system as it is now, and the welfare system as it is now. Some shelters get paid federal money for each individual they have staying there. They don't *want* anybody to become independent because the homeless have become a billion-dollar industry.

After the march on Washington was over, everybody went back home on buses, except for me and Karen. She was determined that she would get to her senator's office to speak on behalf of her son. I wanted to hold onto the atmosphere of the march, and maybe see some of the repercussions.

We tried to get hold of John Danforth, one of the senators from Missouri, because Missouri was the state where Karen's parents were living and had Ethan. We talked to one of Senator Danforth's aides, who took notes.

"We'll certainly pass this on to the senator," said the aide, but we never heard back from the senator.

Back home in New York, the struggle continued. Although we had the letter from Mr. Kemp and HUD, we now had to make that letter work for us. Throughout the country, people were trying to get their ten percent from HUD. We were supposed to have a meeting with Kemp in October. But every time we got a meeting set up, he disappeared. He did it very well. He is a professional—give him credit for that. At the HUD meeting all he had done was pacify us for the moment because there were a thousand people at his door. It would soon turn out that the letter was not worth the value of toilet paper.

***

Public School 105 was an old four-story brick school at 269 East 4th. It had been an abandoned building for about ten years and had degenerated to the point that by the fall of 1989 it was a shooting gallery. The squatters we knew moved into the building, chased out all the junkies and cleaned out all the old sets of works and thousands of needles. Then they moved in and called themselves the "ABC Community." The city even let them know that the building was at that time zoned for housing.

In those days I was staying some nights with Karen at her apartment, which was on 12th Street, right around the corner from Tompkins Square. At her place I could take a bath and sleep in a bed. Come morning, I would head out to the park and then to ABC. As far as I was concerned, I was still homeless because if Karen and I broke up, I would be back on the street.

"But Cas, you can stay here," Karen said.

"It's not mine." I said. "Mine says 'Casanova' on the lease. Mine says I pay the rent. Mine, mine, mine. I don't want yours. I love you, but I want mine. That's why I'm in the streets."

But some people in the park got after me for staying with Karen, accusing me of copping out.

"If you are angry with me because I have a woman who has an apartment," I told them, "you need to think. Why are we in this fight? I'm in it so I can get off the streets. I'm not fighting to live in Tompkins Square the rest of my life. I go stay with her because I'm fighting to have a sense of stability, a relationship, a home, a decent way of life, and that's what I'm getting with Karen. That's what we're trying to do: get out of the fucking park!"

At the invitation of the squatters, some of the Tent City people came to move into ABC. This was a good strategy because the neighborhood around the school was black and Puerto Rican, and with Tent City there, you didn't just have white squatters in the building, you also had blacks and Puerto Ricans. At first we had a problem, though, because the people at the school wanted everybody in the school, and the people at the park wanted everybody in the park. It was ridiculous. Wherever I talked, I tried to emphasize the need for both factions to stay united.

So some of us went in with the squatters and proceeded to start setting up living quarters and a community center. The old school was a big building and it would hold a lot of people. We had an influx of people helping with renovating the building and getting the program going.

We didn't get any money from the city or state or federal government to do this work. It was a grassroots project. Emmaus Haus brought food. The White Lung Association (which deals with asbestos-related lung disease) collected money for us; so did the Democratic Clubs. I and a few others from Tent City had speaking engagements, and we would get some money for that.

One of our supporters, David Green, a teacher at a young adult education school in Harlem, more or less got me started speaking at different places. He had me speak to his students. I did a lot of the talking for Tent City because I was getting warmed up to being a public speaker at that point. My first real public speaking had been in the park at the Squatters' Rights Festival back in the summer. During the elections I was asked to speak at a Democratic Club that was working to get Dinkins elected mayor. I spoke at a high school down in Englewood, New Jersey. I spoke to the School of Social Welfare or Social Workers, I forget exactly. I even ended up going to speak at the Columbia School of Medicine. Each of these speaking engagements was arranged by people who were not homeless, but who were supporters of Tent City. Every now and then I would get an honorarium, but all proceeds went to Tent City, to help what was now an organization associated with the ABC Community. ABC was also getting money from neighborhood boosters and the Law

Students Anti-Poverty Project. They were helping us fix up the building, make the office spaces, put in new walls.

The police knew we were there. They used to watch us come down and fill up our buckets at the fire hydrant and carry them back in. They watched us renovating that building with our own manpower and did nothing to stop us. We had our own plumbers working on fixing the water and carpenters doing repairs and renovation. We had homeless people or squatters who were electricians rigging up the electricity.

You walked in the front door of the ABC Center and that was the place we turned into an office for social services. We invited different organizations that were going in their own directions to have an office in our building. We had a group from Homeward Bound who wanted to open up an office. Not only did we set up a filtering system of getting people off the street and into ABC, we were also getting ready to teach about AIDS and drug and alcohol abuse. Soon the community center opened another office with a phone and a person who worked throughout the community helping the homeless. On the ground floor there were about ten different office spaces. Interested organizations were vying for space. What we intended to do was to put them all in one huge office and share their resources.

Some of the people in Sabotage, the anarchist group, were teachers, and they started teaching reading and G.E.D. classes on the second floor. We found a doctor who was willing to open up a clinic in the school. She wanted to come and open up a clinic and help get a staff going. We wanted to open an art center because a lot of us in Tent City were artists. We planned to let people come there and display and sell their art. One woman who was an artist wanted to open up not only an art studio, but also an art school.

The next flight up was the residence area. That floor was our floor, for the people living there. We had a big communal kitchen.

Our community center was open to people in the neighborhood. On the top floor was a gymnasium. We tore down some walls and made it an even bigger space. That was going to be turned into our community recreation center. We were going to have a karate class for self-defense. A band called Mass Transit was scheduled to play a benefit for us there. Sometimes at night you would hear neighborhood bands practicing up there.

Those were exciting weeks to me. We had a community growing at P.S. 105. We were getting people out of the parks and off the streets. Pretty much every other night we met to talk over how things were going. We were becoming self-sufficient, and we were being accepted by the community. Not everybody in the neighborhood loved us, but we had the majority on our side.

What remained was for the city to give us the building legally. We didn't want money; we wanted to get started helping people. I liked the squatters' strategy because they went right in doing something that needed to be done. On the other hand, I didn't want to be worrying about the police coming to my roof or coming in my basement to throw me out any time they wanted to. I wanted a piece of paper saying this belongs legally to Casanova or to the Tent City Union of the Homeless or the ABC Community. I didn't want to be a squatter, I wanted to be an owner. All of us want our own things, all of us.

We intended to set up the ABC Community to deal with the issues of housing and tenant rights, but most importantly, with the issue of poverty itself because poverty relates to all the other causes of homelessness: drugs, alcohol, little or no education or job training, no family.

This frightened the city. Make no mistake, the folks in charge did not want us doing things for ourselves, did not like the fact that poor people could do things on their own. In the minds of the bureaucrats, that set a dangerous precedent.

If once we could get legal control of P.S. 105, then we could consolidate and continue to branch out. And this strategy would spread. Instead of being puppets of Donald Trump and the real estate tycoons, and the landlords, we would be our own landlords. Now you might think that would make the city government happy because we would save them the social services money. Unfortunately, the bureaucrats didn't see it that way. Instead, they cried out that homeless people were criminals for taking a neglected public building and making it work for the public.

Welfare pays the rent for a lot of bureaucrats. Our independence would hurt the poverty pimps in city government and in the shelter system because then they would no longer get as much social welfare income from the Federal government. Every time the rich and powerful throw somebody out of a building and tear it down, the price of real estate goes up. To the tycoons and landlords, our success would mean there was property they couldn't charge outrageous prices for. To the city it would mean they wouldn't get that bonanza of real estate tax dollars.

To tell the truth, I think that the squatters might have been left alone a lot longer had they not invited Tent City to move in with them. The cops knew us—we had a long-term battle going on.

First the city started sending people from the Housing Department to say that we could not stay there and that they would find us other housing. The establishment tried to pacify us with a program aimed at getting people out of the park. City Councilwoman Miriam Friedlander made a lot of promises to us, first at Karen's apartment, and then at a meeting in the school.

Friedlander promised us that we wouldn't have to deal with any shelters. That had been her say ever since she got involved with the homeless situation: "No shelters. No shelters. No shelters." And I agreed, because if you take people out of the park and put them in a shelter, all you're doing then is pulling them out of one graveyard and throwing them into another. I emphasize that because Tompkins Square Park literally used to be a cemetery at one time long ago.

Unfortunately, Friedlander was the type of person who always got very vocal to people and the press about the need for housing, but no progress was ever made. This was the way I felt about her, but people told me to leave her alone. So I left her alone.

By this time, Tent City had become the New York Tent City Union of the Homeless, and I was president. The Philadelphia-based National Union of the Homeless would contact me either through David Green or Shigemi, who both had telephones. Sometimes I would also get calls at Karen's place.

When I wasn't staying with Karen, I stayed in the back area of the rec room on the top floor of ABC. As president of the Tent City Union of the Homeless, I had a room to myself. My bedroom had once been a room used for storage. In the big room next to mine four people had sleeping bags. We had plans for making rooms so couples could have privacy.

Karen was great. She brought a bed to ABC. She also came up with an electric heater. Before that, the only heat we had was in the kitchen, where we cooked in a barrel. That's where we watched tv, mostly football and basketball.

One day I read an article in the *New York Times* which indicated Kemp, Mitch Snyder and Barry Zigas had been holding meetings with no homeless people there. Barry Zigas was supposed to be mediating this thing for us.

I phoned HUD in Washington immediately.

"Just like we spread the news of this letter with all the commitments and all the promises," I told them, "just like we were able to do that, we're going to spread the news that you're reneging on everything, that you're not keeping appointments with us, that, if fact, you are doing things behind our backs, and totally disrespecting homeless people again."

Half an hour later I got a call from HUD. The meeting was on.

Many of us who arrived in Washington for the meeting (Union of the Homeless paid my way) were the original people who had met with Kemp in early October. We were expecting to meet with Kemp again.

A man came through the door and said his name was Ron Rosenfield. He was the financial director of low-income housing at HUD in Washington.

"You're not coming in here and changing any rules," he said quickly. "What we say goes."

Rosenfield acted as though he felt that it was beneath him even to be in the same room with us. I raised bloody hell right then and showed him the newspaper stories. He said this was politics. He said something along the lines of "You have to learn the language. When immigrants come to the United States, they know that they have to speak English. Well, you're in Washington, now."

They've got a language of their own there, I guess.

We had an agenda we wanted to talk about. But Rosenfield only wanted to talk about the ten percent Kemp had said he would give us because Rosenfield was from the financial department, and he didn't want to talk about anything else. We said that we were there not only to discuss housing, but everything pertaining to the poverty level because there are interconnections.

"HUD is in the insurance business," he told us. "We are in the business of making money."

After several more unproductive minutes, Mr. Rosenfield stood up and ended the meeting. He walked out of the room talking about how he had to go home and put his feet up on the couch and relax.

We had been naive, and Kemp had tricked us by addressing the letter to "Housing Now," leaving him an out on a technicality, letting him only deal with the status quo homeless advocate groups.

Tricking is the same thing as lying.

Mr. Kemp, with all his smarts, knew what he was doing when he addressed the letter "Dear Housing Now." At the meeting he led us to believe the things in that letter were negotiable with the homeless, but when Kemp wrote "Dear Housing Now," that said right then and there, Housing Now! and nobody else. That meant the exclusion of the Union of the Homeless, the Anti-Poverty Organization, and all the grassroots groups and individuals. That was his way out.

Know your enemy. Any time you stop fighting your enemy simply because he says things that sound like what you want to hear, you are making a mistake. You have got to pay attention to exactly how he says it.

Looking back, I believe CCNV, Housing Now! and Coalition for the Homeless were all in line, all together on the issue. The advocates used that march to say to the media, "See, we are helping the homeless people, the homeless accept us as their leaders, the homeless people obey us."

And what did we obedient homeless get for our acceptance of the advocates? Stories of Donna Brazile going to Africa using money made from the march. That's why I hate the word "advocate." That's why we call advocates "poverty pimps." Many people in the world think these organizations are God's gift to the homeless, but, in reality, too many of these organizations are doing little but ripping us off.

Looking back, I think we should have insisted that the letter read "Dear Homeless of America" or something more open like that. If we had been on top of things, we would have had Kemp address that letter differently. But at the time we were so glad to get a letter we didn't pay enough attention.

Nevertheless, the letter was important as a morale booster, a good thing to take home to the people. Homeless people all over the United States then had ammunition they could use to deal with the HUD organization.

We left Washington very angry, feeling very disheartened. When we got back to New York, some of us lodged a bias complaint against Mr. Rosenfield because his statements to us were very bigoted, very racist, and very degrading. We wrote a letter to the *Washington Post*, Cable News, and HUD. Leona Smith, Alicia from Dignity Housing, and David Hayden continued trying to get hold of Kemp. They would set up meetings and spend their money going to Washington, and then no one from HUD would show up.

Meanwhile, the city of New York wasn't liking the idea of a grassroots community center at all. In New York, if squatters occupy an abandoned building for at least 30 days, they cannot be evicted without a hearing. So as we got closer to the end of that 30 days, the city turned up the heat.

First the city tried to kick us out of the building, saying it was not a residence. But then they turned around and told the press and the court that they had given that building in 1988 to a non-profit organization called the New York Foundation for Senior Citizens, which intended to convert it into a *residence* for 82 homeless senior citizens. Whether in fact that was true is questionable. This was November 1989, and the only citizens living there when the squatters took over were junkies. The only improvements that had happened to that old school were the ones made by us.

Old people need housing too, but this location was hardly Mt. Freedom Retirement Resort. This was a drug-infested area, and the city was proposing to put a lot of defenseless old people there? They would have needed a 24-hour police guard at the front door. They would have needed officers to escort these elderly residents to the grocery store and the health clinic. The city's story about the old folks home was just another way for them and the establishment media to play public opinion against us.

Across the street from the ABC Community Center was a vacant lot. Another one of the city's tactics to get us out of ABC was to come up with the idea of letting people stay in the lot. So a lot of people pitched tents and were living there. I guess the problem there for the city came when somebody figured out the lot was more valuable to them when it was empty than it was once there were a lot of homeless people living there. The "property value" deteriorated because people that society said had no value were living there, and so the city changed its mind: the people had to go, period.

The Housing Department finally decided they needed police help and began coming to the door of the ABC Community flanked by officers. We responded by barricading the doors. We also set up an emergency phone tree. We had a secret exit for the eventual time when the police would come to break the door in. At that time, one person would go out the secret exit and make a couple of phone calls. Each of those people would in turn call several other people to come support us, and so on.

Meanwhile, the struggle continued in Tompkins Square Park as well. On October 24th, at a meeting of Community Board 3 in the Alfred E. Smith Parks and Recreation Building, certain factions put forth a proposal to re-establish the 1 a.m. to 6 a.m. curfew. The arguing got raucous, which they probably expected, since a dozen police in riot gear happened to be there. The vote came in 15 to 3 against re-establishing the curfew, with six abstentions and 23 members absent.

On October 26th, I was in Philadelphia for a Union of the Homeless demonstration. We called it our "Halloween Civil Disobedience." This was the brainstorm of Leona Smith and Marian Kramer, from Detroit. I was not there for the strategizing, but let me tell you, when those two women put their heads together, they came up with some grand ideas.

We went to Philadelphia City Hall and into the City Council chambers to protest the lack of housing. Under our clothes, we all had Halloween masks and banners and placards with slogans. Once we were in and sitting down, we waited. When the council started talking about housing, we began pulling out our masks one at a time and putting them on. The council members noticed a few people in the gallery had Halloween masks on. Next time they looked up, a whole row of people had on masks, and there were banners. Finally we had a couple of rows of people all in Halloween masks.

When we were finished and came out of the Philadelphia City Council meeting, I got the word that Tent City had been trying to get hold of me all day:

More than a hundred police had come down hard on the ABC Community.

Around noon, a dozen cops and about six city workers had come to the school and tried to evict the residents of the school. The people in ABC dropped plastic bags full of debris from the third and fourth floor windows to scare off the invaders. It worked. The authorities retreated.

Stanley Cohen and Ronald Kuby, our lawyers, got us an injunction at 4:25 p.m. based on the fact that the squatters had been working in the building more than 30 days, which meant according to the law that we had a right to a hearing.

By about 7:30 that evening, the city lawyers had gotten the injunction thrown out. The police claimed they had made a sweep of the school on September 28th and nobody had been in the building. Once again, the courts believed the cops over the people. It is odd that they claimed nobody was there, since even before we were in it junkies had been living there. And if the squatters hadn't been there, then where were the so-called renovators of The New York Foundation for Senior Citizens?

Word got out to the neighborhood and to our supporters about what was going on. Our friends and supporters quickly began gathering outside of ABC. Shortly after midnight, around a hundred police in riot helmets with billy clubs got together on 4th Street, made themselves into a wall and came toward the crowd, pushing them back. Many people left. Some threw bottles and firecrackers at the police, who were surrounding the building and pushing people, beating up people, tearing down the walls inside that we had built. In the end, 42 people got arrested that night, including Karen.

There was nothing I could do at that point, so I spent the night at a friend's house in Philadelphia. On the Amtrak to New York the next day, I was angry. When I had left, everything was shaping up good. Everybody in the school was getting along, the community was there.

Evening was falling as I walked down 3rd Street in New York toward the ABC Community, and I saw the aftermath. Police barricades and smoldering garbage cans had been set on fire and knocked over. On the block where the school stood, I came to a manned police barricade. They wouldn't let me pass. I could see some people on the other side still protesting, but the authorities had won this battle. The city workers sealed the windows and doors and that was the end of the ABC Community. It was back to the park.

***

After the ABC Community was raided, I moved in full time with Karen at her apartment on East 12th Street. But it still was not my home. As far as I was concerned, even a person who was paying rent was a squatter. Any time the rent goes up and you can't afford it, you are going to get kicked out.

I didn't want squatters' rights. People deserve their own housing. The United States, and I am talking about the federal government as well as the state and city governments, has enough monies and resources to initiate and support programs like the ABC Community, like Dignity Housing. What the city did not realize, and still does not realize, is that if the homeless were to get what we were asking for, the city would be winners in the long run because we would become, in fact, business people. We would have to pay taxes on the property value. In the long run, we would be making money for the city all over again.

The politicians always say they don't have the money for social programs, yet their campaign against the homeless at ABC and in Tompkins Square Park used a tremendous amount of police force, a tremendous amount of the Parks Department personnel and resources. Every time they had a raid against us in the park, they paid people overtime. Now they had a drug-shooting gallery at P.S. 105 to protect—overtime again.

Nevertheless, raiding ABC was a smart move for the city politicians strategically because of their agenda. We had been gaining support every day. But with their attack, the city authorities scattered us. For a while we were like fish out of water, floundering around, bouncing around, not knowing which direction to go or what to do.

But we were and are persistent.

Almost immediately we began to make new plans. Mass Transit's planned ABC benefit performance was changed to Judson Memorial Church. Dinkins had won the mayoral election but would not take office until January. We needed to do something to make him realize that his being inaugurated was not enough. We needed to do something extraordinary. Somebody came up with the idea of taking over the city shelters. Actually going in there en masse and taking a shelter. There was another suggestion that we block or walk down Wall Street. But everybody had their own fight, their own reason for being in the struggle. That caused enough animosity that none of those numerous plans ever solidified.

We should not have allowed a separation between what had been happening at ABC and what was going on at Tompkins Square Park. But because ABC had become more visible for a while, more people paid attention to ABC and directed their energies only to the ABC community. However, people should not have been thinking of ABC alone. This was a mistake on our part. ABC, Tent City, Tompkins Square Park, Homebound, Squatters—they were all about the same thing.

What happened was that Tent City got rebuilt again and a handful of people got back into the ABC Community. All through November 1989 between six and eight each evening at Tompkins Square, those still living at Tent City had been getting visits from the authorities, who put out their fires. Finally, one day we got word that around December 11 they intended to raid us and destroy Tent City again.

After all the mouthing from politicians about how they would not fall back on the discredited shelter system as a public relations "solution" to homelessness, it turned out that one of the first things that was offered to the people in the park was, in fact, shelters. One night in November, 500 homeless and community activists had a meeting with Friedlander, Stern, and the Deputy Borough President. Friedlander and her group came up with a plan to select 150 housing spots which they said they would guarantee to anyone from Tompkins Square Park. Anyone living in Tompkins Square who wanted that housing, Friedlander said, would have it available to them.

Here the authorities were trying to divide and conquer us by telling those from Tent City "we're not even going to allow other people who are homeless, who are on a waiting line, to have first dibs on this." I know the reason they offered this was because the only place in New York City where people fought back regularly was Tompkins Square.

Two people from Tompkins Square Park took the city up on their offer. They went through the city's alcohol detox program and came out and said, "I'm ready for the home."

They were then told, "There is none. You know, we have a housing crisis." Tent City resident Keith Thompson went through the city program twice. The first time they offered him welfare and any shelter in the city he wanted. He refused to go into a shelter.

The second time they offered him welfare and tried to convince him Wards Island was a safe shelter. Wards Island is a shelter where people are robbed by the security guards, where you are not allowed to bring food into the shelter, so you have to eat whatever they offer. Finally they offered Keith welfare and a church program on Beaver Street. Then the church program refused to take him because he had been an activist for homeless people.

Now all this time, Friedlander had been going around telling people that we were agreeing to what she proposed regarding the shelters. She was telling the *Times*, how "today we serviced 60 people." You know what that "service" was? Someone going in and getting a sandwich. The previous summer we fed more people than that every day in Tent City.

In the end, a lot of people went to the shelters, but came back to the park; went through the detox program, but came back to the park. Some of what Friedlander and others had done for people in the park helped us, but the critical point that Friedlander and the rest seemed to forget was that once you send a person through detox and they come out, you have to have some idea what they are going to do then. If they just come out to no job and no housing, then they come out to the park again, they come out to drinking again, and you are back to square one.

During the hard, hectic weeks of that fall and into winter, I hardly had any time to myself or any to spend alone with Karen. My life seemed to be one long strategizing session. Yet I also got energy from those around me because we were fighting for what we knew to be right. We worked to make the community aware that it was not only our fight; it was the fight of all people. We were not fighting to stay in the park; our fight was to get ourselves and other people out of poverty. At the park we were still ready to go to jail if necessary, but we did not want the cops to come down there thinking the only people they had to deal with were the people living in the park.

It is unfortunate that it often takes a catastrophe to wake people up. For example, in New York we had trouble with bridges. Many of the city's bridges were old, old bridges and already people knew they were in dire need of repair. Yet neither the government nor the mayor did anything about it. Only when the earthquake hit California on October 16, and the bridge in San Francisco fell down, part of it on people's cars, crushing them, did something get done about the New York bridges.

It's the same with homelessness. When the earthquake hits your home or when you have a fire, or something happens to you, *then* you become aware. It is unfortunate that sometimes the very walls themselves have to fall down before people realize what is right in front of them.

There are some good homeless organizations out in California, and we were staying in touch. In December they called me to see how things were going in New York and to let me know the situation out there. Homelessness out there had intensified due to the October quake. A lot of middle-class people lost their homes. What happened was that the new influx of well-to-do homeless in California was being taken care of by relief funds and organizations, while the people who had been homeless all along were still being ignored. The middle-class homeless were getting the support that *all* the homeless should have been getting. There was a saying going around that you are but one paycheck away from becoming homeless yourself. Maybe some middle-class people have two or three paychecks to go yet. But the point remains: if not you, then your brothers or sisters or your friends could quickly become homeless.

CHAPTER 18

The Gun to Our Heads

Stanley Cohen was slender with curly hair, curly beard, and gold wire-rimmed glasses. Stanley was an activist lawyer, which I thought was weird the first time I heard of it. Before I met him, I thought a lawyer and an activist could not exist in the same person. I thought you were either one or the other; either you handled the law or you handled activism. But Stanley and his partner had been getting us out of jail for months now. Stanley was cool, but he got it confused sometimes, not intentionally, when he tried to take leadership. He did see things we didn't see, but he was our lawyer. When it came to decision-making, the decisions could not come from the lawyer.

But Stanley sure knew how to be a lawyer. He got the court to order that the Parks Department leave our fires alone. The court ruled that the Parks Department could not interfere with fire law enforcement—that that was the responsibility of the police and fire departments. Still, one of the Parks Department people was quoted in an article as saying, "If you let them have the fires, they will never go away, and that's going to destroy our authority."

The police department wasn't messing with our fires in the park and had no intention of doing so. One man from the fire department got on WBAI radio and said he had been ordered to put out the fires in the park but refused to do so.

"I will go when called to put out fires," he said. "But I will do so to save somebody's life, not to kill them."

None of them wanted to deal with it. A couple of people in the Parks Department got fired. One of the head guys lost his white shirt because of incidents that happened. I heard of a few people who quit the Parks Department because they did not want to work for them anymore. Even in the Parks Department and the Police Department, people were beginning to realize they too could be homeless. They too could lose their jobs. Firefighters know from experience what happens to people when they lose their homes.

By the time December rolled around, the Parks Department would not even talk to us anymore. Before, even when they were coming in and destroying our tents, we were communicating to some extent. Now there was no communication at all. Commissioner Smith, Henry Stern and his cohorts were figuring a comeback. We had thwarted them so much since June that they were furious. Green Meanies would come by in their cars, and they would see you and then look in the opposite direction. We knew something was in the wind.

Meanwhile, some people had gotten back into P.S. 105 and were holed up in the school. They should have been working because they were on the verge of losing their apartments. They should have been out making an income to keep what they had, but they believed what they were reaching for was worth the risk.

By this time, people outside of New York City knew about our situation at the ABC Community; it had become national, briefly symbolic of the whole homeless situation. So on the day in December when the police planned to go into the school and get our people out of there again, the officers found movie stars and tv cameras down there. That day nobody got arrested and people were allowed to take food into ABC because of the news coverage. Even the next day, when the movie stars were gone, the police didn't take us out of the school. I was surprised.

A police officer told tv news reporters, "You know, it's Christmas, and we didn't want these people to be homeless."

Based on what came down later, I know there was no kindness involved in this. It was a strategic move. The only reason they prolonged the situation was because of the publicity and the movie stars. Even after the stars left, the media were hanging around, aware of possible conflict. Unfortunately, the publicity at ABC Community took away attention from Tompkins Square Park, where more people were still living, and where the police did intend to move against us.

Looking back, I see we made a mistake by not emphasizing to the media over and over and over that the issue was not P.S.

105 or Tompkins Square Park; the issue was poverty and homelessness. Tompkins Square Park was where we were, and ABC was where we wanted to go. People wanted to get out of the park. We had no intention of living there the rest of our lives. ABC Community would have been one step out of the park, out of the subways, out of the rundown hotels. At ABC there could have been a training period before moving on to more accommodating housing. ABC was never intended by us to be permanent housing.

Even though I was staying with Karen, I got a dome tent and was looking to get hold of a couple of sleeping bags because Karen and I intended to stay in the park waiting for the cops along with our friends in Tent City. We asked anybody and everybody to come sleep in the park. I emphasized the urgency and I prayed and I begged people.

"Come on down there with your sleeping bags and join us in the struggle. If you think homelessness can't happen to you, you had better start waking up to the fact that it can."

At various speaking engagements I gathered information as well as giving it out. Tent City Union of the Homeless wanted the names and phone numbers of any people who might be our allies. We needed assistance from people familiar with the laws pertaining to housing, welfare, and child care. We urged people to come down to the park on December 9th to be part of our vigil until the cops came. A Festival of Resistance.

Artie Wilson and I were asked to speak at a meeting of the Law Students Anti-Poverty Project at the City University of New York Law School. We told our story to these law students. I also warned people what they would be getting into if they did decide to become involved.

"The past two years they have been beating us publicly," I said. "Kent State and Tiananmen Square can happen here at any time, at any given moment."

We still had some community support. The pastor and a group from the United Church of Christ in Brooklyn were down there with us on the front line. We had some unions. However, it still bothered me that we had not been able to pull together a dramatic civil disobedience after ABC had been shut down.

On December 7th, I moved back into the park. The next day we met with representatives from mayor-elect David Dinkins' office. David Dinkins' representative was a pudgy, bearded black man named Bill Lynch, who had been campaign manager for Dinkins. Now I am not one to be superstitious, but a black man named "Lynch" made me think twice. This Lynch wore glasses and was dressed in a white shirt and tie. A heavyset black woman sat with him. He faced about two dozen of us and our supporters around a big conference table. Standing room only. We had people videotaping the proceedings. That meeting contained an example of the dynamics between the groups who were trying to work together in this struggle.

Our lawyer, Stanley Cohen, sat at the opposite end across from Lynch. Beside Cohen were some of the squatters and some of the members of Sabotage, wearing dark clothes and smoking cigarettes. In back of Cohen, people were standing, and "No Housing No Peace" had been put on the doors of the conference room in letters of tape. To Cohen's right was Keith Thompson of Tent City wearing a sheik-style burnoose. I sat at the corner of the table to the right of Keith.

We started out with Cohen telling Lynch that we had six demands. The primary demand was no eviction of the homeless.

"I would like to put that as the last demand," said Lynch.

Terry, the Minister of Madness, jumped up.

"*You* want to put it last, but they're coming for *us* Monday!"

I think the heavyset woman beside Lynch said something to Terry. You couldn't hear what. Cohen insisted that eviction was to remain the first demand. Terry was all worked up, though, and he yelled back at Cohen.

"I live in the park! She's not going to tell me—!"

"You'll have your turn to speak," one of the squatters said. Terry turned on him.

"Fuck you, you've got a squat."

Terry walked alongside the table toward Lynch.

"I *live* in the park," said Terry. He was intercepted by a smiling, nervous white dude with long hair and a beard and by another white guy who looked like he was in college.

"Stop. Don't touch me," Terry said. He turned to the rest of us, poking his finger at different people. "*You're* not in the park. None of you is in the park! *I'm* in the motherfucking park!"

Terry resisted, but was gently pulled away by a Tent City guy who put his arm around Terry's chest and steered him back away from the Dinkins people.

Stanley stood up. He was getting hot.

"Terry, who are you working for now?" he asked. "Terry, are you working for us now? Or are you working for the other side? We're having a hard time telling that."

"Yeah, no joke," someone said.

"Terry, if the other side had sent somebody in here to do this stuff, they couldn't have asked for better."

Terry jabbed his finger at one of the white squatters.

"You live in the park?"

"I don't care if—"

"No! Fuck you!" Terry jabbed his finger at the guy's face. He turned back to Lynch. "I live in the park! Now, answer my question. What you going to do about the park to stop them Monday?"

Lynch looked somewhat nervous, but he spoke calmly.

"I'm not ready to answer that question until I hear some more about your concerns."

Terry was ready to walk out.

"Terry, it's not over," I said. "I'm still here."

I waved him over, and Terry leaned over so I could tell him to just hang on and I would talk to the guy. Terry clapped me on the leg.

"At this moment," Lynch said, "we support the eviction—not the evictions, the taking down of the structures in the park."

Hearing this, Terry climbed onto the conference table and lay down across it. He slapped his hand down.

"What are you going to do for me?" he said to Lynch. I went up and got Terry off the table.

"Terry, who do you work for?" asked Stanley.

"I work for the FBI," he said.

"I believe it," someone muttered.

It was a hell of a performance. Yet while Terry was agitated from his drinking, he reflected the anger many of us in reality felt but held back for the sake of negotiations. His anger was legitimate. For years, Dinkins had stood in the public claiming to be a supporter of the poor and the powerless, and now here sat his well-fed mouthpiece saying they supported clearing us out of the park. Unfortunately, Terry's behavior played into Lynch's hands because Lynch then had the excuse he needed.

Lynch got up and walked out.

Once we managed to get Terry settled down, we were able to convince Lynch to come back and sit down with us again.

Lynch came back in with the same tired claim about how shelters were available in New York City. Barbara Henry, who had been in the park for a long time, spoke up about how lousy she had found the conditions in shelters.

"Why don't you go live in shelters and come back and let us know?" Barbara said to Lynch. She also let Lynch know that at the raid on the ABC Community she had gotten "busted over the head for no reason by the police" and left with her head bleeding.

Keith Thompson told Lynch that he voted for Dinkins believing that Dinkins would make a change for people who were living out on the street. Change did not mean moving them to a shelter. Keith told him that Dinkins could get people out of the park if he could promise them "that they will get *housing*, not shelters, not the low, degraded shelters that I've been through." Keith had been stabbed in the back and robbed at the shelter.

At this point I had to have my say. I was tired of explaining to people like Lynch who were always pretending they had no choice.

"We need housing," I told him. "No matter how you sugarcoat it. We can't get around this game. We gotta stop playing this game," I said. "People are out there dying in the streets. And more people are going to die every day. And as long as you guys keep playing these games, it's going to get rougher."

But I sensed this meeting would go nowhere. Again, the talk of the suits was just to pacify us.

"You are but a flunky," I said to Lynch. "You have no pull. No matter what we do here, or what we talk about here, all you're going to do is relay it to your boss and nothing is going to get accomplished."

Now all this time Lynch was getting quietly irritated at the flak I was giving him. Then Stanley went to work, first smoothing things over, then launching into his next comments, comparing the sweeps of the park to Nazi Germany, a war zone.

"Call for a moratorium on park raids," he urged Lynch.

Lynch crossed his arms.

Stanley Cohen noted that politicians and press had been describing the Lower East Side as simply a drug haven and a place for criminals. Stanley told Lynch he had represented more than 200 people who had been arrested in the past eight or nine months: squatters, homeless, homesteaders, political activists. Of those, only two of the arrested people possessed drugs. One had marijuana and the other person was someone walking through the park with one hit of LSD.

"Now I dare say if the police of New York were to make a sweep in the *Upper* East Side of New York, in the West Village, anywhere else, and grab 200 people, your stats would be 75 percent," said Stanley. "So I think it's important to keep in mind...what I am saying is that there's drug activity in the park, just the way there's drug activity at Wall Street, just the way there's drug activity in this building right now today, and you know that. Yes, drugs are symptomatic of other problems, and yes there is drug activity throughout the city. But what I'm saying is that the forces of disinformation and the people that have an agenda on the Lower East Side are using legitimate public concern and fear about drug problems as an excuse to attack the Lower East Side....You've got to distinguish between the campaign of disinformation and the reality of the park."

Lynch sat there like a sphinx, not committing himself, letting us get everything off our chest. He kept saying he wanted to find a middle ground, but you don't find a middle ground by threatening people. Yet the city used that tactic first. Lynch told us he could not negotiate with a gun to his head, but he had it the wrong way around; we had no guns. Their police had the guns.

Stanley told Lynch we wanted a moratorium on raiding the park until Dinkins and his staff had time to study the complex situation. Stanley told Lynch that as a gesture of good faith, we might be willing to narrow the encampment. In that way, Dinkins could prevent a blood bath, save millions of dollars, and tell critics that he had gotten a narrowing of encampment. That would give Dinkins a chance to continue working toward other solutions.

Of course, Lynch would commit to nothing.

"I want you to understand," Lynch said, "that David Dinkins is true to his commitment to trying to do something to alleviate the problems of homelessness and the lack of affordable housing. The question is the road we take to get there....I think I can say unequivocally that David Dinkins is going to try to represent all the people of this city. So I've got to be concerned about all of those entities, constituents, users of the Lower East Side, and of the park in particular, when we look at this issue. Finally...I come from a tradition of sitting down wanting to talk it out. I hope we can avoid what happened in August and that that does not happen again."

"It's a question of how much of a moral leader he is," Stanley said of Dinkins, "and how much of a politician he is."

We would get the answer to that question soon enough.

CHAPTER 19

A Dinkins Christmas

The dawn of Thursday, December 14, 1989, came cold and gray. The temperature was in the mid-teens, and snow was coming. You could tell from the air.

We were all waiting. They had not come on Monday. Or Tuesday, or Wednesday. Some people felt we had won again. But what I feared was that we had so angered the powers-that-be that something like Kent State or Tiananmen Square might go down. I feared the National Guard being called in the way they were at the Watts and New Jersey riots.

Deputy Inspector Julian came through the park warning us they were coming in. The Green Meanies passed out plastic garbage bags for people to put their stuff in. One of our people beat on a big drum, and we had banners and signs that said things like "SIEG HEIL!" and "NEW YORK CITY, YOU CAN'T HIDE; WE CHARGE YOU WITH GENOCIDE," and on my tent was what had practically become our motto: "NO HOUSING, NO PEACE!"

Assistant Parks Commissioner Jack Linn directed the raid, what one supporter of ours called "the military solution to homelessness." Scores of police and almost 200 Green Meanies and maintenance workers swarmed into the park with 15 of the big Parks Department garbage trucks. They photographed us at our tents, but we, in turn, had people videotaping the raid. The authorities told us if our stuff was too heavy to carry out, it could be recorded and stored with the Parks Department for three days. But they still shoveled belongings into garbage trucks and flatbeds. People scattered. The Tent City fire was knocked over, and it flared up in blazing orange. As they started tearing Tent City down, we set it on fire.

Two fire engines came and helicopters clacked overhead as firefighters closed in on our fire to extinguish it. It was not yet noon when smoke clouded the air like a fog through the park.

They kept throwing our belongings in the trucks again. Barbara, one of the women who had been at the meeting with Lynch, cradled a teddy bear and had managed to save a scrawny Tent City Christmas tree.

That made a nice photograph for them in the *Times*.

Eleven people from the park headed over to 343 East 10th with the intention of taking over a vacant apartment, but the police arrested them. They also arrested Father George Kuhn of St. Brigid's Church (which faces the park) and two clergymen who went with Kuhn across the police barricade to deliver food to the people who had got back into ABC.

New York is one of the richest cities in the world. But apparently the "city leaders" are comfortable with the poverty and homelessness that exists in New York; they are comfortable with thousands and thousands of people living in the streets and eating out of garbage cans. Any time the city, state or national government truly wants to put a stop to what's happening, they could do it. The minimum wage went for years without being raised, and when they did raise it, it was pennies, nowhere near what is needed to live on. Yet the authorities raise their own checks annually.

The official excuse for the destruction of Tent City this time was a claim that they had had increasing complaints from residents in the area, and that "the encampment had become a center of drug use and prostitution." That very same morning the *New York Times* carried an article with the headline "Dinkins Supports Removal of Tents In Tompkins Park." Dinkins had been elected by a lot of people who thought he was progressive because that's what he misled people to believe. He would not even take office until January, and he was already turning out to be more of the same business as usual. Parks Commissioner Stern said as much when the *Times* quoted him as saying that Dinkins' policy would be a "continuation of the course set by Mayor Edward Koch." That is to say, pure Scrooge.

Dinkins said, "It is important to note that, while the tents will be removed, homeless people will still be able to sleep in the park, on benches, under blankets and on the band shell." He might just as well have said, "Poor people will still be allowed to freeze to death in the park."

He also said, "I support the Parks Department's effort to return Tompkins Square Park to use by the entire Lower East Side community."

That statement infuriated me. In fact, the places where we were in the park already had fences, and we were inside those fences, not in the whole park. Any talk about how we were stopping kids from playing in the park was a lot of bunk. Kids came to the park in droves with their schools at lunch time. The kids, even though young, understood what was happening because the part of the neighborhood that had not become Trumped up, yuppiefied, was pretty cool, very activist. That park was shared and appreciated by the homeless and by much of the neighborhood, and any talk to the contrary was just part of the police and government propaganda.

Sunset came early that day. Three people had gotten arrested in the park. We only had a couple of dozen people left. We had not been trampled or shot this time; you could not see our wounds, but we were hurting just the same. We were disheartened, outnumbered by the police and PD workers who were watching us. Midnight came and we pulled our blankets and coats tighter and stood close around the fires we had made in trash barrels.

On December 18th, Karen, myself, and several other people met with people from the local HUD office at 26 Federal Plaza. We tried to introduce the Dignity House concept to these people from HUD. They liked the idea, but said that they had no HUD housing for that purpose in New York City. They suggested that we get involved in negotiations with city departments. I even asked them about warehouses, anything that we could renovate ourselves. That seemed to pique the interest of the HUD people, but still to no avail. They kept pushing us back at the city government. I tried to remind them the only conversations we were having with the city or the police department was over barricades and billy clubs. What made it funny was that they gave us a lot of information about different organizations to get in touch with. They gave us Housing Now! and Coalition for the Homeless.

We came out of that meeting very disgruntled. We decided not to try to arrange any more meetings with Mr. Kemp and HUD.

The letter from HUD promising ten percent of HUD housing for the homeless became important because of the anger it provoked when people realized that piece of paper was not going to do anything for us. And once we realized we couldn't even use that letter for toilet paper, it made our movement more intensified. There was not enough money to do a decent job of helping people, but there was plenty to call out the police and the helicopters and even the National Guard.

We realized that we had to turn the heat back up in the streets. That meant doing more things to raise the level of consciousness of our government. That meant tearing down doors, pushing into offices, taking over buildings, not letting the government sweep us aside any longer.

My youngest daughter Tonya was living only two blocks away. She came by the park once during that winter.

"They should take a bomb and blow up this park and all you people," she told me.

That hurt me right to the core; she did not understand. The only way the homeless had ever gotten serious attention for their plight was by raising hell in the streets.

Merry Christmas, New York. I had never had a good one before, but this one was even worse. They came, they destroyed, they conquered. The government's rejection, at the federal and city level, of our attempts to bargain and work with them in good faith, marked the beginning of a process that would lead in the coming year to the takeover of buildings all across the United States.

CHAPTER 20

Takeover

During the winter of 1989-1990 we began strategizing a nationwide takeover of HUD buildings. A gentleman donated the use of a retreat camp he owned outside of Philadelphia for a three-day planning summit. From all over the U.S. we came and sat down and had our meetings, planning what to do about Kemp's letter. The government says it is a crime for homeless people to take over buildings; we were preparing to say very loudly that it is more of a crime for the powers that be to allow people to die in the streets.

I was elected as spokesperson for the National Union of the Homeless, to go all over the United States to help organize the simultaneous national takeover in 40 cities. Our planning focused on the offensive for May of 1990, but when the Detroit and Chicago homeless reminded us how cold the winter of '89-'90 was turning out to be, we decided a quick winter offensive was called for as well. We needed to get people out of the cold and into some housing quickly. So some hasty plans were made, and people went back to their cities to immediately launch the winter takeover offensive.

In New York City, we had planned to take a building across from the shelter on East 3rd Street. Our idea was to get people involved who were living in the shelter. However, to do that meant we had to tell our plans to people, including some we didn't know. Somebody informed the police, and the police began following us wherever we went. Once we realized what was happening, we took those cops on different walks all over the place. They let us get on the block where the building was, but then they cut off traffic with barricades. We headed for the building with sledgehammers and tools. But there were cops there waiting for us. They snatched our sledgehammer and tools and took them to jail. So instead of a takeover, we staged an all-day protest across the street from the shelter.

Our friends in other cities did succeed in occupying some HUD buildings, but the whole operation was scarcely noted by the press, or if it was, it was with the attitude of a woman who wrote for *The Amsterdam*, a large-circulation black newspaper. She used to buy alcohol for homeless people in the park and then pump them for information. She professed to be good because she gave them money, too, but she was very derogatory toward the homeless in her articles. She showed up while we were protesting that day.

"Watch this woman!" I shouted. "She's a fink! She's a crook! She always lies!" I spent most of my time that day exposing her to warn the other homeless about talking to her.

Because of negative or nonexistent coverage of our actions, we made up our minds that for the spring offensive, we had to do our own media. Through our grapevine, through all the activist organizations, we put out a call to amateur camcorder operators all over the United States to be with us and videotape the takeovers in the various cities and then send the clips to Skylight Pictures in New York. Peter Kinoy and Pamela Yates, the directors, had been doing documentaries for years, always part of a socially progressive movement. In fact, they had produced a video of the 1989 National Survival Summit which they titled *Street Heat*, and another movie they called *Home Girl*, which tells the story of Leona Smith and how she started the National Union of the Homeless.

Around January of 1990, Karen moved to Kansas City, Missouri, in her continuing effort to regain legal custody of her child Ethan. I told her that when I could, I would come visit her in Kansas City.

In the meantime, I began going around the country as a national field organizer for what we were calling our "Up and Out of Poverty May Day Campaign," sharing our strategies with the people who were going to be with us in May. I took with me a book called *Mayday: No Housing, No Peace* that had been done by some people in the homeless movement about how to do a housing takeover. It told, step by step, how to locate houses, how to hook up electricity, how to find out how long you might be able to stay there, knowing that eventually the Feds would come for you. Our goal was enormous, and my job was to share the knowledge in that book and to help our allies figure out a way they could do their housing takeovers on the same day as everybody else. For the Takeover Tour I went to Philadelphia, Chicago, Detroit, Minneapolis, Oakland, Los Angeles, and Long Beach. Mostly I traveled by plane, with the group in each city I went to paying my way. On that trip, the National Union of the Homeless was also paying me a small salary. At each city we talked and planned and introduced our May Day strategies and formed local committees to deal with news, food, lawyers, and other items.

The city that made the most impact on me was Los Angeles.

Knowing we would be in Los Angeles, we contacted movie director Michael Moore through Pam Yates, of Skylight Pictures. Moore directed the award-winning documentary *Roger and Me,* which details the plight of auto workers put out of their jobs by greedy corporate bosses. We explained to Moore what we were planning and asked if he would come to our news conference, and if he would wear a May Day button in support of us.

I arrived in Los Angeles at 9:15 one morning and was picked up by David Silva, who had been with us on the march to Washington, D.C., and who was part of the National Organizing Committee out in the Long Beach area. I unpacked and was taken on a tour of homeless sites. What I saw in that city frightened me, turned my stomach, and raised my anger almost to the point of no return.

On March 26th, 1990, I sent a report back to the Union of the Homeless that I made on an audio cassette recorder. I told them how I was feeling.

"Dear Brothers and Sisters and supporters," I said, "I know that homelessness is a problem, a very disgraceful one in New York, but the filth, the despair, the ignorance, the death, the hunger, the fear, the total disregard here, in a city and state where a lot of my dreams and fantasies came from—this is unforgivable. I cannot explain to any of you the plight of the living dead, but one sees it every day in this area."

I think I must have fallen into a kind of daze at what I was seeing. I was amazed that my brothers and sisters of the streets in Los Angeles felt life was so useless that they no longer cared about their oppressed way of life, that they would rather lie down and die in the streets than die fighting for the right to live as decent human beings.

What I saw that day in Los Angeles made the picture of our plight, the plight of the poor and homeless, even clearer in my mind than I had ever before imagined. To see the beauty of Los Angeles, the money in L.A., and then to see the despair and disgrace of the city, infuriated me to the point of fear. Yes, fear. Fear of my own anger and how to control it.

Then I remembered the way it had been for me at one time: I did not care; I felt life as it was handed down to me was not worth fighting for. Even in Tompkins Square Park, at first we had been numb to the pain of our brothers and sisters, wrapped in a shell of our own fears, pain, and helplessness. When that happens for too long, to too great an extent, we forget the pain of others, or else refuse to acknowledge it for fear of being overwhelmed.

I had been awakened by billy clubs, by helmeted police and Green Meanies, but it took the help and support of a lot of caring people such as my lady Karen, as well as Leona, Willie Baptist, Shigemi, Marian Kramer, Alicia, and my brothers and sisters in Tent City, to open my eyes, my heart, and my concern for my brothers and sisters everywhere. They helped me understand my plight, and their trust and faith in me helped me have trust and faith in myself that I had not had before. When I saw the condition of people in the streets of Los Angeles, I realized how far I had come. At that moment, I felt a tremendous pride in my friends and loved ones. They were the finest group of people I had ever known or ever would know.

Yet I kept wondering, how do I reach my brothers and sisters who are still isolated and lost? How do I tell them I feel their pain, their hunger? How do I reach them with enough understanding to incite them into political action?

The next day we had our news conference and evening dinner rally at a tent that had been set up through the efforts of a man named Ted Hayes, a tall, slim, dark-skinned brother. Hayes was connected with some people who were trying to get cities to build little individualized domes for the homeless. "Homes, not domes" is the way I feel about it. In L.A. that day Hayes had a huge tent set up for us, with a couple of smaller ones around it, and portable toilets.

For me, the highlight of the long and successful day was the enthusiastic and supportive response of our many brothers and sisters of Skid Row, Hollywood. Their interest and their desire to become more involved with helping themselves was very gratifying. They were the greatest reward my heart could ask for.

It was the time of the Academy Awards. Michael Moore had grabbed my emotional enthusiasm with his movie and the political stance that he took, but what made me more impressed with Michael than the movie was the fact that he responded to our invitation. The studios gave Michael Moore a hard time that day. They did not want him to hold the news conference with us. Michael and Pam Yates had to sneak him out the back door of his hotel in order to participate in our presentation.

We were right across the street from where the presentation for the Academy Awards was. Michael came in a big white limousine that the studio had lent him. As he drove up, he smiled, very happy to see our rally and all our signs. He got out, a heavyset person with glasses and a smile. The press and the fans were going over to say hello to him, but he came across the street to us instead.

We presented him with an award from us for his movie and his efforts to keep the plight of the impoverished before the eyes of the world. Things got a little tight because people kept crossing between us and the news cameras, but we managed to keep things going and keep the focus of the interview on the issues. Michael talked about his reasons for coming to speak to the homeless. Although he can be very comical, he pointed out that the conditions in the United States are serious; conditions such as unemployment, jobs being cut by the thousands while executives make millions in bonuses—all the issues that he talks about in the film *Roger and Me* have an effect on the homeless population. When people lose their jobs and they lose their property and they lose their income, a lot of times they end up homeless. Michael Moore understood that connection and supported the efforts of homeless in organizing themselves.

It was a long, long day, but the end result made it all worth while. Michael Moore got to my heart so much that I did a cartoon painting of myself and him, and I called it "Michael and Me." I left him with that; I hope he still has it.

The next night we met with a homeless committee in Long Beach, and they were ready for the May Day Action. I talked with a man named John, who had been at the rally the day before. John said he was ready and angry. He, too, was trying to understand why a lot of our homeless brothers and sisters refuse to struggle against their condition. I told him it is hard for us to get up and fight. A lot of us are tired of being beat up, tired of going to jail, just plain tired. I told John that sometimes it takes something real bad to happen to them to shock them into realizing the need to fight. It is a tricky issue getting people to fight and risk getting beat up and going to jail. What I told people at that meeting was that we who are already in the fight have to stay consistent in the struggle, continue to get involved, continue to tell our brothers and sisters that the only way we are going to make a change is if we get up, take control and leadership of this struggle and our lives. We, the people of poverty, need supporters, but only we know just what it is we need at this time.

The Long Beach meeting was very moving to me. If, when I spoke, only one person decided to join in the takeover, then I felt like I had done my job. But when we could get 10 or 15 people involved to help make change, I knew we were on a roll.

***

Karen had entrusted me with the care of her place at 527 E. 12th Street, so when I got back to New York, I used that as a base of operations. On WBAI public radio in New York City, we continued to do shows in which we were able to discuss the conditions of living on the streets and gather support for people all over the United States who were preparing to take housing that HUD would not open up, that HUD was auctioning off to speculators only interested in making money.

"I know it is hard for you to put your life at risk," I told my brothers and sisters, "but remember this: all our lives we have been living at risk, we have been letting other people tell us why we are homeless, why we need help, and just what help it is that we need. We continue to let the powers that be control our lives.

"Well, it is time to put a stop to this...The risk we are taking now is needed, and is not difficult when we compare it to the risk of putting drugs into our arms, putting that pipe in our mouths, or drinking ourselves to death. I say our fighting to stay alive and live a decent life in a home of our own is a risk I, and pray you all, must take. I'd rather die trying to get myself and others the right to our own basic human rights—homes, food, clothing, and higher wages—than die of drugs.

"Don't you know, brothers and sisters, that for everyone here who refuses to get up and fight, we become weaker... As long as we do not care what happens to us, as long as we keep buying our oppressors' drugs, as long as we just give up and lie down, we will be helping a corrupt system keep us down, we will continue to help our government keep us down.

"They keep us on welfare and make it hard for us to get off of it. Any city-run shelter operates to keep us in them. As long as the beds are full every night, the city receives funding for those beds.

"What do I say to this? Take the shelters, take the abandoned buildings and abandoned houses, and turn them into housing for every man, woman, and child in need!"

In New York City we planned to take city-owned housing, as HUD had no properties in the main city. By April all our organizing with the National Union of the Homeless and the other activists had come to a point. The National Housing Takeover was set.

***

On May Day, 1990, we had a celebration in progress at Tompkins Square Park. We had tables in the park set up with literature about the struggle. Hare Krishnas were chanting and banging a drum and tambourine. A concert was playing in the band shell. A banner on the stage read: "FOURTH ANNUAL SQUATTERS MAYDAY." There were other banners around the park:

"NO CURFEW."

"REBUILD TENT CITY."

"SQUAT ALL WAREHOUSES AND APARTMENTS."

"NO MILITARY CAMPS FOR THE HOMELESS. FIGHT BACK."

The anarchists in the park had the job of distracting the police while we took buildings. They were supposed to prolong the music. We had not been absolutely certain of the anarchists in the past, but in this c.d. action they became our brothers.

The place we had targeted stood on 9th Street between Avenues C and D. Our walk over there was documented by a still camera and a video camera. I was wearing my black t-shirt with white letters spelling out "Up and Out of Poverty."

Somebody had painted "Homes Not Shelters" on the vacant warehouse. Larry and I hefted a big pair of cutters around the lock and squeezed. Sparks snapped as we cut the lock off the metal door. Our supporters cheered and applauded as we raised up the sliding metal door.

At about the same time, we had a half dozen people taking a building on 3rd Street and one on 9th. While we were taking housing, the job of our friends in the park was to distract the police, which they did. Unfortunately, the police had an ulterior motive in mind. Their job was to kick butt.

At the warehouse we could hear sirens. A brother came to us.

"Something's jumpin' at the park," he said.

"Yeah, the band," someone said.

"No, no. I'm talkin' about heat. Police are racing over there to the park."

Helicopters, chaos, people tackled to the ground by police and Green Meanies. Bitter shouting against the police. People got beat up and responded with bottle throwing and rock throwing.

You fight back when you're hit by an armed force. Our friend, the cartoonist Seth, got his nose broken. People went to the hospital. People got arrested. But takeovers were simultaneously happening, not just in New York, but also in other major cities across the United States—Tucson, Minneapolis, Detroit, Philadelphia, Oakland, Chicago, Los Angeles, and Washington, D.C.

In New York, the actual takeovers, going into the buildings, got a little coverage from Channel 5, but they, and any major media I know of, would rather see people getting beat upside the head than taking over abandoned buildings. So when they heard about the ruckus happening in Tompkins Square, the media left us.

When we walked into this building we had taken, we shined our flashlights and saw devastation. Where once there had apparently been a retirement home or some sort of center, the floor now had dangerous holes and the stairs from the ground floor to the second story were gone. Everything above that, furnished apartments, was in pretty decent shape. But we had to climb up there by rope, which is cool when you're dodging the police, but if you want to make a home, you aren't going to do it with a rope ladder. Although we cleaned up and did the best we could with that building, ultimately it proved a disappointment.

***

All that year we had been sneaking back in to the ABC Community and hanging out our banners. We continued to have protests in the park. We had support from ACT-UP and the gay community. They had done a parade protest in front of St. Patrick's Cathedral, and when they were finished, knowing we were having an activity in the park, hundreds of people from ACT-UP marched all the way down to the park to join us. The park was jam-packed.

The word went around the crowd "Let's take over the ABC Community again!" So ACT-UP and all their supporters went and ripped down the barricades and surged past the few startled police. Lee Grant was one of the celebrities there. More police came and threw everybody out, and this time when it was over, the authorities cemented up the windows and they welded the doors shut.

In another sense, however, we had achieved our objective. One thing I learned that night is that it *can* be done, if people take the initiative. Forget about it being against the law. I don't care. People are dying in the streets. I think *that* should be against the law.

The takeover movement should not have been unexpected by the authorities. There are between 400,000 and 3,000,000 people without homes, and a hell of a lot of empty houses. We had one common goal in the Takeover, one thing we could not disagree on: we needed houses. We needed buildings opened up for people of poverty and for people who were homeless. That was the uniting factor. Although I have come to hate the word "coalition" because of the double-crossing that has happened too often in such organizations, with that uniting factor, we were able to bring to the fight all types of people and organizations.

Soon after the Takeover, the building on 9th Street where I had donated my Mennonite cross burned down. The news media always blames squatters and homeless people for building fires, and I'm sure that some of them may be due to the carelessness of someone who is drunk. But I also suspect that police and owners of these deliberately abandoned buildings sometimes send in arsonists to destroy squatter buildings.

***

At the Young Adult Learning Academy in New York City, I gave a talk about homelessness, about how I am a firm believer that the United States government does not know how to run the United States. I told them the history of what was happening in Tompkins Square Park and how Tent City came about, I told them of the march to Washington, and the ABC Community, and what the city had done to us when we started doing things for ourselves. They heard about how the Takeover went down all over the country, and about the plan we had for buying a building for Tent City. We wanted to raise money by having artists around New York donate work and having an art auction.

During the question and answer session, a good-looking young black man asked me in a somewhat challenging tone why didn't I just get a regular job? I told him I had nothing against work, that I liked work. I had worked as a drug and alcohol counselor, as a juvenile counselor, as a psychiatric attendant. When I worked I didn't want minimum wage, which is so low that you can't live off it.

"Am I going to school for nothing?" he asked bitterly. His friends tried to shut him up. "I want to know."

"The only wrong question is the one you don't ask," I said, and went on to urge him not to write off a college education. I was not intending to discourage him; I was there to explain what was happening in the streets to other people besides myself.

The black students did not pull their punches that day. One young lady in sunglasses and a Raiders cap had a harsh, and I believe oversimplified, view of the homeless.

"I want to know why," she said, "with all these services out there willing to help homeless people, why they still lay on their butts and don't do nothing for themselves. They've got all these services that they could take advantage of, and they don't want to do anything."

Her question touched on the flip side of the bureaucracy issue. Many people in this country have the idea that getting welfare is as easy as falling in the gutter. I am here to tell you that is not the case.

"In order to get on welfare, if you really need welfare, you're put through a number of hurdles," I explained to her. "First of all, you have got to have a whole lot of ID. The majority of people who try to get welfare do not have the necessary ID. They do not have birth certificates, they do not have Social Security cards."

I did not want these kids to think I was putting down every government social program.

"Some of them do work," I said. "Not every program that is out there stinks. But the majority of the system's programs that are out there are not doing anything but collecting monies for the program.

"I believe in the concept of drug and alcohol rehab, I believe in helping people....but the way it's being done now is not working. Most people when they go to any kind of place to ask for help, they've got to go there on their knees. A lot of people don't want to ask for help. Now when you go into these places and ask for help and you're treated like a dog, that turns you off. When you're treated like an animal, no matter what kind of services they are, you're going to react in a different way. I don't like the shelter system. I don't like the welfare system. When you walk in there, they dehumanize you."

Unfortunately, a lot of these students had bought the propaganda that the system puts out about the homeless, about laziness and about drugs. The fact is, a substantial portion of so-called new jobs out there are only part time and minimum wage. If you simply do the math, you'll see that living on the minimum wage as it is now, even after the pathetic raise, is not possible.

"It's not always drugs that gets people in the streets," I told them. "Say your house burns down and you have no insurance. Even if you have a job, you don't keep that job very long when you're living on the street."

Though I did not say so that day, I could also have pointed out that you can't keep yourself presentable to an employer if you are living on the street. And if you're looking for work, most employers will not hire someone who does not have an address. After a certain point, many people simply give up.

I still was not getting through to some of the kids in the classroom. Another young woman, again black, was critical of people who did not want help from others and did not want to help themselves.

"That's why a lot of people dehumanize them like you said," she told me. "If they're not going to help themselves, ain't nobody going to help them."

"I'm glad you're saying that because it's very important," I answered. "Before I got involved in this movement, I was one of those homeless people who didn't give a damn. Before I got involved with this I used to be a social worker and a counselor and I felt like I was butting my head against the wall. I wasn't accomplishing anything.

"The welfare system is good for certain people," I said, "such as people who have lost their jobs or even those going to school to learn a profession or get a degree." I pointed out that welfare is needed for those who cannot do for themselves and cannot be taught, such as the physically disabled, the mentally disabled.

"There's real old people that can't handle work," I pointed out. "They have to go on the welfare system. But even they are treated like animals by the system in too many cases."

The system as it is now has many flaws. But I told those students that does not mean that you should blame everybody on the street, treat them as if they are all by definition criminals just because they are on welfare. Even street people pay taxes. They are contributing to the system to that extent. Even if they don't have a job, they pay taxes every time they buy a pack of cigarettes or a quart of beer. A sales tax is a regressive tax. This means poor people pay a greater percentage of what little money they have when they buy something. If I only have five dollars, a 40-cent tax is a lot to me. If you're making $50,000 a year, that same 40 cents is nothing.

"I don't agree with the tax system," I told the students. "But seeing it's there, we need to utilize it in a way that can benefit everybody who puts money there.

"When we started getting raided in the park," I said, "we started realizing there were changes that we have to make ourselves, so we had to re-educate ourselves, and as we re-educate ourselves, we do so with other people."

I informed these students of organizations such as Welfare Rights, which educates people about the welfare system, how to get what they are supposed to get, and how to get off the welfare system. Dignity Housing in Philadelphia was another organization I told them about. Dignity Housing takes families out of the shelter system and puts them in decent housing at a low rent. Dignity Housing helps these people *buy* those houses.

"Get educated," I told them.

"But I'm not only talking about academic education; I'm talking about the political education...." I told all those kids they should go down and see for themselves what the story was. Take the time and talk to somebody down there in the park.

"Find out exactly why they're down there," I said. "Find out why they gave up on life. A lot of those people are like you and your family and friends and all of a sudden something happens.

"If they have given up for a long time, simply being nice to them is not going to do the job. A lot of people in the streets have been homeless for 15 years and more. They don't know how to come back into society. They don't know how to work. Just telling them to go to work and that they are bad if they don't is not going to succeed.

"One of the things we're going to do," I reminded them, "is buy a building. We're not going to wait on the city of New York. That's what this art auction is all about. In that building we're going to have programming where it's going to be for homeless people themselves to come and learn how to be part of the system all over again.

"For some people," I admitted, "it's never going to work. They're probably going to end up back in the streets. But that doesn't mean that we can't continue to help them. Now I'm not saying that you're supposed to go and pay their rent. But I do say that it is our obligation not to ignore them."

The other speaker at the school that day was a dude named Bruce Parry, who was a writer for the *People's Tribune*. He did his talk about the economy and the way it was changing, about how we are coming to a stage where robots are going to replace human beings at jobs.

"We are coming to be obsolete," Bruce said.

Bruce used car manufacturing for his example. At one time you used to have people bolting these parts together. Now you don't need a person. Now you put it on a conveyor belt and the robots do the work. What happened to the people?

"More and more people are being pushed out of work and onto the streets," said Bruce. "And it's not a choice that anybody makes, it's a squeeze that's happening to lots and lots of people."

Even in McDonald's some of the people who take orders are being replaced by computers. According to Bruce, this has been a predictable run of events to anybody who has looked at the history of industrialization.

Bruce also pointed out the lack of affordable housing.

"One third of the people who are homeless," he said, "who have no place to live, work at full-time or near full-time jobs. That's an important concept. They're not just lying around, they're trying to make a living, but they can't afford housing in New York City, for instance."

I noted that the military's neutron bomb is a fine example to illustrate the attitude the government has about people. When exploded, the neutron bomb will kill living matter but will not destroy buildings. It will not destroy real estate. Everything else, every living, breathing thing would be extinguished, but property value would still be there.

Now Bruce had some important things to say, but Bruce was a communist. As I was growing up, I used to have a problem with the word "communism." I was told that a communist was somebody that wants to overthrow the government. But Bruce and I hit it off pretty good because I believed wholeheartedly that everybody in power at that time deserved to be thrown out of power. The government was not working for all of the people. Now if saying that you have got to get rid of these people and put in people who would do the job correctly makes you a communist, then a communist I was. I believed our government was sick. It was depraved. I don't know why I even called it "our" government because it was not our government. It was their government, the bankers and the real estate men. It wasn't for us.

**

We gathered a number of New York artists together and had a benefit art show where we sold their art and raised over $8,000 for the Tent City Union of the Homeless. Although the purpose of the fundraiser had been to raise money to buy a building for us, a fight ensued about what to do with the money.

To get to the point where we could think about buying needed housing and then wind up bickering about the money disgusted me. Unfortunately, I believe it came back to a basic problem of so many homeless, which is alcohol and drug abuse. Until people dealt with that, no matter how much we were fighting for the right things, it would always undermine our efforts. In the end I got fed up with that.

But I had also gotten fed up with New York City. Too many different organizations that should have been working together were fighting each other instead of the system.

In the summer of 1990, I went to visit Kansas City, Missouri. My main purpose was to be with Karen and help her in any way possible to win back her son Ethan. But I also went to Kansas City to get away from the disappointment of all the fighting between groups in New York City.

CHAPTER 21

The Kansas City Union
of the Homeless

After the court proceedings, Karen ended up getting Sundays-only visiting rights with her son Ethan. Her parents got the rest. As her father had been a judge for decades, I was not surprised by this outcome. I got to Kansas City motivated to help support Karen and Ethan because I knew they deserved a hell of a lot better than they had.

Karen introduced me to people who were working on the poverty situation amongst the homeless in that city. Through her I met Ken West, the director of the Homeless Information Center for the Metropolitan Lutheran Ministries. He had a friend who was a teacher at the University of Missouri at Kansas City, and the teacher had me out to the school to speak. There I found out from talking to people that there were no homeless organizing themselves in Kansas City.

The *New York News* and a couple of other newspapers called me in Kansas City wanting comments about Mitch Snyder's recent suicide.

"I really don't have anything to say," I told them. "I didn't like him when he was alive, so I don't feel it would make any sense to say anything about him when he's dead."

Now I know a lot of homeless people who disliked Mitch Snyder, but I also know a lot of homeless who did like him. When most homeless organizers do a demonstration or a civil disobedience action, they don't have the money, so they don't have the attention-grabber of feeding the multitudes. Mitch Snyder was able to supply food, money or marches to get things going. When he did things, he did them with a spectacular preview and review.

In the beginning Mitch Snyder was activist, he was cool. His fasting brought the attention of the public to the homeless, and he used to stay out there in the streets, be with the homeless. Mitch Snyder had wrestled this gigantic building from the President of the United States. He got a tv movie made about his life, starring Martin Sheen. However, once he got the building in Washington, and that notoriety, he no longer made that much of an appearance with the homeless people he theoretically represented. I think Mitch Snyder lost his perspective. In the end he had become more of a media attraction than a leader of homeless people.

***

One day Ken West told me that if I came to live in Kansas City I could have a job working with homeless people. So that clinched it. I officially moved to Kansas City to become the assistant director of the Homeless Information Center. Soon I was also working as an AIDS outreach counselor for the Swope Parkway Medical Center.

Whenever I got the chance, I would paint pictures. I was hoping that painting scenes from my life would help me get rid of some of my nightmares, some of my fears, some of the confusion that I felt about my life in the streets. When I was painting them, I had to go through a lot of the same emotion again. That hope and those nightmares go into my paintings. But what really helped me was people accepting the paintings and my life, and understanding it and caring. You can do a painting, and if nobody likes it, all it is is paint on a board or canvas. It might as well be blank. If I can do a painting, and people understand it and appreciate it, then they can understand me. They can understand who I am, what makes me tick, what makes me go on. And homeless people who look at my paintings can see themselves there because we've lived the same life. When that is recognized, it helps relieve the pain of the nightmares.

Although I didn't always agree with the Metro Lutheran Ministries' methods, I was fairly satisfied in my role as assistant director of the HIC until an offer was made to us by a property owner who wanted to donate three houses to the Center so that we could house homeless people.

To me it sounded like a dream come true. But the director did not see it that way. He told me that Metro Lutheran Ministries didn't want the responsibility of dealing with the single people of the homeless population—our primary clients—in that type of single-family dwelling.

I could hardly believe my ears. It became clear to me that the philosophy of not only the HIC, but also the city government, was that the best way to deal with the single population was to just let them keep going to the shelters and getting food stamps and going to soup kitchens. Nothing was being done, or even being contemplated, about dealing with the situation of single homeless people, about working with these people to change their lives.

Fortunately for me, at the time I also had the job with Swope Parkway as an AIDS outreach counselor, so I quit my job with Metropolitan Lutheran Ministries with some pride. At Swope Parkway a good part of my time involved dealing with the homeless population, giving them information about HIV and AIDS, and helping arrange medical attention for them.

With Leona Smith's blessing, in the spring of 1991, I started the Kansas City Union of the Homeless. Karen and I began by holding meetings with homeless people every two weeks on Saturday mornings at the Metropolitan Lutheran Ministries Homeless Center at 10th and Wyandotte.

"The Union of the Homeless," I would say, "is an organization of homeless people. *Of* you, not *for* you. The language is important."

We would provide donuts and coffee, and show people videos about the homeless. Pamela Yates and Peter Kinoy of Skylight Pictures in New York had finished putting together a very good documentary called *Takeover*, which showed the national May Day action and the events leading up to it. The documentary included footage from every city where HUD housing was taken over. Skylight had gotten support funds for the movie from people such as Michael Moore and from Bruce Springsteen.

The appearance of Will Sales in the video was a happy coincidence. We did not plan for his poetry to happen. He was part of Hobo Theater, out of Jersey. The whole crew at Hobo Theater was pretty good. They had a space in New York City on the top floor of a building on 7th Street between Avenues C and D. They used to let us have meetings there. In fact, we did some of our strategizing for the winter offensive there. One day, prior to the Takeover, we had a planning meeting at the Hobo Theater. Will Sales saw the cameraman as we were walking from there to Tompkins Square Park. He got hold of Peter Kinoy.

"Hey, man," said Will. "I've got some poetry I could read. I got some things I could say that would probably go real good with what you're doing."

By the time we got to the park, we decided, yeah, let's go with it. So Peter filmed Will, who was wearing a black leather jacket and a leather cap, reciting his poetry in the park. Will's poetry was one of the best things that happened to the video.

After showing the videos in Kansas City, I would talk with the homeless about the need to break the cycle of poverty. Then I would open the floor for discussion. If a person who has only seen homeless people on the street, and looked away from them, avoided them, or become angry and scorned the homeless, never listened to them, if such people could hear the stories these people told, I believe they might find their hearts softened, their minds opened. Young and old, the homeless in Kansas City told tales of being beat up by shelter security, of having to pretend to adopt certain religious beliefs in order to get social services, of how hard it was to get a job while living in a shelter because of not getting messages left there by potential employers. Then there were the stories about the simple human acts of showering, shaving, and going to the bathroom, that become indignities when you're homeless.

The Union needed a location that could be open and accessible to the homeless 24 hours a day, seven days a week. For a time we tried a building at 27th and Troost that gave us twice the space. But many of our regulars could not make it to that location because of the distance from their camps and the shelters, plus the building turned out to not be as available or affordable as we originally thought.

Rosemary Pritcherd, a homeless single mother with children, showed up regularly at our meetings. One day she found a billfold somebody had lost. It had a name in it and she returned it to the woman it belonged to. That woman ended up giving Rosemary a house as a reward for her honesty.

When I organized the Kansas City chapter of the Union of the Homeless, I thought at first that our main support would come from the national office of the Union of the Homeless. But I had not thought that through carefully enough. We are a union of homeless or impoverished people, even at the national level, so the national office did not have the money to keep us operating in Kansas City. We had to do most things for ourselves. So we had fundraising pot-luck barbecues and homeless art shows. By my continuing to speak out and make contacts and work in the community, gradually the Union of the Homeless began to be known around Kansas City.

Fortune then smiled on us when the Reverend Stanley Counts gave us a house at 3410 Garfield, and it became the property of the Union of the Homeless. It had once been a crack house and was boarded up, with holes in the roof and the porch, but to me it looked beautiful. It was ours. It would be a place for people who had no place. We would call it "Empowerment House One."

The theory of the Union of the Homeless was and is that a person has to have a place to start. For a person who has been homeless for a long period of time, the place to start is not a job. Let them move into a house, *then* work on getting them a job and income. It is very difficult to get a job if you do not have a place to live. Our strategy was get them moved in first, then from that base of privacy, plentiful food and clothing, work on everything else that's necessary, whatever it may be. Most important, you have to talk with the person who has been homeless. Very rarely do people listen to what a homeless person thinks or says. That someone will listen and not put them down, that in itself is empowering.

We began working on Saturdays with homeless and volunteer supporters to repair and rehab the Garfield house, but we needed funds. Although PBS would not accept the movie *Takeover* for several years, one of the ways I continued to raise money for the Union of the Homeless was by fundraisers where we would show the videotape and follow it with a talk about the issues.

At one such showing at the Kansas City Friends House, a Quaker church, I met a young man who said he wanted to work with us. I will call him Kenneth, though that is not his real name. He was white, but had dreadlocks. Raised in a semi-middle class Quaker family, Kenneth told me that he had been homeless for a little while at one point in his life. He had done a lot of traveling all over the country and had worked for Greenpeace as a canvasser. Soon he was helping us raise money door-to-door.

A contemporary band called the Sin City Disciples gave us a lot of help by performing a benefit at Harling's, on Main Street. Then the Midwestern Musical Company also raised some money for us. At last we had a stake to work from. On September 27, 1991, we incorporated "the Kansas City, Mo., Union of the Homeless" as a non-profit agency.

Around that time, a woman named Kai Alvetero, who was a deejay for KKFI, the local community radio station, agreed to let us use a house she owned at 27th and Olive rent-free for five years. Unfortunately, the huge three-story house was in very bad shape, and we calculated it would take something like $10,000 to rehab the place, plus months of labor. And then, at the end of five years, she was going to want it back. All that invested effort and money and we would really have nothing to show for it when our time was up. Still, it was a generous offer, and we felt we were moving forward. Additionally, we got the use of another house as well, off of Warwick, at 119 East 34th. The house on 34th Street was a property we got through the Missouri Housing Development Commission. Suddenly, our plate was very full.

***

A Kansas City artist named Jeff Robinson had decided to put on a big no-strings-attached, no-sermon Thanksgiving dinner for the homeless at Pierre's, a fancy restaurant down in an area of the city known as the River Quay, which is pronounced "key" by the locals.

As it turned out, another bounty was to be ours that Thanksgiving as well. ABC News came to town wanting to do a story about homelessness and poverty in the heartland of America. They contacted Rosemary Pritcherd, the homeless single mother who had returned the purse and got a house, because they figured that would make an upbeat story for their Thanksgiving broadcast. Instead, Rosemary, who liked what we were doing at the Union of the Homeless, sent ABC to us, and so the network ended up getting a story with a little more of an edge, that had its upbeat moments, but which also reminded people of the hard realities.

On tv Thanksgiving night, ABC's *Nightly News* ran a national story about Jeff's generous dinner and through that, the Union of the Homeless ended up getting good national exposure about our work and our philosophy.

"It's not all about putting dollars in a donation can," I told the reporter. "It's about going out there in the streets and getting involved with the people.

"We became an organization because we believe our government is not doing enough to help people in need," I explained. "We say that, given the opportunity, like this house being donated to us, given this opportunity, that *we* will be the ones to make this house work. There *are* homeless people out there who are honest, you understand, who are willing to work hand in hand with the neighborhood... It's not about other people doing for us, it's about us taking the initiative. For changes to be made, people have to make the changes themselves..."

Coincidentally, on Thanksgiving Day we found our first residents. At the dinner there were three guys who were hitchhiking throughout the country, and they did not have a place to stay that night. I told them about our house at 2644 Olive.

"It's in bad shape," I said, "but you guys can go in there and sleep for the night."

They went in and cleaned out the whole house. That told me they wanted to stay. By the following Tuesday, we had five other homeless people move in as they heard by word of mouth. Things were rolling. We just took people as they came.

I began staying at the house on Olive, as well as maintaining my apartment on Armour Boulevard, paying utilities at both places. That was draining me. However, my on-site presence was necessary at the Olive house, so I gave up my apartment and moved into the house, making my office on the ground floor, near my bedroom.

Oh, I had grand plans for the house on Olive Street. I wanted to set up a cultural center there, to open up the basement for homeless people as a place where they could come to do their artwork, their crafts, and feel secure that their work and supplies would not be stolen. I wanted to give other people the opportunity to express themselves through art. By December we had come far enough along with fixing up the building that we held an Open House in the basement on the 21st.

In the next few months, any chance I got to speak on the homeless and poverty issue, I jumped on it. I talked on KKFI community radio, and was quoted in the *Pitch* and *The New Times*, which were alternative papers. I talked on cable public access and on the local PBS affiliate station. On a Kansas City public television program called *Kansas City Illustrated*, several people involved with the homeless in the area, including myself, told viewers what the reality was for the homeless of the city. A lady named Ruth Schecter, who was the director of an organization called the Housing Information Center, which attempts to find affordable housing for low income people, made the point that there had been an increase in poverty during the Reagan and Bush administration. She was also right on the money when she spoke about the kind of work that seemed to be the only type available.

"Anybody who tells me the recession is over, I will fight them," she said. "It is *not* over.... Unemployment in Kansas City is 4.8%, and that may be wonderful, but what kind of jobs are these people getting? They're fast-food, service-connected, part-time, low-wage, no-benefits jobs. You can't raise a family of four on $4.75 or even $6.00 an hour. It doesn't work."

I explained proudly how the Union had 15 residents and three houses. Each resident was expected to pay $70 a month, which was simply to cover utilities. Some were working; some were going to school. In order for people even to get into our program, they had to come into the house and work. If they wanted a room, they had to agree to work on improving that room, and also help fix up the other houses of the Union.

Few of the major political candidates in that election year had so much as mentioned poverty, homelessness or hunger. Thus it was not even an issue. The mayors and the governors and the presidential candidates did not and do not want us to exist. That's why we were also registering our residents to vote. That's why in the homeless movement around the country, we were starting to work to get homeless people jobs within the social service delivery systems, and to put up homeless candidates for city council. In Boston that year a welfare mother with several children was running for Congress.

In the beginning, everything was working in Kansas City. All over the city, as either I or Karen would be out doing business, people were seeing our blue, beat-up Ford Ltd station wagon with our name, KCMO Union of the Homeless and our motto "Each One Teach One" painted on it. Kenneth, who was effervescent and vivacious, was a good canvasser and knew how to set up the streets. We began publishing the *K.C.,MO. Union of the Homeless Newsletter*, and professional writers Danny Alexander and Mike Warren later joined in the effort to improve the layout.

Things were working at the houses, as well. In short order, Kenneth had become vice-president of the Union and was in charge of the house on Garfield, where he was living and working with six people. The house had been built for a single-child family, so it was more crowded than I liked. Meanwhile,

Karen was taking care of the house at 34th and Warwick. The residents in that house were receiving HUD funding, which helped support the house.

But coming up with enough money to pay the utilities at the other houses tended to be a problem. Sometimes we still had to buy food with food stamps. Our volunteer support ran in spurts, a problem that continued to dog us. Sometimes it seemed like I had to be in each house 24 hours a day. You know what they say: "Be careful what you ask for—you might get it!"

Eventually I moved my base of operations to the house on 34th Street with Karen. I felt glad that Kenneth was running the house on Garfield because one of us needed to check at each of the houses to make sure they ran according to our ideals: No drugs or alcohol; counseling about drugs, alcohol and AIDS; political education; and shared, co-operative responsibility for the household.

Unfortunately, Kenneth scorned any interest shown in sports, to the point of not even wanting a tv in any of the Union of the Homeless houses even though people wanted to watch football or basketball games. Kenneth also became very disappointed when the homeless would not go to antinuclear meetings.

"Listen," I told him, "you can't expect homeless people to get into the battle against nuclear weapons when they are worried about the battle for day-to-day life. The only way homeless people are going to pay attention to the atomic bomb is if you can connect it to their everyday struggle. Until you can find and point out that common ground, you're not going to get the support you're looking for."

That did not seem to satisfy Kenneth. He had homeless people helping do the carpentry on the Garfield house, but the way he talked to the homeless was too harsh and bossy. After a while, when it came to repair work on the house, nobody wanted to work with him.

Although he was a good canvasser, Kenneth was not a good teacher. We would send homeless people out to learn how to canvass and to help him, but it had to be done his way and his way only. Here it was, the first time for many of these people to go out knocking on doors and asking for money, not just for themselves, but also to help others. Yet he had no patience with them. Worse, he discouraged them.

On top of everything, Kenneth began to grow secretive.

"This is not *your* organization," I told him. "This is not *my* organization; this is *our* organization, a union of homeless people. You need to share information so we can work together."

On February 21, 22, and 23 of 1992 the Kansas City Union of the Homeless was proud to help organize and cosponsor the "Break the Blackout: Pro-People's National Media Summit" with other groups, including the Greater Kansas City Coalition Against Censorship. The President of the Coalition Against Censorship was Danny Alexander, one of the writers helping me with the *Union of the Homeless News*. He helped bring writer Dave Marsh as one of the keynote speakers, and one of the producers of *Takeover*, Peter Kinoy, came also. Most important, though, socially concerned people of all colors, homeless people, and people of poverty from all over the United States convened at St. Stephen's Church by the I-70 highway to discuss the neglect of issues of poverty and social injustice by the monopolistic corporate media of the country.

We began in the morning, before the dew had lifted, with an outdoor prayer circle by our Native American brothers and sisters. Then we had our open forum. People from the Up and Out of Poverty grassroots organization reported on various national actions by homeless people. Marian Kramer, president of the National Welfare Rights organization, talked about budget cuts and how they would affect the needy. I outlined the progress of the Union for the Homeless in Kansas City. But it was not just leaders who spoke. Anybody who wanted to speak got their chance. Later, people put on workshops explaining various aspects of organizing. At other meetings we began to hash out plans for more coordinated national efforts.

The focus of the gathering was the concern that our news does not reach the general public. For example, Channel 5 in Kansas City did a story about the local homeless. But they focused on panhandlers, and many homeless are not panhandlers.

Some well-dressed woman was quoted as saying panhandlers were making more money than people who were working. First, where does she get that statistic? The tv news didn't say or ask. I say, Lady, even if that is true, what does that tell you about the economy? If you can make more money panhandling than working a minimum-wage job, why the hell go to work? If you can make more money selling drugs, why work a minimum-wage job? Because of stories like Channel 5's, at the summit we strategized ways using our own camcorders, our own newspapers, such as the *Union of the Homeless News*, to get our story out to the public's eye where it could be seen and not hidden or distorted.

The Break-the-Blackout Summit was a good time of national brotherhood and sisterhood. We got to reacquaint ourselves with old friends and to know new people. We had a number of people there who had been among the many laid off from Allied Signal, a defense contractor in the Kansas City area. Generally, people who work for defense contractors tend to be conservative about the status quo government. Yet here were workers from the "defense" industry now booted out of their jobs, in attendance at a conference discussing how to radically change the way the status quo is perceived. So long as people remain ignorant of how hard life truly is for many of their fellow citizens, they will remain complacent until they lose their own jobs or their own homes. So long as people remain ignorant of the truth—that, given opportunity and diligent compassion, underprivileged and impoverished people can and will change themselves for the better, people are always going to believe the worst of their less fortunate brothers and sisters.

Sad to say, shortly after the Summit, Kenneth and I parted ways, and he left town. Unfortunately, we had come to the point where we could no longer work together. Still, I was sorry Kenneth was gone. Hopefully, we both grew from the experience.

CHAPTER 22

A Time to Reassess

With Kenneth gone, the workload for Karen and me increased. We had three houses, only to discover that we didn't have enough community supporters to keep these houses functioning along the lines of our program of training and education.

To be fair, most of the homeless who moved into the Olive house were really energetic about attempting the necessary changes in their lives, and we did all we could, with the resources at hand, to empower them. For a while it worked. But then the realities of changing from homelessness to responsibility hit home, so to speak. Becoming a member of the Union of the Homeless means not only getting yourself together, but also starting to work toward helping other homeless people accomplish the same thing. Along with becoming ex-homeless comes the responsibility of *staying* ex-homeless, off drugs and alcohol, and paying bills, and being part of the community, and being a good role model. At that time even I felt it as a very heavy load. Sometimes I would sit in the house when Karen was gone and the responsibility of keeping the organization going felt overwhelming. I would think, "Aw, man, why did I want this?"

All three houses were in need of various repairs. For example, the roof of the back storeroom of the Garfield house leaked. But the support crew we had in the beginning, people from the community who were activists or who were not homeless, but who wanted to help, began to taper off. People either lost interest or just did not follow through, and in the end the rest of us were spread too thin. It's all right to talk an ideal, but putting that ideal into practice is another long battle altogether.

On top of everything else, I learned that I am HIV-positive.

There was a time in my life when I didn't give a damn, but could not bring myself to stand out in front of a bus. My addiction to heroin had been a suicide attempt over a long period of years, and now it turned out that I did in fact kill myself, by getting the HIV virus as a result of sharing needles. The doctors started me on AZT, which made me sick to my stomach.

Looking back, I think we moved too fast with people who were not ready. To go directly from living in the streets to having the kinds of responsibilities we were requiring was a little bit more than our residents were prepared for. People at the Olive Street house began drinking and drugging again, and we had several instances of theft and of guys falling asleep drunk with cigarettes in their hands and almost starting fires. Many of the residents were no longer holding up their end of the bargain in regards to sharing of chores and paying their part of the bills. Finally, the city was threatening to close the house on Olive because too much of the house still did not meet city codes for safety.

It hurt when I made the decision to shut down that house and even the tremendous house on East 34th Street with its beautiful wood trim and seven bedrooms.

***

On the white front door of the Garfield house I had painted with black paint a portrait of Malcolm. Everywhere I went around the house, there were other reminders of who I am and what my life is about—my paintings. I paint to get rid of the nightmares, but I also keep many of the paintings around me because I don't want to lose the nightmares entirely—they are part of what keeps me going. Sitting in my house in Kansas City, I closed my eyes and focused, and I was back. Look! Tompkins Square. Old Man John, Terry, Red Wolf. The tents....

The very hardest part after I had to shut down the two houses was walking the streets with some of the people whom I had to put out of the houses.

"Aw, man, we should've listened," they would say to me.

When they came to me and asked for food, I still gave them food. When I had extra clothing, I gave them clothing. But there were certain points beyond which I would no longer go with those individuals because I had been there and I learned I had to do it another way.

In light of our setbacks with the empowerment houses, I began to reassess my goals, give a lot of thought to what I was doing and how I was doing it.

My job is to find out what makes people tick, to find out *how* we can best help people make a change *if* they choose to make that change themselves. Unfortunately, in this job you often find yourself not only in battle with a government that does not care about people, but also in a mental battle with those among the homeless who cannot and do not want to realize that we can help each other help ourselves. You can show somebody how to get out of the predicament, but it is still up to the person to make the choice to get out of it.

Sometimes homeless people can be tough to motivate and activate. They may be enthusiastic in a meeting, but once they walk out that door, they go back to just figuring out where they are going to eat and sleep that night without any thought of the future. The sense of pain and hopelessness that comes when people lose their home drives so many homeless people to the depths of not caring what happens beyond the next meal or warm place to sleep. When you live like that for too long, it is hard to return to a more normal life.

I had to make up my mind—was I going to worry about the lack of participation from the homeless population and from the community at large, or was I going to continue to work at making the Union of the Homeless a model for other homeless people and homeless organizations? Do I give up, I wondered, because people who are well off won't put in the time and effort to work with their less fortunate brothers and sisters? Do I give up because homeless people don't get involved as much as I would like? Or do I keep at it in hopes that people will see that what we are talking about is actually working, so that they can realize that it is possible for them to become part of this movement?

I made up my mind. You don't stop helping people because they don't want all the help you offer. You keep the door open.

The key word is "consistency." When you go to the park to help feed people, and a person comes up and asks you for food but does not want to change his life, that does not mean that you don't give that person food. You still give him or her food, you still leave open the door for them to make the decision in their own time.

The hard lesson facing me was that I could not afford to take anybody fresh off the streets. I had taken anybody and everybody who was homeless. I should have made the stipulation that if you are an abuser of alcohol and drugs, you have to go through detox and rehab before being eligible to move into Union of the Homeless Housing. I do not believe that such a stipulation is against what the Union of the Homeless is working for. The program we were trying to run promoted permanent housing—with homes, not shelters. In a program of our type, some of those homes are going to have children in them. In those homes there are going to be people who are in recovery one way or the other, myself included. Why should we put ourselves at risk?

But let me make this clear: not every homeless person has a substance abuse problem, but I believe the longer someone stays homeless, the more the odds go up that the person will develop one.

***

The Kansas City Union of the Homeless was helping feed twelve families once a month, each family getting big boxes of groceries. Sometimes our help seemed like a very small drop in a very big bucket of need. In 1993, there were 160 camps of homeless people in Kansas City, Missouri, many of them along the river. I would go out there, walking along the railroad tracks and the banks of the Missouri, talking with people. Those camps were *communities* of people helping themselves help each other. That's how Tent City started out. That's how it is all across the country. No longer can a thinking person accept the claim or the theory that homeless people are not doing anything for themselves. Homeless people *are* feeding themselves and

242 EACH ONE TEACH ONE

clothing themselves. They may not be doing it very successfully, but they *are* feeding and clothing themselves, as well as is possible with their resources.

That is why I must emphasize that the words "help feed" as opposed to "feed" are very important. Saying we "help clothe" is better than we "clothe." Once you get used to the language, you'll get used to the idea. It's an important concept. I make myself repeat it. We have got to start changing the way we talk because *we* are not doing it all for *them*; we are helping each other make it. Our *helping* them makes life a little bit more bearable for them. That kind of philosophy has to be incorporated into the way we speak. Living in the streets is not the most desirable way to exist, but for many homeless, that life is preferable to the institutional way of life. Far too often, life in the streets offers more dignity than life in an institution.

***

No matter how bad life seems at some times, a good majority of the time some decent things are happening. Every now and then I have to remind myself that there is beauty.

Whenever I could find time to myself, I liked to sit in the front bedroom of the house on Garfield, smoking my pipe and painting. My body had started aching all the time and the medicine made me sick, but I still had some scenes to paint from my life. I would get baseball caps and paint things on them, and slogans and logos, which I would sell at activist conventions, using the money to get more canvas and paints.

I love animals, and I guess I like painting animals more than people and other things. Animals and beautiful park scenes and woods—I like to paint those because there *is* beauty in the world. So I also keep pictures around me that I've done of my "Beach Bum Bear" and of Marilyn Monroe.

My Marilyn Monroe is a copy of Hirschfield. I'm a good copier, but I only copy styles I like. I learn from copying the masters. I've done the Mona Lisa a few times. I like Van Gogh.

I had on my bedroom wall a pencil drawing, a copy of one of Van Gogh's self-portraits. He's an inspiration.

I'm not a very humorous person most of the time. Most jokes make me angry rather than amused because most jokes are at the expense of another person. I don't see the humor in that. I believe there's enough humor out there so that you don't have to use another human being as the butt of your joke. But I draw and paint a lot of cartoons. I like to do cartoons because of the lightness that goes into them. Painting something happy helps me have that mood.

I also got a lot of pleasure painting for Ethan. Ethan loves trains. At the time he had several kinds of toy trains and knew them all by name. So I stretched a t-shirt over a canvas on an easel and painted on it each of the toy trains he had, with their names. And I had to get the details right because Ethan was cool; he checked things out. I made sure I had the right color train with the right name because if it was not the same, he wouldn't like it. I painted the name of the whole shirt "Ethan's Trains," and to my joy, he liked it.

***

In 1993 I was honored by being made the Organizational Director of the National Union of the Homeless, and Senior Editor of the *National Union of the Homeless News*. I started expanding the newspaper, not seeking news from the regular sources only. I sought stories from homeless people who were actually living in the streets, who were fighting as they were living in the streets, fighting to make a change. And for those accepting the shelters, I attempted to find out *why* they accepted the shelter system.

For a couple of years, on June 11, the Kansas City Union of the Homeless held an Artists Against Homelessness benefit sale. That was my birthday present to myself. We always got good support from Keith Coldsnow's art supply store. At the benefits I always included my happier paintings as well as the more serious ones.

"You must have really been feeling weird here," a man said to me after looking at one of the scenes from my life.

"That is what I see most of the time," I would answer. "But the happy pictures are what I like to see—the beauty of the world, and even the humor."

Besides art from homeless people, we also showed work from some Art Institute students. I had a few of those kids come over to the house as teachers for the neighborhood children. So in addition to Karen teaching neighborhood kids to read, we had art classes, too, and that July Karen and I took some of the kids on a field trip to the Traco Kenpo karate school on Broadway, in the historic Westport area of Kansas City, for the opening of "Whips and Scorns," a show of painting and sculpture by an artist friend of mine, Nancy McGalliard, who now works in London.

But during the summer of 1993 I mostly traveled around the United States on a speaking tour sponsored by a group called the National Organizing Committee, which was working to bring together the efforts of the various socially conscious organizations in this country, such as the Union of the Homeless and Up and Out of Poverty.

This is the right track. When I was living in Tompkins Square Park, a lot of people, people like Terry, the Minister of Madness, used to ask me, "Cas, why do you go to Washington? Why do you go to Philadelphia? Why do you go to Detroit? That ain't got nothing to do with what's happening in New York."

Such questioners did not understand the full picture. Such questioners did not understand that what's happening in New York is happening in Detroit and in Philadelphia, in San Francisco and in Los Angeles. As long as homeless and impoverished people keep themselves isolated, we're in a dilemma. But when we reach out, contact, and embrace people who are struggling for the same dignity, we all gain—in resources, in ideas, in strength.

Likewise, homelessness respects no race. In Kansas City, some of the black people in my neighborhood did not care for the fact that some of the people coming to the house for help were white homeless people. I had to tell my neighbors I don't believe in prejudice of any kind, shape, or form. I don't believe in an all black world or an all white world or an all red or brown or yellow world. I believe in a multicolored world because that is what we live in.

On the speaking tour, the people who wanted to hear me speak paid my way and gave me places to stay. What I saw was that things were bad for a lot of people all over the country. Homeless people were and are being aggressively harassed. In San Francisco, the police were constantly after the squatters, many of whom are young, white and gay. On the other end of the spectrum, in Bartlesville, Oklahoma, a town of 34,500 people, north of Tulsa near the Kansas border, the Phillips Petroleum employees I visited never thought about homelessness until they started losing their jobs.

It hurt me to see the bewilderment of those company men suddenly faced with no source of income. We spoke about ways they could organize and share resources.

The Bartlesville politicians denied that homelessness existed in their town. These officials were claiming proudly that there were no homeless people in Bartlesville, Oklahoma, even though they had just opened up a new shelter and a pantry for the homeless!

CHAPTER 23
Dilemma

My joints ached like the flu 24 hours a day. My feet were swollen
and numb, my toes especially. After talking to a number of
friends with AIDS or who had friends with AIDS, I quit taking
AZT and my other medication, DDI. They made me sick all the
time, and from what I could see and what I heard from others, it
was not worth it. I began taking a multivitamin designed for
pregnant women, and also I took a daily painkiller used for
people with arthritis. Without the painkiller, I could not and
cannot function.

Yet in October of 1993 I went on the road again, this time
with some other folks, to Chicago, Philadelphia, and New York,
representing three groups: Empty the Shelters, the National
Union of the Homeless, and the umbrella group, the National
Organizing Committee. Even though I was still quite active, I had
become more conscious of having to conserve my energy. I knew
when I had to say to people: "Hey, listen, I'm tired, man, I gotta
lay down" or "I gotta eat something."

I went to New York. It was always good to get back there.
Pam Yates and Peter Kinoy let me hang out at Skylight Pictures,
the company that made *Takeover*, and use it as my office to make
phone calls. I stayed with them, too, at their house. I spoke at the
NYU Law School, and to a group of NYU film students about
Takeover, and to students at Cornell University. We were able to
recruit more students for Empty the Shelters, and got the NYU
law students to start a program on the Lower East Side to teach
homeless people the law as it affects homeless people. Our old
friend Stanley Cohen was helping with that.

At Tompkins Square Park, I got together with some of my
old friends from Tent City and some of the squatters, and we
cooked hamburgers and frankfurters with the homeless people on
a hibachi just outside the entrance to the park. The authorities let

us do our thing for about an hour and a half, and then they arrested six of us on the charge of having an open fire. They had us in jail for about nine hours. In the holding pen there are no chairs, so we were on the floor. My life was so hectic at that time that I took jail as an opportunity to rest. I went to sleep.

When I got back to Kansas City, I plunged into the ongoing task of getting the Kansas City house and base of operations functional and safe and into writing and editing the *National Union of the Homeless News*. On top of that I began writing this book, and then came more speaking engagements in Chicago, New York, and Philadelphia. One day I looked up and found myself in a dilemma. I realized it had been some time since I had made the opportunity to get out in the streets to talk with the homeless, to organize the homeless face to face in Kansas City, the town where I lived. This made me feel a bit hypocritical, since I had been going all over the country telling people that is what they must do. First and foremost, I am a homeless organizing activist, and I believe what that entails is getting out in the streets and dealing with the homeless population on their turf.

Yet I must communicate, I must express myself—it's a key part of how I make a difference, of how I do my work. Still, I worried that I was not doing enough in my own local area, plus I was disappointed over my slow progress with the homeless in Kansas City. Finally, I was disheartened by the uneven support I got from most of the people who said they supported the Union. Unfortunately, my frustrations carried over to my personal life, where Karen seemed increasingly dissatisfied. We argued more than either of us wanted.

In early July of 1994, a trip I made to Raleigh, North Carolina, helped me come to a decision about what to do. In the past, whoever had asked me to come and help organize would make the arrangements for my travel and housing. This time, however, the Annie Smart Leadership Development Institute came up with the money to send me to North Carolina. The ASLD Institute is a combination of the Empty the Shelters organization, the National Union of the Homeless, and the

Welfare Rights Union. They raise funds to teach people grassroots organizing and political education.

On behalf of those groups, I went to Raleigh to provide support and to advise Home Street Home, an organization of homeless and former homeless led by a woman named Mary Ubelgunne, who was once homeless herself. During the summer of the 25th anniversary of the famous music festival Woodstock, Home Street Home was holding an awareness "sleep-in" which they called "Homestock."

One day while I was in Raleigh, the city council was presenting Mary with a proclamation honoring her efforts to help the homeless, and I was invited by Mary to come along. Before the presentation, Mary introduced me to a woman who had once been allied with Mary and had been very helpful and supportive of Home Street Home. But then the woman won a seat on the Raleigh City Council, and suddenly she began treating Mary like a political liability, probably because Mary has these ways that some people don't understand or appreciate, and therefore they call her "crazy" or "stupid." Yet even the word "eccentric" is too harsh to describe Mary, who is a dynamic woman in her own right.

After Mary introduced me to the woman politician, and Mary and I were walking away, I heard the councilwoman and the guy she was with start laughing about how Mary had said something. I turned around and made sure they knew that I saw them.

The proclamation the city gave Mary was a certificate saying that the city agreed to proclaim July 4th to July 9th "Homeless Week" in Raleigh. To City Hall it was no big deal, you know. It made them look like good guys. But Mary had truly earned it and I was happy for her. She made a little speech and then introduced me as a representative of the National Union of the Homeless. I spoke to the council and said something like:

"We appreciate this paper. I want you to understand one thing, though. To us this paper is not a joke. You give us this paper and shrug it off because you give these out to a lot of people. And some of you think it's funny. Actually, it's time for you to *wake up*. We're not something to be laughed at. This paper, though you may not understand it, can be the tool to help us organize people here within this city. We know you think we're a joke, but we ain't no joke, you understand?"

The councilwoman lost her smirk.

"We're going to use this paper to help homeless people and poor people get out of poverty," I said.

That night Mary and I were at the Homestock festival site. We had been talking, and I mentioned my 49th birthday had happened the month before.

"Forty-nine years," Mary said cheerfully. "In another year you can get a senior citizen discount."

For the first time, my age really sank in.

Four a.m., July 10th, 1994. Homestock. "Homeless Week" was over. I was sitting awake. My body ached and I was very tired. About 64 homeless people lay sleeping. All is well, I thought. Or as well as can be, sleeping on the concrete ground. Shades of Tompkins Square Park. At times that night I couldn't help but expect the mounted police, the helicopters, and the storm troopers that they sent at us in New York. I could just see the situation develop right there in that Raleigh park.

I counted one, two, three—four ways the police could get in to where we were sleeping, and no way, no way for us to get out. I worried because any storm-trooping tactics from the police would not only hurt the homeless in that park, but also devastate the efforts of Home Street Home and the Union because the homeless would carry a grudge if we got them into a situation they could not get out of. So, tired as I was, I sat awake with my anxiety. Around 4:25 three more people showed up to sleep. I did a lot of walking around, making sure people were all right, picking up trash.

It was very important for me to be in Raleigh that night, not only as a representative of the Union, but also as a way of getting in touch with myself. Every now and then, the leaders of any organization should go out and experience the hardship of their past again, to re-energize, to get that shot of adrenaline. For me that meant camping in a park again. It was a pain in the butt, but the experience rekindled the fire of my activism that had been getting smothered in day-to-day business.

Every now and then, somebody would raise their head and look around. You see, when you're homeless, every now and then you open up your eyes in the night and remember where you are, who you are, and what's going on. When they saw that I was walking around keeping an eye on things, they felt the peace, and then at least for that one night, they felt safe enough to be able to lie back down and go back to sleep again.

It was then I realized that even had I not been worried something might go wrong, I would have wanted to be awake. I treasured the opportunity to watch over my brothers and sisters.

***

When I got back to Kansas City, Karen and I needed to sit down and talk. We had been preoccupied, but now we could no longer keep putting this off, and she understood that. So we sat down and talked about where we had been, where we were, and where we knew we were headed.

Though we realized my decision to move to Philadelphia was the best for Karen and Ethan and me, and for the overall movement, it still was not easy. No matter what, it's never easy to say good-bye.

CHAPTER 24

America Street

December 1995. The weather outside was ice-cold. Though I was inside the Philadelphia Employment Project volunteering as an HIV and AIDS counselor, between clients my mind was with my friends and colleagues out in the freezing, winter streets. A takeover was going down.

Cheri Honkala and the Kensington Welfare Rights Union linked with the Philadelphia/Delaware Valley Union of the Homeless to make this takeover happen. Kensington deals primarily with homeless mothers and their children who are on welfare. I wanted to be there with my friends for the actual takeover, but actions in freezing conditions are dangerous for my health these days. That's why last summer I made the most of the warm weather, living in a tent city camp we set up in a vacant lot at 4th and Lehigh Street. Then there were organizing trips to Boston and New York, to the Albuquerque Union of the Homeless, and to a summit meeting of anti-poverty organizations held in Houston, Texas.

The groundwork for this takeover had involved checking records to locate empty HUD houses, finding out how long these houses have been vacant, and then doing advance work talking to people in the neighborhoods, letting them know more or less what we were planning, so it wouldn't come as a shock to them.

At last word came. A friend phoned and gave me the good news: we were in! Some two dozen vacant HUD houses had been successfully occupied by families. That put me in a good mood for quite a while.

***

In the beginning I got involved as an activist basically to get food, clothing, and housing for myself. I soon realized that in order for homeless people to get the things we don't just want, but need, we have to become part of the political system that makes the decisions. This means that we cannot just go out here and raise hell and take over buildings; we have also got to become social workers, become part of the city councils. Before you dismiss this possibility, keep in mind the fact that in Philadelphia alone there are an estimated 24,000 homeless people. That's a lot of vote potential.

This is not something we can just talk about; this is something that needs to be done. Most people today are working longer hours for less real income. New jobs are mostly lower-paying jobs. Molly Ivins quotes a study showing almost 20 percent of American workers, people with full-time jobs, are still living below the poverty level. Mass layoffs are hitting even upper-middle-class people. More working-class people are slipping into homelessness. When I visit shelters nowadays with college student volunteers, we're encountering more people who have been working, but have lost their jobs, and then their houses as well. If we don't get involved with them now, they'll go through the shelter system and be lost.

It's frightening. The L.A. riots, which could not be ignored by the press, were not just about Rodney King. Wherever I speak, I try to make that point: if you don't want what happened in the L. A. riots to happen in your own town, then you need to become an active part of your whole community, not just your neighborhood.

Most people think that revolution means going out there and hurting someone. That is not necessarily so. Revolution does not have to be violent. I believe it's a revolution when a poor person can help feed another poor person. I believe it's a revolution when a poor organization is within a community helping to feed, helping to educate, helping with health care. That to me *is* a revolution.

***

In the once-empty HUD house I worked with Mari Luz and Elba and their kids at making it into a home. I know it probably won't be my last. We put locks on the door, and we had electricity hooked up, so no more kerosene heaters. Every now and then cops would show up ask what we were doing there. Once we had been at the house for a while, we have paperwork, such as bill receipts and personal mail, showing we lived there. For a while that satisfied the officers, and the authorities left us alone.

My body aches constantly, almost like when I was kicking alcohol. My good time is in the morning. By noon I have to take pain medication to keep functioning. I find myself thinking about the people from my past.

As for my family, I don't even know where some of them are. But my brother Philip has ended up managing a couple of shoe stores.

Terry Taylor, our "Minister of Madness," finally kicked alcohol, but died of AIDS.

Spider is dead, and his lady Barbara got knifed to death.

My brother Hundu died of AIDS.

Hundu died soon after I moved to Philadelphia. When I heard my brother had died, I recalled a day in 1991 when I was back in New York briefly on Union business. He had come around to see me at Tompkins Square. We were on a good note by then. We knew he had the virus.

We got ourselves a little ways off from the Tent City activities. We sat on a bench along 7th street. Hundu told me he had been reading about my escapades as an activist and told me he was very proud. Neither of us said a whole lot after that. We had a silent understanding, just happy to be sharing this companionship with each other. We spent the afternoon drinking coffee and reading the newspaper. Hundu even wrote a little poetry.

I think a lot about my daughters. Until a few years ago, Tonya, my younger daughter, was not even on speaking terms with me. She might see me and say hello, but she never called me "Pops," never said she loved me. My daughters lived two blocks away from Tompkins Square Park, but we didn't connect. They used to be very angry with me, and rightfully so.

Happily, after all these years, my relationship with them is rekindling to an extent. In this past couple of years I've been able to get a little closer to them. I'm glad to say Tonya is in college and working. I try talk to her by phone about once a week. Less often with Yolanda, but they have both learned that what their pop does now is his life's calling. They understand that if somebody comes knocking on their father's door and is hungry, all they have to do is say they're hungry and he will give them food. Yolanda seems to have respect for my projects as an activist, and Tonya, who once told me the authorities needed to throw a bomb in Tompkins Square Park to get rid of the homeless, now reads the *Union of the Homeless News*. However, we still have a lot of lost ground to recover.

The human resources in Philadelphia are amazing. In some ways it's easier to do this work here than in other places, because this city has a longer history and tradition of activism than many communities. Yet some days I miss Kansas City terribly.

As it stands today, the Union of the Homeless in Kansas City is pretty much out of business. Unfortunately, part of this is because some people thought "Cas is the Union," so that when I left town, what little support there was dried up. I must emphasize here how much Karen did for the Union in Kansas City. Karen contributed not only in putting up with me, but also in working her fingernails to the bone to make the Garfield house work. I rarely told Karen enough how much I appreciated her and her work. I have a hard time saying things like that. I don't know why. I should have praised her and thanked her more. Karen was my right hand throughout my time in Kansas City, even through our own personal difficulties.

People need to understand that if it wasn't for the organization, no single person could do anything. And if it wasn't for the homeless population helping, the organization couldn't do anything. When you understand the needs of the people, you understand the need for the people to organize. This is an important concept because if what we're building becomes perceived as being dependent on one individual, we are all lost. The Union of the Homeless is not Leona Smith or Casanova or any individual, but an organization of people of like mind working together to make changes in society for the better, whether it be in Kansas City or New York or L.A. or Bartlesville, Oklahoma. We have gained ground together. Together we can gain more. Together we can make a better life.

From my experiences in Kansas City I now recognize that in order to make the Union work, we must achieve and maintain a certain level of volunteerism among people who are not homeless and may never have experienced homelessness themselves. We need to have their support beyond donations of money. It is easy for people to give money and say "I've done it!" That's not it. What's necessary is getting involved at the personal level, as opposed to a bureaucratic level. Each city, each *community,* needs to get involved. The community is what is necessary. No human being makes it entirely on his or her own.

In this kind of work you constantly have to rebuild the organization because the more you succeed, the more you tend to lose your membership. As people become ex-homeless, they naturally become more involved with keeping their own lives on track and tend to disappear from the movement. So we continually campaign among the homeless to interest them in working with us.

Although every day is a struggle, in Philadelphia we have our victories. We have increased our number of houses to around 60. Leona, whose energy is tremendous, constantly goes out and speaks to people at churches, schools and detox centers. Over the past few months she has signed up 200 new members for the Union of the Homeless, and so far they have been fairly active.

I focus full-time on publishing the *Union of the Homeless News*, writing articles with my old Magnavox PC dinosaur of a computer that someone donated, and on organizing at the national level with the National Union of the Homeless as a base. My operation has a crew of four or five ex-homeless people, and seven to ten solidly committed college students who work with me.

On March 30, a group I started here called Artists for a Better America was scheduled to hold an evening art benefit at

the University of Pennsylvania in Houston Hall at the Bowl
Room. College students I work with from the Empty the Shelter
movement did the majority of work putting the show together.
The day of the event, Tonya called to remind me I had missed her
birthday the week before. As we talked, she sensed my anxiety.
She was enthusiastic and very happy to hear about the show and
wished us all luck. Her words of encouragement did me good.
That night I sold a painting. The benefit grossed $1,000 and
made us a whole lot of new friends.

Though I have a lot of pain from the virus, I'm in better
shape than most people who have had HIV for as long as I've had
it. I have a motivating factor that helps: the movement against
homelessness and the fight against poverty is part of my
medicine. The movement is helping me fight the virus by
providing a meaning to what I do. It strengthens my will to live
and fight.

What keeps me fighting is my nightmares. The paintings I
have done, based on my life, have helped me liberate my
nightmares, but my nightmares are not all gone. My nightmares
are still very much alive in my heart, in my sleep, on the streets.
Every time I walk through a town and see a homeless person, it
reminds me of New York, of Tompkins Square, of Tent City.
Every time I hear of the death of a homeless person, I'm on fire.

My life story is similar to that of a lot of homeless people
all over the United States. When I was living in the orphanage,
when I was running the streets, when I was homeless, I needed
help, and I didn't get it. So my 44 years prior to becoming an
activist were ill-spent, wasted. I take that back a little because the
experiences I went through made me who I am now. But at the
time I needed help, I needed persistent and caring counseling. It
wasn't there, so I lived a real hard, nasty life. I don't want what
happened to me to happen to anybody else. While I believe in
self-reliance, I also recognize there are people out there who
cannot help themselves without first being brought into the fold
of a caring community.

This is a lifelong struggle. When I came into this world there
was homelessness. When I leave there is going to be

homelessness. But what we do in the meantime while we are here on this earth does matter.

On Good Friday this year, a day when many people's thoughts are on Jesus, his teachings, his death and life, we marched from City Hall to the Liberty Bell to remind people of the pain that cuts in social programs budgets are inflicting on the kind of people Jesus spoke for.

I don't have a formal religion now. I believe in the spirit of the Lord and the more humanistic philosophy found in Christianity. I believe in the love that's supposed to come out of the Bible, but I don't believe in churches. I will say that any time I hear the song "Amazing Grace," I'm amazed, so I sing amazingly.

Sometimes I believe in God and sometimes I don't. When I see hardship I question the Lord, but when I see beauty I want to put it somewhere, and I guess I put that on the Lord. I believe that there is a spirit which inspires my feeling of love for people, but I don't know if that necessarily has to do with the Bible. One of the things that got me angry with religion is that most of them teach fear of the Lord. The kind of God I think about is a loving God.

***

About the middle of April 1996, HUD gave eviction notices to the people living in all of the houses we had taken at the end of last year. The need for another Tent City to publicize our plight became apparent.

At first we decided to rebuild the Tent City site at 4th and Lehigh, a vacant lot right across the street from McDonald's and a Burger King. We had one tent, lots of chairs, our sleeping gear and possessions. We were just settling about to build the livingroom and meeting space under the tarp, when the police came to move us off the lot. You might expect that the businesses were the ones who called the police on us. Not so, at least this time. It turned out that a poor person in the neighborhood phoned the police on us. What a blow. This really hurt our hearts. Some of our brothers and sisters just do not understand our fight.

At first we considered trying to hang onto the spot, but then we decided not to fight it. Instead we passed out flyers and information. As a result of this spreading of information most of the people in the neighborhood ended up wanting to support us, but we moved to American Street, behind a Cousin's supermarket just off 2nd and Lehigh.

We spent all day cleaning up the lot and building. I stayed that night. At about 10 p.m. I had just gotten some food and was sitting down to eat it when the rain came with a thundering impact. Mari Luz, Hope, and Cheryl were in the tent, while I took cover under the tarp. The rain came in torrents. My food got soaked. Finally I went to the women in the tent.

"Ladies," I said. "I have had enough." The women let me come into the tent, where I slept at their feet that night, out of the rain.

As I write this, people are still living in Tent City on American Street. I visit there every now and then, as my busy schedule and health allow. I cannot afford to get sick. The neighbors in the area have been great. They understand that our plight is their plight. They bring food and whatever they can to the tent, and some of their children have become members of KWRU's youth group. That makes me feel real good. Once the summer comes and the weather changes for the better, I expect more members of KWRU to be living at the site.

***

Some of the shelters we visit used to be churches. The house I come to on this day with my student volunteers has been turned into a shelter for 12 women and their kids. On the outside it looks like a small school building. You can hear the kids inside. I ring the doorbell, and a woman answers it.

"My name's Casanova," I say, "I'm with the Union of the Homeless."

We're invited inside. Inside looks similar to a boarding house, with the women using the kitchen communally. There are a lot of kids at this place.

We sit down and I explain briefly what we're about. I try to make the women comfortable talking to me, let them know I'm not just running my mouth. The key is to not talk *at* the people. The key is, you ask them what they think, and then you listen. The students and I hand out a questionnaire we have put together to help find out what's on the mind of these women living in shelters, what makes them tick.

Just the fact that we are asking their opinion opens some heavy conversations with these women. You'll find nearly any person in the shelter system is going to be enthusiastic about talking to anybody from the outside world. These women have a lot of worries, a lot of subjects they want to talk about, even though they believe they can't do anything about those subjects. They are happy we care enough to come there to let them know about what is being accomplished through the various organizations such as the Union of the Homeless, Empty the Shelters and the Kensington Welfare Rights Union.

At the end, one dark-skinned woman with three kids tells me, "We're so glad that you came and that you're able to spend some time with us."

Finally we invite them to a meeting of the Union.

"We're on blackout," one of the women says. "We can't go."

"All right. Let me go talk to the manager," I say. When you first go into many shelters, they have a thing called "blackout." That means for 30 days, you're not allowed outside the shelter to deal with the world.

The manager of this particular shelter is a light-skinned black woman. I explain what I am asking. Her answer comes so easy it surprises me.

"Sure," she says. "Let them go to your meeting."

***

I don't think I help people out of any abstract political ideal, any religious tenet or even a spiritual feeling. To me it's more basic: when I see somebody hungry, I feel pain, and therefore, the need to help that person.

Even if there is a Lord, it wasn't only the Lord that has kept me alive. I had to take some initiative myself in order to get where I am. Yes, there will always be homeless people, but we have to change the attitudes of people toward the homeless, both the people who have and those who have not. We have got to do something about the housing and the poverty. Maybe there will always be poor and homeless people, but if I can make the world even an inch better than it used to be, I am going to keep on.

The way I look at it, any knowledge I have gained is no good to me if I can't teach it to somebody else. Remember the ancient proverb about teaching people to fish. Some people will read these words who have never been homeless, but will yet experience some type of homelessness in their lifetime.

My hope is that this book will have an impact on people who read it, homeless or not; that this book can give people the courage that comes from knowing they are not alone in their struggle; that this book can be a tool to help people to rise up and out of poverty. That is the objective—that homeless men and woman in poverty learn the tools and form their own organization. Whatever they learn in order to make their lives and their organization work, they need to be showing other people how to do it, too. That's what I believe in: each one teach one. Then, and only then, do I believe we're doing things right.

Through
Peace, Love, & Understanding
Ronald (Newhouse) Casanova
Tent City, Philadelphia
April 1996

Selected Resources

Films and Videos:

I Want to Go Home: A Pictorial Essay of Homelessness in New Hampshire, Video Verite, Attn: Peter Braddock, PO Box 1579, Portsmouth, NH 03802; tel: 603-436-3360. $25 postage included.

Homeless in America, NMHA, 1021 Prince St., Alexandria, VA 22314. $19.95, includes book. 12 minutes.

Takeover: Heroes of the New American Depression. A video by Peter Kinoy and Pamela Yates. **Featuring Ron Casanova**. 58 minutes. Color. Institutions: contact First Run/Icarus Films, tel: 800-876-1710. Videocassettes for home use only are available through Skylight Pictures, tel: 800/724-8367

Books:

Blau, Joel, *The Visible Poor: Homelessness in America* (New York: Oxford University Press, 1992).

Kozal, Jonathan, *Rachel and Her Children* (New York: Ballantine Books, 1989).

Golden, Stephanie, *The Women Outside: Meaning and Myths of Homelessness* (Berkeley: University of California Press, 1992).

Vanderstaay, Steven with photos by Joseph Sorrentino, *Street Lives: An Oral History of Homeless Americans* (Philadelphia: New Society, 1992).

Internet:

"A Short Bibliography on Homelessness," http://thecity.sfsu.edu/~stewartd/biblio.html

"Articles on Homelessness," http://www.miyazaki-mic.ac.jp/classes/compoliss/homelessarticles.html

Organizations:

Artists for a Better America, 3434 Old York Rd., Philadelphia, PA 19140, tel: 215-221-0459.

Homebase, 870 Market St., Suite 1220, San Francisco, CA 94102, tel: 202-775-1316.

National Union of the Homeless, 3434 Old York Rd., Philadelphia, PA 19140, tel: 215-221-0459.

For more information, see: "Bibliography on Homelessness," *Rethinking Schools*, (Summer 1966), p. 23.